12/6

THE SHAKESPEAREAN SCENE

THE SHAKESPEAREAN SCENE

Dramatic Criticisms

by

HERBERT FARJEON

"... or may we cram
Within this wooden O the very casques
That did affright the air at Agincourt?"

Henry V.

HUTCHINSON & CO. (Publishers) LTD

London   New York   Melbourne   Sydney   Cape Town

With acknowledgments to the following papers:

The Bystander
The Graphic
The Sphere
New Statesman
Radio Times
Sunday Pictorial
Shakespeare League Journal
Old Vic and Sadlers Wells Magazine
Vogue
Weekly Westminster

Printed in Great Britain by
William Brendon & Son, Ltd.
The Mayflower Press (late of Plymouth)
at Bushey Mill Lane
Watford, Herts

Contents

FOREWORD

BY PHILIP HOPE-WALLACE

THE value of these collected notices by a critic of the first rank, who served the theatre well and truly for some thirty years and knew more about the Shakespearean problem, *considered as a scholar's problem and the problem of a practical man of the theatre*, than any other critic of his time, is so obvious that of all rôles which might be cut, that of introducer should be the first to go. These notices need no puff preliminary from me. But it might be a good thing to remind readers that they were after all (though they do not read so like it) so many pieces of *ad hoc* journalism, Herbert Farjeon being no despiser of that much-berated craft. They do not therefore scruple to make a second time a point which may have been made at a previous production of the play, if that point was of value (and it usually was); and being designed for immediate public consumption (as they say of certain sorts of food) they had perhaps a slightly sharper taste in the week they were written for than they have now; for like all good criticism, however lasting in value, they took on a little of the mental climate of their date. But what disadvantage there may be in thus re-presenting them is more than outweighed by the extraordinary interest resulting from setting one notice of a play next the notice called forth by its subsequent revival. A most valuable picture emerges of the treatment accorded to any particular play of Shakespeare during the last three decades.

And it is more than the picture that would be given by a selection from a well-kept library of cuttings. For here the critic, to a most unusual degree, remains a "constant". He was surely the most constant —in the old exact meaning of the word—of all the critics of Shakespeare. People who knew him better than I did would explain that quite easily in terms of his personality and character. "Constancy," like his wit and his relish for every kind of thing from cricket to magic-lantern slides, informed all he did as well as all he wrote. But for those who had not the luck to know him personally, it may be worth chasing this quality a little further, for it is a quality fast disappearing in an age when the publicity man and the public relations officer are to the disinterested critic as kings and prelates to some half-lunatic soothsayer! In short the quality of Herbert Farjeon's Shakespearean criticism which will jump at you out of these pages is a quality which was always rare and is getting rarer.

9

"Taste", a tiresome word in some ways, is none the less the word for Herbert Farjeon and it was this indefinable thing which was the touchstone of his criticism. Taste, not prejudice, personal prejudice. It is criticism which is the antithesis of the kind to which Shaw's famous *boutade* gave so unfortunate an impetus, to wit

"Whoever has been through the experience of discussing criticism with a thorough, perfect and entire ass has been told that criticism should above all things be free from personal prejudice."

Which of course leads you to the position that one man's personal prejudice is as good as another's and that the value of acquiring a sensitive palate is very likely outweighed by the value of having a fresh mind! Another result is that though Shaw's criticism, like Herbert Farjeon's revue sketches, still contorts us with laughter, and that though long ago and quite forgotten things live again as hapless victims of his assaults, most of his criticism (to say nothing of his Shakespearean criticism which is fantastically wrong-headed) has very little historical interest other than as a sidelight on Shaw himself.

Herbert Farjeon's criticism was the very opposite. It was a comparatively weak projection of himself and his personal likes and dislikes, but an extraordinarily keen piercing to the heart of the matter under review. This could be a disappointment sometimes; dealing with some fearful rubbish, he could, one feels, have hit harder; but it is all gain with Shakespearean criticism. We really have the feeling that we "get at" the production as it was, and can compare it with what it ought to have been. For Herbert Farjeon always felt, and without anything involving either pride or modesty, that he knew how it ought to be. Instinct or training? Both. The proper analogy is that of the trained musician who kindly but firmly points out that the pitch is slipping or the rhythm failing. (And how right he is!) There was no need to eke the notice out with accounts of personal frets or delights, or only occasionally so. An ear for Shakespeare—or does one say a palate for Shakespeare? Possibly the latter, for it suggests cultivation, and the other suggests only the innate gift. At all events there it was, as the following pages testify. But how so sensitive a man managed to keep his palate in such conditions, seeing what it had to taste so often in the way of the theatre's shoddier stuff, is not for me to explain. He kept it, as he seems to have kept delight in many of the first pleasures of childhood, unimpaired all through his life. Equally mysterious is how a man who held in his hand such a lethal weapon of wit, came to use it so gently and kindly, more often like the pole wielded by the magic-lantern lecturer, pointing out the good bits and the bad bits, than as the pole-axe it might so easily have been. Perhaps because he had so many other outlets. After all, the pen that could, in one of his revues, write the lyric of Les Non-stop Nudes, or that parody of the chit-chat family play, in another, was not going to waste critical energy in smashing the rotten walnut of some feeble "west-end success".

With his Shakespeare criticism the dominant impression remains one of entire but unassertive sureness; that there was "a right way" of tackling any particular Shakespearean problem; that a natural sensibility informed with scholarship would give rise eventually to that taste which was the only sure guide; in short that the essence of a Shakespeare play could, with enough trouble, be distilled and that fantastication, popularization and all the rest were so many wretched evasions. He should be living at this hour!

COMEDIES

THE TEMPEST

THE MESSEL *TEMPEST*
(1940)

THE TEMPEST has always seemed to me the most baffling flight of beauty that ever called for an audience of poets. It has the elusive quality of light; the faint-strong smell of the sea-shore; and the sound, an arcade of sound, is that of a shell against the ear, when all the storms and zephyrs that have ever swept the seas make peace in a cool, echoing whisper. Why is Prospero so cross? Why does he abjure his magic? Why doesn't he keep his word with Ariel? What's all this about hanging garments on a line to vex the louts who masquerade in them? Well, well, little critics shouldn't ask questions. Enough, like Ariel, to drink the air before us. And to thank the Old Vic for a draught of rare loveliness in these violent, mortal and suspicious times.

Of all Shakespeare's plays this, in production, is the most perishable. How to get the flesh and blood out of the actress who plays Miranda? How to get the levity and celerity into the actor who plays Ariel? How to get the fish into Caliban? How to conjure up the miracles conjured up by Prospero between his strange fits of perturbation? To answer this last question Mr. Oliver Messel, most brilliant of all stage designers, has been called in. He achieves many near-miracles by a careful and sensitive consideration of gauze and effect. But miracles they aren't, and that is a worry. It is impossible to reproduce Prospero's magic one hundred per cent; and since it is impossible, wouldn't something more formal, leaving more to the imagination of those who have any, answer the purpose better? If the sound of *The Tempest* is the sound of a shell, might not the formality of a shell, with its exquisite and definite convolutions, serve as the best guide for an artist tackling this proposition? Mr. Messel's costumes are unexceptionable. Given the approach he has chosen, I know no other artist who would have come so near the goal. But I question whether the approach is a wise one. The attempt to make the pageant insubstantial is too challenging.

Acting—well, not too good. Mr. Gielgud does not seem old enough for Prospero, is not impressive enough, or harsh enough, or commanding enough. Miss Jessica Tandy's Miranda looks delicious, but her voice could scarcely be described as harmonious charmingly; and the music of this play must not be marred. Mr. Alec Guiness is preferable to the pudding-Ferdinands so often set before us. Mr. Jack Hawkins has some grand moments as Caliban. If he lacks the embryo-human quality that makes Caliban such a marvellous compound, his "Get-a-new-master" frenzy is tremendous. Mr. Marius Goring's Ariel has

15

caught some of the ominousness that might have been in Prospero. Trinculo and Stephano, played by Mr. Frank Tickle and Mr. W. G. Fay, come out rather like Tweedledum and Tweedledee—an Irish Tweedledee, which, as they say, makes a change.

So does the play, being fire and dew, which are not qualities one would ascribe to most current shows.

RANDOM NOTES

The Tempest is the loveliest of all Shakespeare's plays—like so many of them! It is generally believed to have been the last he wrote, the Epilogue being his Farewell to Drama. Its quality is unearthly. Shakespeare, although he did not die until some years after he wrote it, may well have had one foot in the grave. He certainly had one hand in Heaven. But the date of *The Tempest* (1611) is, like almost everything else about Shakespeare, purely conjectural. If you want to prove that *The Tempest* must have been an early play, you may point to the cumbrous explanatory opening after the storm has passed and assert that here is clearly the work of an inexperienced dramatic craftsman. If you want to prove that *The Tempest* must have been a late play, you may point to the same opening and assert that here is clearly the work of a playwright so advanced that he could no longer trouble his head over the pettifogging niceties of dramatic construction.

.   .   .   .   .

Of this, however, we may be pretty sure: that Shakespeare knew his audience might be bored by the opening, and that Prospero's "Dost thou attend me?" "Thou attend'st not!" and "Dost thou hear?" are breaks introduced to recapture the audience's possibly wandering attention quite as much as Miranda's. For what daughter, hearing the truth about her father for the first time, would not be all ears? Editors suggest that Miranda is really still so deeply concerned with the fate of the poor shipwrecked mariners that her attention wanders to the sea. Here, they say, is another fine Shakespearean stroke, in which the tenderness of his heroine's character is masterfully revealed. But editors will be editors. I would rather leave the preparation of an Authorized Version of Shakespeare's Plays to playwrights and actors.

.   .   .   .   .

Shakespeare is full of slips and the commentators of three centuries have spotted most of them. But there is one in *The Tempest* which seems to have escaped notice. In the second scene of the first act Prospero desires that Ferdinand shall be lured into the presence of Miranda, and this he contrives by means of Ariel, who sings "Come unto these yellow sands" and so draws Ferdinand along. In giving Ariel his instructions, Prospero says:

> Go make thyself like a nymph o'th'sea, be subject
> To no sight but thine, and mine: invisible
> To every eye-ball else: go take this shape
> And hither come in't: go: hence with diligence.

This task Ariel performs, for the stage direction a few lines further down reads:

> *Enter Ariel like a water-nymph.*

And a few lines further down again:

> *Enter Ferdinand, and Ariel invisible, playing and singing.*

Ferdinand makes it plain that he cannot see Ariel, for he remarks:

> Where should this music be? I' the air or the earth?
> It sounds no more.

But why, if Ariel is invisible to every eye-ball but Prospero's, should there be this business of dressing up like a sea-nymph at all? An invisible sprite in disguise sounds like a by-word in fairyland! One can only conclude Prospero to have been such a consummate artist that he made Ariel dress up for his own aesthetic delight.

. . . . . .

Fanny Burney well said that *The Tempest* is "at the head of beautiful improbabilities." How impalpable it is, how subtle, how elemental! And how it smells of the salt sea-shore, an oyster-shell smell, recalling one to the astringent sanity of beauty. The smell of a play! Is it not a kind of test? Might one not postulate that any play of any account smells of something, and that plays of no account betray their weakness by smelling of nothing at all? Ibsen smells—he smells of must. Even on the mountain-tops he seems to be brushing the must from his great-coat sleeve. Synge smells—he smells of peat, a most heavenly and most earthly smell. Shaw smells of anaesthetic. Barrie smells of pot-pourri. Noel Coward smells of rather good pomade. But this, I begin to see, is a fireside game for winter evenings. So for winter evenings by the fireside let it be preserved.

THE TWO GENTLEMEN OF VERONA

SOME RANDOM NOTES
(1935)

OF all Shakespeare's plays, *The Two Gentlemen of Verona* has perhaps made the lightest impression on the public mind. There is no record of any stage production until 1762, nearly two hundred years

B

after it was written. If it has been put on for a run during my own lifetime, my memory is defective. Even at the Old Vic it has not been seen for a decade, and is not likely to be seen for another. Apart from the printed page, there is really but one happy haven for this pretty comedy in the twentieth century, and that happy haven is a dream, being our non-existent National Theatre. Not the least important function of a soundly-based National Theatre would be to exhibit at regular intervals plays which have established themselves as dramatic classics, but which may no longer be seen in the commercial theatre because they are no longer commercially profitable. Such a play is *The Two Gentlemen of Verona*. And since there is no National Theatre to keep it on show as the National Gallery keeps on show the lesser masterpieces of great painters, we may be doubly grateful to the B.B.C. for arranging Sunday's broadcast.

The B.B.C. is not likely to receive any complaints about this broadcast. Shakespeare has made such a name for himself that listeners, even if they don't listen to him, would almost as soon think of complaining about a broadcast by the King. For Shakespeare is something more to the public than his work. He is an Englishman—the Englishman who licked all the foreign poets and dramatists at poetry and drama. Had he been a Frenchman or a German, and had his works, translated into English, been word for word the same as those we now read and hear and see—well, *Hamlet* and *King Lear* and *A Midsummer Night's Dream* might be received by listeners with approval. But *The Two Gentlemen of Verona* would hardly be regarded as sacrosanct.

Nevertheless, you will find *The Two Gentlemen of Verona* full of charm if you accept the romantic conceptions on which the story is based, and if you have enough taste and education to receive a conceit for what it is worth rather than for what it will fetch. And if you enjoy the game of spotting the tunes when medleys of old popular songs are broadcast, you may enjoy a not dissimilar game which may be played with *The Two Gentlemen of Verona*. For this is one of Shakespeare's early comedies, and it abounds in scenes, cadences, and characters which, in his maturer years, he used again to better purpose. You will find bits of *Twelfth Night* in it, and bits of *Romeo and Juliet*, and bits of *The Merchant of Venice*, and bits of *All's Well that Ends Well*, and bits of *Much Ado About Nothing*, and bits of *Measure for Measure*, and the whole of some of the Sonnets. Compare the opening scene between Julia and her maid, Lucetta, o'er-naming suitors, with the opening scene between Portia and her maid, Nerissa; compare the foolish Thurio with Sir Andrew Aguecheek; compare the outlaws in the forest between Milan and Mantua with the outlaws in the Forest of Arden —and you will see how Shakespeare treated the same things in youth and in maturity.

This, however, is not to deny that much of *The Two Gentlemen of Verona* is peculiar to itself and that on some of it Shakespeare never improved in his later versions. Take, for one example, the superb clown Launce—the most vivid and completely satisfactory figure in the comedy. Launce in later life became Launcelot Gobbo of *The Merchant of Venice*. Some of his tricks he even handed down to the First Gravedigger in *Hamlet*. But what have either of these to show that can equal Launce's immortal soliloquy on the grief engendered by his leave-taking from home: "My mother weeping, my father wailing, my sister crying, our maid howling, our cat wringing her hands, and all our house in a great perplexity: yet did not this cruel-hearted cur shed one tear." It is impossible to think of Launce without thinking of his cur, and of all the stories of love for animals in fact and fiction there is none more charming than the tale Launce tells of how he suffered himself to be whipped for the offence committed by his dog.

Shakespeare must have been a great animal-lover. He is always inveighing against blood-sports. Even the snail inspired him to the most exquisite poetry. And I feel sure that he would have been touched to hear Mr. Charles Laughton in a passing moment of enthusiasm declare to me last spring that of all the characters in *The Two Gentlemen of Verona*, the one he would most dearly love to play was Launce's dog—whereupon this amazing actor proceeded to give such a fine, such an adorably sensitive and understanding performance of Launce's dog, as he would act it while Launce was soliloquizing, that I longed for Shakespeare to be there to see.

Nevertheless, Launce is, I suppose, a better part than his dog, and I never expect to see Launce more saltily acted than he was by Mr. Hay Petrie during the days when he was making clown-history at the Old Vic. A remarkable thing happened on the night I was present, for during one of the soliloquies a gentleman in a private box let out one of those sudden, solitary laughs that completely break up a scene by attracting the attention of the whole audience. Mr. Petrie, however, was not nonplussed. On the contrary, he looked up at the box and winked at the gentleman, and the house roared. It occurred to me at that moment that this was probably the first time a Shakespearean clown had winked at an audience since Shakespeare's own day, but the inspiration was unquestionably sound, for Shakespeare's early plays demand clowns who can take advantage of the moment and get the better of the groundlings. Therefore I hoped that this inspiration of Mr. Petrie's would mark the inauguration of a new era in Shakespearean clowning, or the revival of an old one. But my hope was disappointed. Shakespeare's clowns are still direfully respected.

Bernard Shaw has well said of *The Two Gentlemen of Verona* that the best parts of the play are the parts that have nothing to do with the play at all, and this is true. Shakespeare had yet to become a master-dramatist, though he was already a master-poet. Keep your ears open, then, as you follow the rope-laddery plot, for the purely lyrical passages—for the lovely lines about the current that "makes sweet music with th'enamel'd stones", and about Orpheus' lute "strung with poets' sinews"—and that loveliest line of all, "Didst thou but know the inly touch of love". And when the play is over, when Valentine has forgiven Proteus, even as Shakespeare may have forgiven the handsome, high-born W.H. of the Sonnets, perhaps you will agree that even the minor plays of Shakespeare would be ranked among the major plays of anybody else. For my own part, in the absence of a National Theatre, I look to the B.B.C. to give us not only Shakespeare's minor plays, but the best of the "doubtful" plays as well. For if we do not get *The Two Noble Kinsmen* and *Sir Thomas More* from Broadcasting House, there seems little hope of getting them from any other source.

THE MERRY WIVES OF WINDSOR

MISS EVANS AS MISTRESS PAGE
(1923)

THE revival of *The Merry Wives of Windsor* at the Lyric Theatre, Hammersmith, is a very jolly affair. This was almost inevitable, for the play is essentially so jolly, so blithe, and, withal, so thick-skinned as to be practically producer-proof. The best possible description of the mood in which Shakespeare wrote it is to be found in the terms applied by the Host of the Garter Inn to Master Fenton: "He capers, he dances, he has eyes of youth: he writes verses, he speaks holiday, he smells April and May, he will carry't, he will carry't, 'tis in his buttons, he will carry't." Master Fenton does not fulfil the expectations aroused by these exuberant, bouncing words. In the event, he proves himself a weak walking gentleman rather than a triumphant bounding boy. But how the comedy itself capers, dances, has eyes of youth! how it speaks holiday, smells April and May! how Shakespeare carries it, from the pribbles and prabbles of the opening squabble till "candles and starlight and moonshine be out"! how burstingly it is "in his buttons"!

When the curtain fell on the first performance last Saturday night, Mr. Nigel Playfair, answering the clamour for an anti-climax, described the piece as a Christmas entertainment. To make it so, there is no need, as Mr. Oscar Asche apparently thought there was some years ago, to contradict the spirit of every line by providing a Christmas-card setting of snow, and so superfluously adding to the agonies of Falstaff's ducking. *The Merry Wives* will do for any holiday. Its production would, indeed, serve as a capital excuse for a holiday, like the visit of a celebrity to his old school; it does not, like so many of the plays rushed on this Christmas, need a holiday as an excuse for its appearance. We are for ever routing out excuses for the presentation of poor plays. When we are busy, we have become, it is urged, so tired by nightfall that we are fit only for frivolous trifles. When we are idle, we are so carefree that to offer anything but frivolous trifles would be out of keeping. It is a relief, then, to find the Hammersmith Lyric staunchly uncontaminated by the vogue for amateurish puerilities dominant at this season of the year. And it is worth recording that the first-night audience was so hearty in its response that a few encores, after the fashion of *The Beggar's Opera*, would no doubt have been rapturously welcomed.

The honours of the performance fell to Miss Edith Evans. She is that rare thing, an actress with both breadth and subtlety. She is that equally rare thing, an actress who can bring out the full literary flavour of every word. To those who know their Shakespeare before they see him on the stage, how maddening it is to find word after word misunderstood, slurred over, debased, diminished, or subjected to the ignominy of substitution by the performers. But Miss Evans quickens every syllable, recognizes in a choice epithet something as three-dimensional as a living being, reveals new wonders unsuspected and never to be forgotten. Miss Ellen Terry's Mistress Page was more electric, more gallivanting, possessed more animal magnetism. But Miss Evans is more in period, more sweepingly dominant, and, I verily believe, the better actress. Miss Dorothy Green put up a good bold show as Mistress Ford, but comparatively she never stood a chance. Indeed, it is difficult to remember the other people in the play.

Referring to my programme, I am reminded of Mr. Randle Ayrton, who achieved the uncommon feat of making Ford credible without making him too realistic. I am reminded again of Mr. Play-fair's Host, a stout, tough, ample slice of work. And there was Mr. Roy Byford's Falstaff, more nimble of foot, if less nimble of wit, than most Falstaffs, because Mr. Byford is, off the stage as well as on, a man of monstrous bulk, and consequently knows how nimble of foot the corpulent can be in emergency. But Miss Evans would have dwarfed an even larger and better Falstaff than Mr. Byford's.

The production by Mr. Bridges Adams is resolutely reactionary. There is picture scenery of the most undistinguished type; there is incidental music for the various entries of Falstaff and of the Merry Wives, to mark them unmistakably from the minor characters; there are cuts, perversions of the text, misinterpretations of the text, even additions to the text; none of them glaring, but all of them obviously deliberate and indicative of Mr. Adams's views on Shakespearean production. Ford's frenzied search in impossible places, with rag, tag and bobtail at his heels, is infectiously worked up. The duel between the terrestrial Doctor and the celestial Parson is rattling rough-and-tumble. But does not Sir Hugh, counting the stars when he is felled to earth, savour less of Shakespeare than of the less original moments provided by modern musical comedy clowns in cricket caps and Boston garters?

FALSTAFF IN SPATS
(1929)

The production of *The Merry Wives of Windsor* at the Apollo Theatre brings us one step nearer to the logical conclusion of the passing craze for Shakespeare in modern dress. When Sir Barry Jackson put the first of these jigsaw misfits on the stage, it immediately became apparent that to translate the costumes and scenery of old plays into modern terms was bound to create discord if the dialogue and action remained intact. In a setting of curtains, with the actors and actresses dressed as at rehearsal, scenery and costumes might not unsatisfactorily be left to the imagination. But when an attempt is made to represent what was once an Elizabethan soldier by putting him into twentieth-century khaki, it comes as a considerable shock to the audience, if not to his troops, to hear him ejaculate "Od's bodikins!"

If we are to have Shakespeare in modern dress, with telephones and cocktails and golf-clubs *obbligati*, then the only thing to do is to rewrite the plays. A start in this direction has been made by Mr. Oscar Asche, whose production of *The Merry Wives* comes to us with the official approval of the British Empire Shakespeare Society.

Here is Falstaff in spats, here are the Merry Wives in knee-length skirts, here is Shallow in a bath-chair, here is Parson Hugh with a portable wireless, here is Pistol as an old-time "laddie" actor, here are nigger minstrels outside Mine Host's historic pub, here is Robin hawking the latest racing special (yet still referred to as a "page"). To such pranks as these we are already accustomed. As Pistol aptly remarks, "Young ravens must have food." We are also accustomed to the monkey-tricks played by Mr. Asche with scissors and blue pencil, which ruthlessly upset Shakespeare's expert construction and make hay of his dramatic intentions.

What we are not accustomed to are the liberties taken, additionally to the blue pencil, with the black. As soon as the curtain rises, we hear Pistol reciting "Half a league, half a league, half a league onward!" Then a small boy comes on and shouts "Get your 'air cut!" Next Parson Hugh, arriving on a push-bike with trouser-clips, informs us that "Seven *thousand* pounds and possibilities is good gifts." A moment later Slender (with monocle) is recalling that Mister Page's fallow greyhound was "outrun at *Wembley*". Soon after which we hear Falstaff crying "Taxi! taxi!" And so it goes on.

Sometimes I found it hard to decide whether the changes in the text were according to plan, or whether the actors had forgotten their lines, or whether they just didn't think it necessary in the circumstances to learn them. But manifestly it was not forgetfulness that made Falstaff refer to young men who "smell like Piccadilly at closing-time" (instead of "Bucklersbury in simple time"). Manifestly it was not forgetfulness that made him protest to Mister Ford, "You might as well say I like to walk by Billingsgate, which is as hateful to me as a gas-sewer" (instead of the Counter-gate and a lime-kiln). And manifestly it was due to no lapse of memory that references were introduced to Shaw and Tennyson, that a "plain kerchief" became a "plain bonnet", that "gentlemen with their coaches" became "gentlemen with their carriages", and that when Mrs. Ford said, "My maid's aunt the fat woman of Brentford, has a gown above", Mr. Asche as Falstaff cut in with "I want a gown below."

To itemize all the tomfoolery that goes on in this lamentable production is happily unnecessary. It may, however, be observed that in order to give Shakespeare his chance at last, the convention of the soliloquy is overthrown; whenever Falstaff or Master Ford has something to say *solus*, what the blue pencil has permitted to survive is spoken strictly in the presence of a second party, who is required at intervals to nod, shrug shoulders, and generally display interest. This is supposed to make the situation more natural but actually makes it less so. The soliloquy was a convention employed to let audiences know the thoughts characters, for one reason or another, kept to themselves. With anybody else present, these thoughts would not have been uttered. A desperate attempt is also made to secure good "curtains". Thus, at the close of one scene, there is a piece of pantomime in the course of which Falstaff is brought the latest edition of an evening paper. He opens it, reads it, casts it away in disgust. He then proceeds to remove an Oxford favour which he has been wearing in his buttonhole and replaces it with a Cambridge favour, which he produces from his trouser-pocket. And down the curtain comes.

Enough of details. What is important is the generality that, while plenty of liberties have been taken with the text, these liberties are not drastic enough to make it harmonize with the modern costumes. Ann Page may ride pillion behind Fenton on his motor-bike, but the modern atmosphere is completely dissipated when we get a fat gentleman in a frock coat terrified out of his life in a forest at night-time because he believes in the presence of malevolent fairies. If this play, presented in this way, had been written last week by a living author, it would unquestionably be regarded as the work of a lunatic.

The issue is clear. Either this modern costume business must be completely abandoned or the plays must be *completely* rewritten. It is bootless to make Shakespeare's characters say "Yuss!" and "Mister Paige" and "Go on, hop it!" if you still retain such exclamations as "La!" and "Well-a-day!" and "Out upon you!" The task confronting the modern costume apologists is to bring out a new edition of the Works of Shakespeare, in which the words of Shakespeare and the plots of Shakespeare are treated as just so much antiquated rubbish. But what will be fatal to their cause will be to remove the name of Shakespeare himself; for nobody would ever go to see these shows if they were not supposed to have something to do with him.

And so, although it is the apologists for modern costume who launch the most vigorous attacks against what is called Bardolatry (attacks not without justification), it is these same apologists who in fact trade more than anyone else on the name of the poet. Not that we need worry seriously. Their cause is lost. They have routed themselves. We shall soon be able to look back on all this as just an entertaining little spree that provided a lively topic for conversation in the later nineteen-twenties.

STRATFORD-ON-AVON
(1935)

There would seem to be a tradition that, just as one should be kind to animals, so one should be kind to festivals. Perhaps one should be kind to everything; but why festivals in particular? Why more lenient to Shakespeare in Stratford-on-Avon than to Shakespeare in Shaftesbury Avenue?

After all, it's a tough proposition to make Shakespeare pay in Shaftesbury Avenue. Whereas Stratford—well, being Shakespeare's birthplace, isn't it the one spot on the map where you can produce Shakespeare as badly, or even as well, as you like and be sure of making a good profit? Much luck in Stratford.

A new Festival Season opened there last week under a new director —Mr. Iden Payne. Expectation had been whetted by Mr. Payne's profession of faith in Mr. William Poel, who championed Elizabethan methods of production for Elizabethan plays. Was Mr. Payne going to provide at last a special reason for going to see Shakespeare's plays in Stratford rather than anywhere else?

Well, he didn't in *Antony and Cleopatra*. And he didn't in *As You Like It*. These two productions say next to nothing that is really new— or really old. The company is mediocre, the acting uninformed by any original or individual force. The décor is picture-book décor; the sort of realistic coloured-platery to be found in children's gift books issued round about Christmas 1912.

These pretty pictures are presented with ingenious rapidity. Mr. Payne realizes the importance of speed. The only interval is the interval. That is a distinct merit. But in the beginning there was the word. Out of the words emerge the character and the drama. Concentrate on the words and take a chance, if you must, on everything else.

In M. Komisarjevsky's production of *The Merry Wives* the words seemed hardly to count at all. It should have been re-christened *The Good-humoured Ladies of Windsor*, for here was essentially a ballet—

The characters jigged in delicious, period-annihilating costumes. Ann Page waltzed to Strauss. Ford's soliloquies, punctuated by orchestral chords, became recitative. It was entrancing, modern, alive. But the animal brought to life wasn't Shakespeare, nor would it have been one of his pets.

One day someone will buy a field in Stratford. In this field he will construct an Elizabethan playhouse. In this playhouse, with no support and probably much opposition from local authorities, he will run a season (followed by another season) of Shakespearean Shakespeare. What a shock! Then Shakespeare in Stratford will stand for something individual. Then he will again breathe his native air. Then poor old new Memorial Theatre! Speed the day.

MEASURE FOR MEASURE

"HEAVENLY COMFORTS"
(1925)

THE production of *Measure for Measure* at the Old Vic is chiefly remarkable for the acting of Mr. Baliol Holloway as Angelo. With Miss Edith Evans in the small part of Mariana, Mr. Holloway takes all the honours, presenting a beautifully composed picture of an extremely difficult character—extremely difficult because, for the purpose of a happy ending, it is necessary to suggest that Angelo is not such a bad sort, even though he demands that Isabella shall yield her virginity to him as the price of her brother, Claudio's, reprieve, and then secretly orders that Claudio shall be put to death all the same.

The fact that Claudio is saved behind Angelo's back, and that Mariana takes Isabella's place in Angelo's bedchamber, is no excuse for Angelo. His conduct was pretty low. But I prefer him infinitely to the Duke Vincentio of Vienna, who seems to have had a passion for play-acting, and ought to have been a stage producer. Not for one moment does Shakespeare suggest that the duke's behaviour is open to criticism. That is why I am up in arms against him. Resigning the reins of government for a time, he disguises himself, you may remember, as a friar in order to watch the subsequent course of events. He observes all the scheming and intrigue that take place in his supposed absence. He has only to come out of his cowl to bring everyone to justice. But such is his passion for theatricals that nothing less than a great discovery scene will satisfy him, in the contriving of which, he deliberately inflicts on innocent people agonies that would surely soften the heart of the most sadistic sportsman.

Mark, first, how this duke behaves towards Isabella, whom he professes to love. Mariana having spent the night with Angelo, Isabella comes to the duke-friar to ask whether Claudio's reprieve has yet arrived. Claudio, as I said, has been saved behind Angelo's a brilliant piece of fantastication, imaginative, rhythmic, irresistible. back, but the duke-friar, because he must have his great discovery scene, flatly tells Isabella that Claudio has been executed, murmuring to himself the specious excuse that he :

> will keep her ignorant of her good,
> To make her heavenly comforts of despair
> When it is least expected.

Imagine, pray, marrying the sort of silly sensationalist who will go to the length of saying, "Your brother's dead—no he isn't!" for the pleasure of observing, as he explains, your relief! Isabella is, of course, distracted, the duke leaving her for a whole night in ignorance of the true state of affairs. On the day following he returns to the city in his own person as duke, and Isabella, according to advice given to her by him in the friar's habit, prostrates herself before him, demanding justice against Angelo. The duke then pretends to think that she is mad. He orders her to be put in prison. She is borne off, distracted. Mariana then makes her petition. The duke dismisses it. He tells Angelo to punish Isabella and Mariana to the top of his bent. And all in order that he may enter again, disguised as the monk, and at the most dramatic moment reveal the monk and the duke as one, produce the live Claudio like a conjuror producing a live rabbit out of a hat, and inform Isabella that she may now have the pleasure of marrying him, all of which might have been done twenty-four hours before, when he had all the proofs he needed, and all that was lacking was a stage crowd, with limelight.

The truth of the matter is, probably, that Shakespeare has really identified himself with the duke too closely. We may glimpse this identification in the fact that Isabella is not allowed to give herself to Angelo to save her brother, as she does in the original from which Shakespeare made this play, suggesting that Shakespeare wanted Isabella all to himself. We may glimpse it again in the fact that all the noblest sentiments spoken by men in this play are put into the mouth of the duke. And we may glimpse it once more in this transference to the duke of Shakespeare's own love of stage-management—which is all very well in the theatre, but far from well in real life. This does not, of course, mean that Shakespeare, in real life, went about preparing sensations for his friends, and making them suffer for his own enjoyment. It does mean that he was sensationally inclined. If you cannot, as you sit in the audience, pretend that you are the duke, you will find it difficult to enjoy the last act of *Measure for Measure*, because neither the surprises that are sprung on the other characters nor their reactions to them are surprises to you. The only pleasure obtainable is the pleasure (which to most of us is rather tedious) of seeing things turn out exactly as you meant them to.

ISABELLA'S VIRTUE
(1925)

Mr. Sean O'Casey's Irish play, *Juno and the Paycock*, was presented
for the first time at the Royalty Theatre on Monday night, but I did
not see it until Tuesday, for on Monday night I went, rather rashly,
to admire Miss Edith Evans as Isabella in *Measure for Measure* at the
Old Vic. Rather rashly, I say, because when I reached the Old Vic
I found that Miss Evans was not playing Isabella but Mariana—
Mariana of the moated grange, who has that one beautiful line, "I
have sat here all day." Mr. Holloway as Angelo was magnificent, and
Miss Evans as Mariana was good, but she was too large physically
for the part—I am not prepared to back my feeling that Isabella should
be taller than Mariana with reasons since, if we are to be reasonable,
we must, taking into account Angelo's mistake in the dark, assume
something of an equality in height and girth. But it is not because of
this that anybody who sees little Miss Carter as Isabella standing beside
large Miss Evans as Mariana must receive something of a shock.

Perhaps Isabella, with her precious preservation of purity at all costs,
needs to be generously proportioned if she is to be saved from the
suspicion of spiritual miserliness. Had she consented to give herself
to Angelo to save her brother's life, then it might be more easily
possible to regard her as a heroine. But this more-than-our-brother-is-
our-chastity attitude seems to me rather nauseating, and even Isabella,
I notice, is driven to rationalize about it, trying to slip in an unselfish
motive by declaring that "I had rather my brother die by the Law,
than my son should be unlawfully born."

Shakespeare's attitude towards women and sex always seems to
me rather priggish, and nowhere more so than in this play. Purifying
heroines was one of his incorrigible bad habits. Perhaps he stood himself in too intimate a relationship with them to allow anybody with
whom he could not identify himself to touch them. Just as he purified
Portia in *The Merchant of Venice*, so he purified Isabella in *Measure
for Measure*. Turn to the source from which this comedy is taken and
you will find that the original Isabella does give herself to Angelo
to save her brother's life. It was Shakespeare who, with his passionately jealous nature, refused to let her perform this act of self-sacrifice
and who, realizing that he was a bit of a hound for it, tried to excuse
the new attitude by putting Isabella into a convent, as who should say,
nuns will be nuns, or novitiates novitiates. Of course, all the commentators, with the professed morals of schoolmasters, praise the
poet for making heroism safe for the Upper Fourth. "Shakespeare
improves on the original plot by saving the virtue of the sister without
altering the situation." But is a situation anything apart from the
attitude towards it of those whom it involves? It seems to me that

Shakespeare changes the situation completely, taking all the heart out of it for the sake of what he deems to be the soul.

THE COMEDY OF ERRORS

ELIZABETHAN ERRORS
(1922)

THE pace was particularly exhilarating in Mr. Robert Atkins's revival of *The Comedy of Errors*, which was played straight through without an interval in Elizabethan costumes. These Elizabethan costumes gave the performance a pleasant, familiar air and were infinitely preferable to the "accurate" dressing that came in with Charles Kean's management. Yet it is possible that a compromise of classical superficies imposed on an Elizabethan basis might come nearer to the picture in the poet's eye. It is the picture in the poet's eye that matters; for whether its quality was good or bad, the producer who boldly sets out to improve on it will inevitably either mar the harmony of the whole composition or find himself faced with the necessity of making so many little readjustments, one leading to another, that by the time he has finished, there will be little of the original conception left. Mr. Atkins seriously constricted the geography of Ephesus by providing a delightful set, showing the house of Antipholus of Ephesus on one side and the Priory on the other. This set proving too elaborate to be speedily moved, we found the Dromios executing their errands on the very spot from which they were dispatched.

A similar trouble commonly occurs in productions of *A Midsummer Night's Dream*. The action in the wood takes place all over the wood. Up and down, up and down, Robin Goodfellow leads the lovers up and down. If there is no set scenery, there is no limitation to the ramblings and roamings of Helena, Hermia, Lysander and Demetrius. But almost invariably there is one set scene, charmingly foliaged, to which the characters must always return when anything important is about to happen to them, so that the magic of the wood appears to be confined to a few square yards of it. The play loses its freedom and spaciousness, and all for the sake of a pretty picture.

BLACK BUSINESS
(1924)

Mr. Henry Baynton's productions of Shakespeare's plays are among the most unsatisfactory now being offered to the public. The performances he gave of *The Comedy of Errors* at the Savoy Theatre recently were no better than those presented by him at the same theatre a year ago. It is true that the play was acted straight through without a break, but as the play was so heavily cut that it only took just over an hour to perform, the absence of a break in continuity was hardly remarkable. The name of the author of *The Bells*, which followed *The Comedy of Errors*, was omitted from the programme. Mr. Baynton might mercifully have maintained a consistent policy by omitting also the name of William Shakespeare. Having, however, cut the first two lines, he was consistent enough in that respect, scene after scene being shortened and speech after speech scored out, the general impression conveyed being a desire to get through the whole thing as quickly as possible, that there might be no need to truncate *The Bells*.

The scenery and costumes being of the conventional classical Wardour Street order, the effect produced was, we believe, as far from Shakespeare's intention as would be the effect of a performance of *The Merry Wives of Windsor* with Falstaff in a toga and scenery of the temple-cum-forum kind. For *The Comedy of Errors* is no less Elizabethan in atmosphere than *The Merry Wives*, and if ever there were two Elizabethan clowns, those two were the twin Dromios. Mr. Baynton—partly, it may be, in the hope of achieving historical accuracy, and partly, no doubt, to make their resemblance more credible— blacked the faces of his Dromios. Had Shakespeare meant this, he would hardly have allowed it to pass without comment. It might, also, have been obvious to Mr. Baynton, had he given the matter more than a moment's thought, that a Syracusan Dromio who had been black from birth would hardly talk about being pinched "black and blue".

Again and again the comic situations were ruined by the breakneck speed of the performance. The actors should, it is true, look lively in this play, but they should not behave like a retreating army on the run. Matters were made still worse by the absence of any intelligent reference to Shakespeare's intentions as a theatrical craftsman. It must be clear to anybody familiar with the construction of the Elizabethan stage that in the scene where the Ephesian Antipholus and the Dromio are shut out of their house, the Syracusan Dromio and Luce and Adriana appeared on the balcony above and spoke their lines in full view of the audience. The humour of the situation depends largely on the ability of the audience to see the facial expressions and observe the reactions of those "within". When Mr. Atkins produced this play the attackers and attacked were alike visible and the scene proved one of the most amusing. But in Mr. Baynton's production the Syracusan Dromio and Luce and Adriana were not only invisible but, their voices being muffled in the wings, were often inaudible as well. Having become accustomed in the theatre at least either to see what we cannot hear or to hear what we cannot see, we confess this to have been an experience for which we were totally unprepared.

It is, perhaps, worth recording that only one of the critics writing for the public Press commented on the fact that little more than half the text was spoken. Nearly all the criticisms were favourable, and the reception by the audience was, at the first performance, enthusiastic.

MUCH ADO ABOUT NOTHING

MUCH ABOUT MEMORY
(1925)

THERE are times when it seems to me that the most wonderful thing about actors and actresses is not the way in which they subdue themselves to the quality of alien personalities; not the way in which they body forth so convincingly the hypothetical passions of this hero or that: but the way in which they so remarkably manage to remember their parts.

We take their memories for granted, as we take for granted most of the wonderful things in the world. When we are abruptly confronted, in an omnibus or in an underground train, with the spectacle of a fellow-passenger, a little better-dressed than we are, straining over a book, then casting eyes to Heaven and moving lips in silent prayer, then back to the book, then eyes aloft once more, we are quite surprised to remember that the first duty of a stage player is not to forget. However magnificent Forbes-Robertson's performance of Hamlet, to me at this moment the most astonishing thing about it appears to be that the actor should have been capable of learning the part. I cannot take it for granted. And still less can I take for granted the miracle that a mere child should be capable, as all mere children are, of learning the alphabet: which is surely one of the most difficult things in the world.

Think, for a moment, what a feat of memorization that learning of the alphabet represents: twenty-six unmeaning, unrelated sounds, placed in an arbitrary nonsensical order! After all, in the case of Hamlet, there is perceptible cause and effect. Given the first word, the rest may be said to follow, save for an occasional "pajok". You have your reason to assist your memory. But the alphabet! Why on earth should H follow G and be followed in turn by I? Why should I be so far removed from Y? And how did P get between O and Q? Well, there may be half a dozen adults in the world who can tell you, but not a single child. Try yourself memorizing twenty-six strange, unmeaning, unrelated sounds, and see what sweat it costs you. Mark, in the memorization, what queer associations you are compelled to summon to your assistance. Remember how much wider is the area of association from which one can draw in maturity than in childhood. And then pay due homage to the prodigy that once you were!

You may say that it is foolish to marvel at what everybody can do, but these common accomplishments are, surely, the most marvellous of all. Paderewski—Galli-Curci—Cinquevalli—they have won the wonder of the world rather, I think, by surprise than by anything else. In what trifles must they be held to excel the rest of us when it is considered that we can actually procreate and bear children, and walk up and down stairs! If you were the only person capable of walking up and down stairs, how you would pack the variety theatres, what columns the journalists would reel off in your praise! And so I now feel inclined to reel off a column or so in praise of stage players in general, and of stage players at the Old Vic in particular, for the feat they accomplish in remembering their lines—and devil take the acting!

This inclination is perversely prompted by the fact that at the Old Vic on Monday night, when Shakespeare's *Much Ado About Nothing* was revived, many of the players actually forgot their words—sometimes, as it happened, most appositely. Benedick's "Thou hast frighted the word out of his right sense" came very aptly after one over-realistically long pause, and was almost as much relished by the audience as Claudio's "How still the evening is"—spoken while the wind played havoc with a loose ventilator up in the roof. There were times when the performance came practically to a dead stop. "Really!" whispered my neighbours, "Disgraceful! scandalous! outrageous!"

While all the time I couldn't help thinking how extraordinarily clever it was of the actors to remember as much as they did. True, there were embarrassing moments. One player, having lost his words, lost his presence of mind into the bargain, so that I thought he would be running off the stage in a minute, rending the roof with shrieks of agony. But again I marvelled not that actors should lose their wits, but that they should be able so to control themselves that they do not run off the stage when they are overtaken by fright. To see this actor standing his ground like Casabianca, unable to help yet refusing to leave his post while the flames seared him on all sides, was to see such stuff as V.C.s are made of. And I pictured to myself what might happen if all those present in the theatre were suddenly to lose their self-control, if the poor actor were to dash from the stage, and if all the other actors, perceiving their entertainment to be ruined, were to catch the infection of fright and take to their heels, helter-skeltering down the Waterloo Road in full rig, with the frenzied audience in full cry after them, opera-glasses hurtling through the air, umbrellas falling athwart the shoulders of the Paduan grandees, policemen blowing whistles, Mr. Robert Atkins leaping into the Thames, with nobody left in the Old Vic but Miss Lilian Baylis, kneeling in fervent prayer before the picture of Miss Emma Cons.

It is, of course, the first duty of an actor to remember his words, and it was interesting to note at the Old Vic how Mr. Ion Swinley, who was not quite as sure of himself as he might have been, covered up his lapses by adopting a kind of hesitating manner all through, pausing where he would not ordinarily pause even though he might know his next words perfectly well, and pacing the stage during his monologues, so that we might always have at least the motion of his body to watch. And it was interesting to note how well the play came through the epidemic of aphasia, for despite the impossibility of sympathizing with Claudio or of mustering up the faintest interest in his mechanical amour with Hero, the tomboy dialogue and the Shavian cat-and-dog love-making between Beatrice and Benedick are capital fun. Sometimes I think that Mr. Shaw himself would, indeed, be the ideal Benedick, for his attitude towards love, as mirrored in *Arms and the Man* and *Pygmalion* and other plays—oh, what a plague is love!—is by no means un-Benedictine: and is not Benedick voicing Shavian policy when he cries that "it is most expedient for the wise to be the trumpet of his own virtues, as I am to myself"? Mr. Swinley seemed to me rather heavy in the part. I preferred Miss Marie Ney's spirited, sporting, likeable Beatrice which, if it was a little too thin in texture and a little too rapid in utterance, was really first-rate in the difficult "Kill Claudio" scene. And Mr. George Hayes's Dogberry (ably assisted by Mr. Andrew Leigh's flibbering Verges) was a rich monumental ass.

Is *Much Ado* a bad play? No, a thousand times, for, whatever its faults, it is full of entertainment, and every minute there is a searching line that nobody but Shakespeare could have written, and those night watchmen are superb. The best things that they say do not bear quotation, but they represent an aspect of England that only an Englishman can truly understand. You have to see the whole of the play, and you have to have lived in England for twenty or thirty years, to understand the full richness of Seacoal's "Let us go sit here upon the church bench till two, and then all to bed". So, once more, to the Old Vic. There's not a theatre to equal it.

ADO AT THE NEW
(1926)

There never was a playwright so astonishing as Shakespeare. The more you read his plays, the more astonishing they become. It is not only that you go on and on discovering new marvels of wit and beauty and psychological insight which, fool that you were, you never marked before. It is also—well, take *Much Ado About Nothing* and ask yourself whether it is not astonishing that an experienced and skilful playwright like Shakespeare should, deliberately or accidentally, leave out of a comedy what nine hundred and ninety-nine out of a thousand experienced and skilful playwrights would, with good reason, regard as the most vital and not-to-be-neglected scene in the whole piece. I refer to the unwritten scene in which Don John's plot is carried into execution—the scene in which the Prince and Claudio, screened by night, behold Borachio wooing Margaret under the name of Hero beneath Hero's chamber window. It is on this scene that the plot of the play hinges. We may be tolerably sure that the popular audience to which Shakespeare appealed expected it and would have relished it. We may be quite sure that Shakespeare could have written it on his head. Why, then, did he prefer to leave it out? I can only conjecture that he saw three recapitulations looming ahead—first, the recapitulation of the story by Borachio to Conrad, which was unavoidable, since the Watchmen must overhear it; second, the recapitulation of the story by the Prince and Claudio to those assembled at the altar, which was unavoidable, since they must give some explanation of their brutal conduct; third, the recapitulation of the story in the last act, when the whole matter had to be cleared up. But even so, the omission remains remarkable, and more is lost by it than appears on the surface. The difficulty of feeling anything but the utmost repugnance for Claudio is one of the least satisfactory features of the play; but there can be no doubt that this difficulty would be to some extent modified if we actually beheld Claudio's agony in the bushes.

Claudio is one of the weak spots of the play. Since he gets Hero in the end, it is only right that we should like him. But how can we reconcile ourselves to a young man who, not having the pluck to woo his girl himself, gets a friend to do it for him and then promptly suspects that friend of playing false; who, having been satisfied on this point, proceeds to suspect his girl of playing false with someone else; and who then, biding his time, postpones denouncing her until the marriage-service before all the wedding-guests, for all the world as though he had been feed by a Yankee news editor. I can never quite believe my ears when I hear Claudio call Hero a "rotten orange".

Claudio and Hero, however, do not interest us much. Beatrice and Benedick are the engrossing characters. They are inevitably thought of first whenever *Much Ado* is mentioned. Yet they have so little to do with the story that—here is another surprise—they could quite easily be left out of it altogether. True, Beatrice is Hero's cousin, but consanguinity is not drama. True, Beatrice had slept with Hero every night for twelve months before the night of the Borachio episode, but the fact that on that last night, for reasons unstated and hard to guess, they did not sleep together, only accentuates the superfluousness of Beatrice. True, again, after the dust-up in the church, Beatrice extracts from Benedick a promise to kill Claudio, which makes it look for a moment as though they may justify their part in the play's construction after all. But nothing comes of it. Benedick does not kill Claudio. Nor does his intention to do so, if intention it is, in any way influence the plot of this formal, spirited and courtly comedy.

Nevertheless, to enjoy this play, one must concentrate on Beatrice and Benedick, for they are the high comic relief. Miss Madge Titheradge's Beatrice at the New is a mettlesome piece of work. Most Beatrices flounce all over the stage. Miss Titheradge stands her ground refreshingly, delivering every word with point. Innumerable are the

c

actresses we have seen romping through this part on personality, trying to bolster Beatrice up with charm as producers try to bolster Shakespeare up with scenery. Not so Miss Titheradge. She has a good eye—she can see a church by daylight. Every moment of her performance is worth hearing as well as watching, every verbal thrust, every verbal parry, is executed like a duellist of the first class. Only at one point does she fall from grace—where she announces that when she was born, a star danced. At this moment Miss Titheradge becomes as overwhelmingly sentimental over herself as an actress licking her lips over a Barrie titbit. But it is her only lapse. For the rest of the evening she is a perfect thoroughbred.

Miss Titheradge apart, this is a tame production, emasculated by an ineffective gentility that smacks of the 'nineties. There is nothing robustious about it—and there should, I think, be an undercurrent of robustiousness in the presentation of all Elizabethan plays. The settings suggest the taste of a representative Royal Academician. And Mr. Ainley's own performance as Benedick lacks colour, asks too much for sympathy, and lies becalmed on placid waters, waiting for a puff of wind. His delivery of Benedick's lines is much too naturalistic, takes itself too easily, dissipates the flavour of the best words into thin air, so that the delicious "I will be horribly in love with her" speech goes almost for nothing, Mr. Ainley running through the lines like an actor at an early rehearsal, before he has worked up his points. To bring out the best that is in him—and we all know how good that best can be—Mr. Ainley needs, I suspect, a producer who is a bit of a martinet.

But though, taken as a whole, this production has not one quarter of the life of the production at the Old Vic, those who go to the New with their ears will hear wonderful words. "Alas poor hurt fowl, now will he creep into sedges". When Shakespeare's characters drop marvellous casual remarks like this, how hard it is to pay attention to the words of the next speaker!

MUCH ADISNEY
(1934)

The Old Vic is a responsible theatre with a great trust. It is a theatre in which tradition should be respected. It is a theatre in which experiment should not be discouraged. But the experiment should be intelligent, not capricious. It is hard to bear with patience such fooling with Shakespeare as we were given last week in *Much Ado About Nothing*. We have enough to put up with in the world without this.

The gentlemen in this production of *Much Ado* are dressed in Elizabethan costume. That sounds like a good foundation. But it is no foundation at all, for the ladies are dressed like ladies in late eighteenth-century portraits by Gainsborough, and Hero is seen

preparing for her nuptials while she discusses the details of an Elizabethan costume in a boudoir that might have been decorated for
Lady Teazle. Mr. Cass, the producer, says he did this because the
periods chosen seemed to him "the most attractive and suitable for
each sex"—but whether most suitable in this play or all plays, and why
in any case, he does not explain. This, however, is not his only
defence.

"These mixed costumes", says Mr. Cass, "remove the play from
any definite time and place and make it what it really is—a masque."
If Mr. Cass thinks that *Much Ado* is "really a masque", he is mistaken
about masques and mistaken about *Much Ado*. If he thinks that even
in masques there is necessarily no definite time or place, he is again
in error. And why seek to remove from any definite place a piece in
which the opening line runs: "I learn in this letter that Don Peter of
Arragon comes this night to Messina"? Why treat Don John and Co.
like Peter Pan Pirates unless *Much Ado* is "really a play for tots"?
Why dress the Friar like a High Priest of the Greek Church unless
Much Ado is "really a play for loonies"?

As for the treatment of Dogberry and his Watchmen—I will
limit myself to recording the fact that they enter in front of a backcloth
of roofs and chimneypots with cats dangling watches and a general
air of Mickey Mousery that savours of the sort of comic picture post-
card one would blush to receive even from one's old nurse; after which
we are regaled with comic business of the type one associates with
such performers as the Marx Brothers. Mr. Maurice Evans as Benedick
again acquits himself creditably, but I thought Miss Mary Newcombe's
Beatrice something too strenuously joyous.

JOIN THE RING
(1937)

My next recommendation is that you should immediately join the
Bankside Players Society, 32, Shaftesbury Avenue, W.1. You will
then be able to see Shakespeare most intelligently produced by Mr.
Robert Atkins at the Blackfriars Ring as it was in Shakespeare's own
theatre. *Much Ado About Nothing*, his second venture, knocks every
other production of *Much Ado* into a cocked hat. The easy flow, the
intimate relationship between actors and audience, the vivid arena
that vitalizes the actors instead of imposing on them the necessity
of pumping themselves out of a mortifying picture frame—these
things you will find revelations.

The performance of Mr. Jack Hawkins as Benedick is so lively,
humorous and assured that the Old Vic might do well to tackle him.
A remarkable thing happened when, quite unexpectedly, an unknown
actor named John Abbott walked on to the stage as the Friar, one of
Shakespeare's dullest parts, and, by speaking Shakespeare better than
I have heard any actor speak Shakespeare for years, made immediate

sense of every word he said without losing one jot or tittle of the flavour or the rhythm. The difference was so marked that the audience burst into applause on his exit. I don't know where Mr. John Abbott comes from, but clearly no production of Shakespeare should be without him.

LOVE'S LABOUR'S LOST

AN UNDERRATED COMEDY
(1918)

TO the Vic Shakespeare Company for its production of *Love's Labour's Lost* we offer our heartiest congratulations. *Love's Labour's Lost* is probably the least acted of all Shakespeare's comedies. It is undoubtedly the most underrated. To excuse it as a first attempt is like making apologies for April on the ground that it is only a first attempt at August. Its youth is irresistible. Shakespeare, as a young man, came from the depth and freedom of the woods of Warwickshire to the shallowness and constraint of the fashionable life of London. The euphuism and conceit of the city intellectuals roused him instantly to arms. A dramatic comparison was inevitable, and with unerring discernment he hit on the most effective means of "showing up" artificiality. The contrivance had all the simplicity of genius. He simply took a few pedants and set them spouting Latin in the meadows. He took a Spanish Italianate courtier and made him disgorge the scraps he had stolen from the great feast of languages. And then he took a bird and let it sing. The competitors are, in turn, ridiculous and magical. The result is a most ridiculous and magical comedy. And if lovers of entertainment want more than this, they are indeed hard to please.

The performance of this satire by the Old Vic company is the best they have given this season. The two exquisite songs are both delightfully sung, and the concluding revels are as gay as a daisy. The acting is unusually good—especially the Don Adriano de Armado of Mr. John Leslie, a most fantastical and absurd creation. Mr. George Barran is good as the sesquipedalian Holofernes; Mr. Orlando Barnett is Boyet to the life; and Mr. Ernest Milton, who gave us a very clever Benedick not long ago, plays his prototype, Berowne, along the same lines, and well. Of the ladies, Miss Gwen Richardson does best with Jaquenetta. But the whole performance is remarkably fresh—largely, no doubt, owing to the fact that *Love's Labour's Lost* is practically virgin soil to the present generation of actors, who are therefore compelled to explore it for themselves instead of following in the traditional track beaten out by predecessors. Everybody who can should go to the Old Vic this week, not only because they will then be able to say that they have really seen *Love's Labour's Lost*, but because they will be able to say that they have seen it really capably done.

SHAKESPEARE CALLS CUCKOO
(1925)

It might be rash to proclaim *Love's Labour's Lost* the best of all Shakespeare's comedies, but since it is the most grossly underrated, the Fellowship of Players deserves especial thanks for giving us a chance on Sunday night to appreciate its mischievous austerities. This mocking pastoral is a cuckoo-call to scholasticism: cuckoo to the fasting lovers of Ferdinand's Academe, "quaint votaries of science"; cuckoo to the sesquipedalian Spanish fantastico; cuckoo to the syntactical pedagogue who would construe a daffodil and dares to Latinize in the long grass under the sun—with young Shakespeare holding his haunches on the other side of the hedge. This is one of the few plays, perhaps the only play, in which Shakespeare had, quite definitely and consciously, "something to say":

> Small have continual plodders ever won,
> Save base authority from others' books.
> These earthly godfathers of heaven's lights,
> That give a name to every fixed star,
> Have no more profit of their shining nights,
> Than those that walk and wot not what they are.
> Too much to know, is to know naught but fame:
> And every godfather can give a name.

This, then, is a comedy of name-giving godfathers in which the characters "climb o'er the house to unlock the little gate." Shakespeare was well qualified to tilt at the ambassadors of affectation since he himself was so astonishingly free—in his plays, at all events—from affectation of any kind. Nor was he envious of the thing he pilloried —a malady most incident to satirists. Nor, again, was his attack tainted by the truculent, sadistic, I'll-give-'em-what-for-ism of Jonson who, when the lords and ladies ridicule the Braggart's ridiculous appearance as Hector, would never have permitted the poor fellow such an exquisite retort as "The sweet war-man is dead and rotten, sweet chucks, beat not the bones of the buried: when he breathed he was a man." It is interesting to note that in this, probably Shakespeare's earliest comedy, the word "sweet" occurs nearly twice as often as in any other play: sixty-one times in all. If *Love's Labour's Lost* is satirical, it is never cynical. There is the sap of youth in every line.

On the scenery and most of the performances in the Fellowship production at the Strand Theatre it will be kinder not to dwell. Enough that Miss Jane Bacon made a very gracious, well-poised Princess, and that Mr. Hay Petrie's Costard was a real salt-mine, for which he deserves "better than remuneration".

CADENCE VERSUS WORDS
(1932)

Shakespeare's first play has been produced at the Westminster Theatre. For so *Love's Labour's Lost* is expertly believed to be. Here, say the critics, is the work of a very young man. Yet Shakespeare was at least twenty-eight years old when he wrote it. By the time Noel Coward was twenty-eight he had written not one but fifteen plays and revues. And if anything is to be deduced from that, well, I'll leave it to you.

Love's Labour's Lost is one of the most delicious of all Shakespeare's comedies. It is a light-hearted satire on pedantry and bookishness. A king and his courtiers vow celibacy at the shrine of learning. A princess and her ladies upset their apple-cart with a glance. A peda-gogue spouts Latin under a blue sky. A cuckoo calls and Latin becomes a laughing-stock. The parade of curious-knotted academics culminates in the loveliest nature lyric in the English language. No comedy, not even *Twelfth Night*, ever had a more exquisite ending than this one.

At the Westminster Mr. Tyrone Guthrie, one of our astutest producers, has presented *Love's Labour's Lost* as an Elizabethan masque. Elizabethan it is. Masque it is not. His setting, with its elegant little pavilions and elegant little terrace, is entrancing. But trances are transient. When we come out of this one, we realize that Mr. Guthrie's treatment postulates more songs and dances than the play contains. It insists on rhythm at the expense of words.

Words, words, words. These, where a Shakespearean producer is concerned, should be his first, second, and third consideration. Let him think of Shakespeare dipping his quill. Let him think of Shake-speare choosing one epithet rather than another. Let him extract the essential salt and sweetness from the words Shakespeare wrote. The matter against Mr. Guthrie is that he was taken with the manner. In going all out for an artificial lilting cadence, he has too often obliterated the sense. I had to strain my ears, even though I have read the play twenty times.

Nevertheless, this production is a gallant venture. The accessories of scenery and costume are in unexceptionable taste. And the last ten minutes of the piece, when it turns from gay to grave, are overwhelmingly lovely. Of the performances, Mr. Evan John's Holofernes has most fibre. Mr. Richard Goolden's Costard is intermittently amusing, but he throws away too many of his sentences. The ladies and gentlemen of the Court are all pretty to see. The whole thing is, in fact, most pretty and pathetical.

A MIDSUMMER NIGHT'S DREAM

MR. DEAN'S MENDELSSOHN SEASON
(1925)

I

IN writing of the production of *A Midsummer Night's Dream* at the
Theatre Royal, Drury Lane, I propose to leave for later consideration the acting; the décor; the mass-attack on fairyland, which Mr.
Basil Dean seeks to overwhelm by numbers; the many mechanical
contrivances with which he conducts his assaults on acorn-cups: and
to devote my first article to the music. I propose to do this because
the music is really the dominant feature of the production, the centre
from which all radiates, Mr. Dean, like many of his predecessors,
assuming that the first thing *A Midsummer Night's Dream* requires,
to bring it back to life, is an extra heavy dose of orchestra. The reason
for this assumption is, I suppose, that *A Midsummer Night's Dream*
is an intrinsically musical play. You have only to read Shakespeare's
words to realize the truth of this. But surely the more musical a play
is, the less it needs an orchestra? One might almost as well try setting
to music a Chopin Nocturne. Tunes, of course, there should be where
they are indicated in the text—a tune for the ousel cock, a tune for
the spotted snakes, a tune for the blessing of the bride-bed. But for
the rest, are not the melodies composed by Shakespeare as all-sufficing
as the pictures which he paints in words and which make the most
expensive scenery a vulgar, pretentious mockery?

When, before the production of the *Dream* at the Lane, it was
rumoured (incorrectly) that Mr. Herman Finck was composing music
additional to that already provided by Mendelssohn, one critic,
greatly perturbed, declared that, with all due respect to Mr. Finck,
the music of Mendelssohn should be regarded as sacrosanct. And in
the eyes of Mr. Dean it apparently is—far more sacrosanct, indeed,
than the music of Shakespeare. For, in order that we may not lose
a pretty commonplace bar of Mendelssohn, we are deprived of many
of Shakespeare's most exquisite lines. Because it would take up too
much time to give *all* Mendelssohn and *all* Shakespeare, and because
it is Mendelssohn's *Dream* that he is bent on producing rather than
Shakespeare's, Mr. Dean condemns us to sit through the Wedding
March while his prize blue pencil gets to work on "irrelevant"—
because so purely musical!—passages in the text. Having engaged
Miss Athene Seyler to play Hermia and Mr. Leon Quartermaine to
play Lysander, he bereaves them of their most musical duet. Having
engaged Miss Mary Clare to play Hippolyta, he takes away her one
clarion speech. And having engaged for the part of Titania Miss
Gwen Ffrangçon-Davies, an actress capable of speaking Shakespeare's

verse with a real sense of its harmony, he proceeds to deprive her of her loveliest speech, which I must give here in full, to redress the balance:

> "These are the forgeries of jealousy,
> And never since the middle summer's spring
> Met we on hill, in dale, forest, or mead,
> By paved fountain, or by rushy brook,
> Or in the beached margent of the sea,
> To dance our ringlets to the whistling wind,
> But with thy brawls thou hast disturb'd our sport.
> Therefore the winds, piping to us in vain,
> As in revenge, have suck'd up from the sea
> Contagious fogs: which falling in the land,
> Hath every pelting river made so proud,
> That they have overborne their continents.
> The ox hath therefore stretch'd his yoke in vain,
> The ploughman lost his sweat, and the green corn
> Hath rotted ere his youth attain'd a beard:
> The fold stands empty in the drowned field,
> And crows are fatted with the murrion flock,
> The nine men's morris is filled up with mud,
> And the quaint mazes in the wanton green,
> For lack of tread are undistinguishable.
> The human mortals want their winter cheer,
> No night is now with hymn or carol blest;
> Therefore the moon (the governess of floods)
> Pale in her anger, washes all the air;
> That rheumatic diseases do abound.
> And thorough this distemperature, we see
> The seasons alter; hoary-headed frosts
> Fall in the fresh lap of the crimson rose,
> And on old Hiems' chin and icy crown,
> An odorous chaplet of sweet summer buds
> Is as in mockery set. The Spring, the Summer,
> The childing Autumn, angry Winter change
> Their wonted liveries, and the mazed world,
> By their increase, now knows not which is which;
> And this same progeny of evils comes
> From our debate, from our dissension;
> We are their parents and original."

And this Mr. Dean sacrifices on the altar of Mendelssohn, because he feels that the play needs music and has not already got music good enough. Can it really be that Mr. Finck's orchestra playing the Wedding March is more worth listening to than Miss Ffrangçon-Davies speaking the above lines? If Mr. Dean thinks so, then may Heaven be merciful and send him a new pair of ears.

What calls for the attention of the producer before all else in *A Midsummer Night's Dream* is not the story, or the setting, or the music of Mendelssohn, but the music of the words. The more I think of the production at Drury Lane, the more it grows upon me that Mr. Dean, whom I have never met, must be stone deaf. For the part of Helena he engages Miss Edith Evans. He arouses our expectations by presenting her alone, in front of a curtain, to speak the long "How happy some o'er other some can be" soliloquy. And then, while she speaks it, he sets his stage-hands behind the curtain diabolically bump-bumping scenery about—because scenery, as well as instrumental music, is more important than Shakespeare!

Mr. Dean may know that it is the duty of the actors in this play to interpret Shakespeare's music faithfully and self-effacingly. But if he does, he has been too much occupied, I fancy, with his mechanicians—with making his fairies really fly on wires, so that they may seem like "real" fairies—to pay enough attention to this important point. Puck, in this respect, is a great sinner. He has lovely things to say, but so bent is Mr. Petrie on maintaining a consistent character, that you lose their beauty in his sustained vocal antics. It is possible for Puck to be too Puck-like. Of what avail are squeaks and jerks when he comes to that heavenly speech after the clowns have rolled home in glory and the bridal couples have retired to rest—when, stealing into the deserted chamber, he chants:

> "Now the hungry lion roars,
> And the wolf beholds the moon:
> Whilst the heavy ploughman snores,
> All with weary task foredone.
> Now the wasted brands do glow,
> Whilst the screech-owl, screeching loud,
> Puts the wretch that lies in woe,
> In remembrance of a shroud.
> Now it is the time of night,
> That the graves, all gaping wide,
> Every one lets forth his sprite,
> In the church-way paths to glide:
> And we fairies, that do run,
> By the triple Hecate's team,
> From the presence of the sun,
> Following darkness like a dream,
> Now are frolic; not a mouse
> Shall disturb this hallowed house.
> I am sent with broom before,
> To sweep the dust behind the door."

At this point the actor must not worry himself about Puck. He must concentrate on the mystery-music. When I returned home and read these words to myself, I realized how many wonderful words I had lost at Drury Lane. And these had not even been sung!

And what nonsense Mr. Dean endures for the sake of Mendelssohn! "I know a bank", says Oberon. And then, half-an-hour or an hour later, Titania, who must have a song at all costs, sings the words we have already heard spoken. She, too, knows a bank. Why not, to conclude, a grand chorus of fairies and mortals: "We all know a bank"? But there is no Mendelssohn for that. We must be respectful to Mendelssohn. Mendelssohn, who wrote his music for nineteenth-century productions! Mendelssohn, whose music, pretty and jolly undeniably, is no more Shakespearean than "Horsey, Keep Your Tail Up!" is Mendelssohnian! Mendelssohn, whose music is like the best art illustrations in two-guinea Christmas editions-de-luxe of the *Dream*, editions in which nobody ever thinks for a moment of reading the text! If we are to get *A Midsummer Night's Dream* in its full beauty, the first thing we have to do is to get rid of Mendelssohn's music. It is such stuff as concerts are made of. Or *Iolanthes*. But not dreams.

II

Having preferred the music of Mendelssohn to the music of Shakespeare, and having slashed Shakespeare's text in order that Mendelssohn's score may be preserved intact, Mr. Dean has certainly been consistent in providing his production of *A Midsummer Night's Dream* with a setting favourable to the intention of the nineteenth-century composer rather than to that of the sixteenth-century poet. Leaving aside the classical, wedding-marchy, Alma-Tadema palace of Theseus, in which the idea of Puck's besom seems almost as much out of place as would the idea of a vacuum cleaner, let us consider for a moment the heavy, many-planed, elaborately built-up forest: a forest designed for the accommodation of masses of fairies, because masses of fairies are clearly demanded by Mendelssohn's *chichey-chichey* fairy motive.

Shakespeare, being a practical playwright, visualized the resources of his stage and cut his cloth according to his measure. He saw that he must create the illusion of a forest full of fairies in words, and so effectively did he accomplish this purpose that, when Titania summons her sprites to attend on Bottom, there is nothing absurd in the First Folio stage direction, which reads: "*Enter Pease-blossome, Cobweb, Moth, Mustard-seede, and foure Fairies*": eight in all. Mendelssohn's music, however, calls for eight fairies a bar, and eight fairies a bar at Drury Lane it gets—fairies grown-up and small, who are dressed in costumes convenient for post-show engagements at Blanchard's Club or the Savoy, who play Old Harry with the rhythm of Shakespeare's play by punctuating it with ballets undreamed of in Shakespeare's stage philosophy (they actually open the last scene in the Palace of Theseus), who fly about the stage on wires (like amateur reciters who think it necessary to illustrate every other word with an action), and who, we may be sure, would have crept into acorn cups and engaged in aerial warfare with humble-bees before our eyes, had the resources of Drury Lane run to it.

For Mr. Dean's production is a Beerbohm Tree production, and his forest is Beerbohm Tree at his most arboreal. It overlooks the important fact that Shakespeare's loveliest lines were written through sheer necessity, and that to give them a production by which the necessity is removed, turns the play into a succession of disregarded superfluities and redundancies. We do not describe the things before our eyes to the companions by our sides. When we are in a moonlit forest with a friend, we exclaim "How lovely!" and it is enough. But if we return to a third person to whom we would communicate our experience, it is no longer enough to exclaim, "How lovely!" Then we must describe the picture that is not there. That is why Shakespeare's characters said such lovely things about nature, and that is why the utterance of these things in the presence of Mr. George Harris's scenery is about as sensible as it would be to stick up a placard on one of Mr. Harris's banks, announcing: "This is a bank."

There is another important point which must be urged against such scenery as we are given at Drury Lane. It limits the field of action. Shakespeare can no longer count himself a king of infinite space. In *A Midsummer Night's Dream*, as in many of the other plays, we are continually being transported to what editors describe as "Another part of the forest". Victorian producers tried up to a point to follow these instructions, which were true to Shakespeare's imagination, but since they employed pictorial scenery, the result was a desolating succession of waits, while the scene-shifters made the journey. Then came the outcry against waits. We have now reduced the waits by employing a single picture forest scene, and so conveying the impression—and this is in no way true to Shakespeare's imagination—that the action all takes place on one and the same spot. "Up and down, up and down, I will lead them up and down", chants Puck. The lovers stumble mazily through the tangle of the wood, now here, now there. Yet always—at Drury Lane—they are in the same place, cribbed, cabined, and confined by the same trees. And though Mr. Dean exclaim, "Ah, but what trees!" when I can't see the dream for the trees, I remain dissatisfied.

The truth of the matter is that production has gone to Mr. Dean's head and has so intoxicated him that, unable to see the stars, he embraces a lamp-post. The introduction of Puck by means of a trap-door may be great fun for the mechanically-minded, but Puck was no mole. And all the hydraulic contraptions of Drury Lane will never make him one.

And now, turning to the acting, and congratulating Mr. Dean on presenting the West End with a male Puck and a male Oberon, I must chronicle the failure of both these parts in interpretation. Mr. Petrie is a fine comedian but, having wound himself up, he ticked out Puck's lines, and was so intent on not running down that, while he was better than any female Puck, he lost the full flavour of the lovely words. As for the Drury Lane Oberon, it was a most unintelligent conception. Mr. Robert Harris played the part as though Oberon was subject to, rather than the creator of, the spell of the forest. He lolled and lay about the stage less like a Fairy King than like a spoilt boy on camp not doing the washing-up. The real Oberon, surely, was erect. He bent no knee. He had a backbone. He was no Prince Hal sporting with a Puck-Falstaff, but a King Harry, issuing commands.

Miss Ffrangçon-Davies's Titania was, on the other hand, delicious, in spite of her "Come-and-see-the-caves" cave: imperious, petulant, and pale as mist. The mechanics, too, were good without exception. Mr. Malleson's Snout, keen as mustard, stuffed with amusement at the idea of playing in a play, and on the verge of laughter listening to Pyramus and Thisbe as one is on the verge of a sneeze, will always remain in my mind as a superb piece of comic acting. Mr. Walter's Bottom, if a little subdued, was humorous and well-spoken and most yokelishly credible. Mr. Cellier's Quince, Mr. Nicholson's Starveling, Mr. Mollison's Flute, Mr. Clark's Snug were all admirable. Of the mortals, I liked best Miss Seyler's needle-minded Hermia, a beautiful performance, and Mr. Quartermaine's incisive Lysander. Miss Evans seemed to me to have tried to read too much into the part of Helena. I fancy that she is not content unless she can pluck the vitals out of a character. She must get to the very core of it: and Helena is without core. She is not far, indeed, from a nonentity.

A well-acted *Dream*, certainly: but a disappointing *Dream*—for good dreams are not begotten, as Mr. Dean would seem to think, of magnificent bedrooms, any more than good hunting is begotten of the singing of Tally-ho choruses. If only Mr. Dean had spared us his Tally-ho chorus, together with the prolonged sunrise which preceded it; if only he had spared us some of the ballets and the musical interludes; if only he had spared us Greek costumes for mechanics named most un-Greekly Bottom and Snout; if only he had spared us his scenery and his lighting and his flying effects and his blue pencil—then the hunting might have been very good indeed.

He has assembled a first-rate company of actors. Why not give them a chance?

PUCK AND SEX APPEAL
(1936)

To-day George Bernard Shaw is four score years of age. Everybody is wishing him many happy returns. Everybody is saying nice things about him. And everybody, surely, should. Reading his encomiums, he may well laugh to remember the very different things that were written about him half a century ago by those who looked upon the beard when it was red. Then he was a puppy, a coxcomb, a self-advertiser, a blow-hard, a clown who merely delighted in saying the opposite to everybody else. Not that he cared. Let them. For no one had a higher opinion of Bernard Shaw than Bernard Shaw. Which is true, I fancy, even to-day.

If Shaw *has* been a bit of a clown, he has been so of set purpose. I sometimes think that his favourite character in Shakespeare must be Jaques, whom he resembles among other things in being a militant humanitarian. "Invest me in my motley," said Jaques after meeting Touchstone, "and I will through and through cleanse the foul body of th' infected world." For a clown is given licence to utter truths for which a grave man might be crucified. So Shaw, desperately serious at heart, has wagged his cap and jingled his bells and not once has he been put in prison.

Though Shaw is the most famous playwright alive, I shall always maintain that it is as a platform speaker that he has most excelled his contemporaries. To hear Shaw speak has been an even greater joy than to hear Dame Madge Kendal. Moreover, he has been, in my opinion, the finest dramatic critic since Hazlitt. Sitting in the Open-Air Theatre at a performance of *A Midsummer Night's Dream* last week, I wondered what Shaw would have said about it all. Compare the following vigorous passage from his brilliant notice of *A Midsummer Night's Dream* at Daly's forty years ago with the stuff we poor pusillanimous pygmies write nowadays.

"Mr. Daly", writes Shaw, "has trained Miss Lilian Swain in the part of Puck until it is safe to say that she does not take one step, strike one attitude, or modify her voice by a single inflexion that is not violently, wantonly and ridiculously wrong and absurd. Instead of being mercurial, she poses academically, like a cheap Italian statuette; instead of being impish and childish, she is elegant and affected; she laughs a solemn, measured laugh, like a heavy German Zamiel; she announces her ability to girdle the earth in forty minutes in the attitude of a professional skater, and then begins the journey awkwardly in a swing, which takes her in the opposite direction to that in which she indicated her intention of going; in short, she illustrates every folly that still clings round what Mr. Daly no doubt still calls 'the legitimate.' "

Had he been present at the Open-Air Theatre, Shaw would, I feel certain, have approved of Mr. Leslie French's Puck, which has spirit, variety and other-worldliness. It is alive with mystery and mischief. It is impish and poetical. It is as quick as a needle and as light as a feather and responsive to Oberon's slightest movement. But I fancy Shaw would have had some pretty tart things to say about the dance Puck executes with one of the fairies—a dance including scraps from the alms-basket of *L'Après-Midi* and preposterously suggesting a sex-relationship not for one instant dreamt of in the philosophy of Robin Goodfellow. What Shaw would have written of Miss Phyllis Neilson-Terry's Oberon, which insists on silvery high notes that would seem extremely improbable even in a female fairy, you may deduce from what he wrote of the female Oberon at Daly's.

"Another stroke of Mr. Daly's", wrote Shaw, "is to make Oberon a woman. It must not be supposed that he does this solely because it is wrong, though there is no other reason apparent. He does it partly because he was brought up to do such things and partly because they seem to him to be a tribute to Shakespeare's greatness, which, being uncommon, ought not to be interpreted according to the dictates of common sense. A female Oberon and a Puck who behaves like a page-boy earnestly training himself for the post of footman recommend themselves to him because they totally destroy the naturalness of the representation, and so accord with his conception of the Shakespearean drama as the most artificial of all forms of stage entertainment."

I wish I could quote the whole of this notice, which, after nailing down various defects, declares that "at such moments the episode of the ass's head rises to the dignity of allegory". At the end of it all, we find Shaw saying, "There is only one way to defy Time; and that is to have young ideas, which may always be trusted to find youthful and vivid expression." This is characteristic, for has not Shaw always been defying Time, with his vegetarianism and his swimming exercise and his amazing five-play pamphlet on the importance of living longer, entitled *Back to Methuselah*? And as for having young ideas, has he not surprised his followers, if not by his admiration of the New Communism in Russia, by his admiration of the New Fascism in Italy?

After which I have no room left to give my own views. But this, as I reminded you at the start, is Shaw's birthday. It is, perhaps, a tiny tribute to him that what he wrote about a performance of *A Midsummer Night's Dream* given forty years ago should still be so much more interesting than anything I or anybody else could write about one given to-day.

A DREAM FOR QUEEN VICTORIA
(1938)

Here is a thing, and a very pretty thing, and whether the owner of this very pretty thing is Shakespeare or Mendelssohn or Mr. Oliver Messel or Kirby's Flying Ballet, let us not worry to inquire. This much, however, may be told at a glance—that *A Midsummer Night's Dream* at the Old Vic has gone appropriately Old Victorian. You can almost see our young Queen leaning forward in one of the boxes. And it is nice to be able to approve the transports of underlining into which she would surely have been plunged when writing up her darling diary on her return home.

Mr. Tyrone Guthrie has clearly enjoyed himself. A tendency to produce Shakespeare's comedies "just like ballets" has here developed into a full and life-size *corps de Sylphides*. These so fill the forest that it is only a small exaggeration to say you can't see the wood for the wings. When they invade the Palace of Theseus, they prove such an imposing crowd that what should seem spacious seems more than a little cramped. But that the wood is as pretty as a transformation scene, the palace as superb as pre-Victorian Inigo Jones, Mr. Messel is permitted to reveal during less congested intervals. For beauty, for humour, for the magic that is the life-stream of theatrical art, here (though it's produced all wrong!) is *the* Christmas pantomime.

Certainly, no comedian now dame-ing it at the Adelphi or the Lyceum or the Prince's succeeds in being half as funny as Mr. Ralph Richardson in the part of Bottom. But Mr. Riscoe, Mr. Rose and Mr. Lupino may well answer, "Look at his material!" That this Bottom should drop his aitches seemed so much more Early Victorian than late Elizabethan that I found myself waiting in some alarm to hear whether he would "Beseech your *vorship's* name" or announce that he had had "a most rare *wision*." It was, too, a little startling to see Theseus and Hippolyta joining hands with the mechanics in their rowdy bergomask—would our young Queen quite have approved of *that*?

But the rustic rehearsals are excellently fooled, and with Miss Agnes Lauchlan—the best Helena I have seen—to liven the lovers with her plaintive wit, no one could be unhappy for long—not even those who realized that, the mistakings in the forest at an end, Helena was getting back at Lysander by stealing some of his lines. Just before this, another interesting novelty had been introduced, Hippolyta in the morning dew serving the awakened lovers with brew from a bowl with a ladle. No doubt they were glad of it, but I don't think Shakespeare's verse was.

Miss Vivien Leigh looks delicious and behaves every inch like a nice young Victorian miss playing the part of Titania. Mr. Robert Helpmann, making his first appearance in legitimate as Oberon, speaks his verse better than almost anyone else in the company—a majestic, ominous and most romantic figure. To see the part of Puck acted by a little boy is usually more satisfactory than to see it acted by a little girl, but not, I submit, in a Victorian production. Miss Chattie Salaman would have been a more suitable choice than Master Gordon Miller. But then Miss Salaman would not have been able to appear as the First Fairy, which she did so entrancingly that one day she must certainly be promoted to Titania.

Altogether, a diverting evening. But it remains to be demonstrated how they did *A Midsummer Night's Dream* in periwigs, or how (if it had been written then) they would have done it in the Stone Age.

RANDOM NOTES

Shakespeare wrote two great pastoral plays: *As You Like It*, the scene of which is laid in the Forest of Arden, and *A Midsummer Night's Dream*, with its Wood near Athens. Of these two plays *A Midsummer Night's Dream* is the more magical and mysterious; and if you would inquire the reason, you might find it in the answer that, while the Forest of Arden is the Wood near Athens, and while both are English to the last acorn, night is more magical and mysterious than day. The Forest of Arden is for the sun-worshippers. Here it is perpetual high noon. We shall never know what sleeping accommodation the Banished Duke provided for his contented followers. We shall never know how Rosalind behaved by twilight—whether she maintained her triumphant buoyancy, or whether, when the horn of night had sounded in the glade, she subdued her wit to a gentler quality.

We shall never know how Oberon and Puck would have rung the changes on the love of Silvius for Phebe, of Phebe for Ganymede, of Orlando for Rosalind, and of Rosalind for no woman. But just as the Forest of Arden is governed by the sun, so is the Wood near Athens governed by the moon. This wood is wet with night. The tiniest sounds prick as piercingly through the darkness as the stars prick through the vault of heaven. And as you thread your way between the trees, stumbling over a root or a shoot or a lover, to where Titania in a cup of light decks her gentle ass with coronets of flowers, the smell of a century of dead leaves rises with a strength and sweetness unknown to-day.

. . . . . .

If a psycho-analyst were to ask me to "associate", as I believe it is called, beginning from the starting-point of *A Midsummer Night's Dream*, my first response would be "Wet woods at night"; and after that perhaps I should blab out, "Three-legged stools", for Puck, you may remember, plays pranks with three-legged stools, and the immortal fairy-stuff in this play is made firm and fibrous because it is not merely of the air or even of the earth, but of the cottage.

When he created, or perhaps one should say when he reincarnated, Puck, Shakespeare was not so much fairy-conscious as kitchen-conscious. What a loss we should have sustained if, in the last scene of all, Puck had come to bless the house with a wand instead of a besom! We must remember that it was the housewives who invented the fairies, and that the true fairyland is therefore to be found, not in the hazy nowhere to which timid fancies gravitate, but between four solid walls of brick and mortar. The Wood near Athens is the home of the newts and the bats and the screech-owls and the spotted snakes. It is not the home of the fairies. It is their playground. When their revels are at an end, they vanish, but not into thin air. They

vanish into the linen-press of Mistress Quince, into the oven of
Mistress Flute, into the milk-pan of Mistress Starveling. And it is
because Shakespeare understood their origin and because he had
grown up with them under a thatched roof that he made them so
much more alive than Theseus and Hippolyta. Hippolyta may have
been an Amazon and Theseus a mighty hunter before the gods, but
it is in Oberon that we see the man of action and in Titania the mate
who must be won with more than wooing.

· · · · ·

Perhaps there is no comedy by Shakespeare containing more
beautiful music than *A Midsummer Night's Dream*. It is for the nose
and for the ear rather than for the eye, and if you wander through
the woods on a summer night, you can scarcely fail to smell it and
to hear it, though you may fail to see it. But it would be a mistake
to infer from this statement any sympathy with the objection to stage
representations of *A Midsummer Night's Dream* which is based on
the mathematical calculation that fairies five, or even four, feet high,
could never drown in the honey-bag of a humble-bee. A playgoer
who cannot imagine that four feet are half an inch can never have
looked at the stage through the wrong end of his opera-glasses and
should give up the theatre altogether. This particular objection may
disappear when the play is broadcast, but even so he may be troubled
to account for the fact that Pease-Blossom has a mouth like a Loud
Speaker. The playwright uses his imagination to the best of his
ability, but all his efforts will be vain if the audience does not bring
its own imagination to his support. After all, it entails little effort.
For as Theseus says, at the close of his famous speech on the lunatic,
the lover and the poet:

"How easy is a bush suppos'd a bear!"

· · · · ·

What *is* to be done about those fairies? What did the Elizabethans
do about them? What sort of a spectacle did they present in Shakespeare's time? Nobody can say for certain. But is there not an illuminating suggestion in that most illuminating pamphlet by Mr. Ernest Law
on *Shakespeare's "Tempest" as Originally Produced at Court*? Mr. Law,
considering the problem of Ariel, suggests a costume similar to that
described by Ben Jonson for Jophiel in his *Masque of the Fortunate
Isles*. Here is Ben Jonson's direction:

*Enter, running, Jophiel, an airy spirit . . . attired in light silks of
several colours, with wings of the same, a bright yellow hair, a chaplet
of flowers, blue silk stockings, and pumps, and gloves, with a silver fan
in his hand.*

Pumps, gloves, and a silver fan! Not an ideal flying costume

D

according to the lights of Drury Lane. Yet Jophiel was a flying fairy
It is with these words that he opens the Masque:

> Like a lightning from the sky,
>   Or an arrow shot by Love,
> Or a bird of his let fly;
>   Be't a sparrow, or a dove:
> With that winged haste, come I,
>   Loosed from the sphere of Jove,
>   To wish good night
>   To your delight.

In some such way might we not formalize the retinues of Titania and
of Oberon into diminutive courtiers and ladies-in-waiting, with capes
and ruffs and wings and chaplets? It might not be an entirely satisfactory solution, but a charming diminutive effect is achieved when
children are dressed as grown-ups. And it would be better, I swear,
than presenting these fairies like choristers out of *Iolanthe*, or tricking
them out in the customary gauzy flummery, which makes them look
like secondary schoolchildren who have temporarily abandoned their
spectacles to give a Christmas breaking-up entertainment. If you believe
in the gods and the heroes and the little people, they are as solid as
goats. It is only the doubters who dress their fairies in gauze.

THE MERCHANT OF VENICE

MISS EVANS AS PORTIA
(1925)

THE Old Vic reopened its doors on Saturday last with a performance under Mr. Andrew Leigh's direction of *The Merchant
of Venice*: a comedy in which the expected order of things is curiously
reversed, Jewish lust for blood (not a characteristic of the race) being
countered at the eleventh hour by Christian sharp practice. However
preposterous the premiss of the "merry bond", it cannot be denied
that Shakespeare has illuminated the story all through with flashes
of marvellous poetry and psychology, from Salarino's "rich burghers
on the flood" (always massacred by the worst actor in the company),
and Shylock's "wry-necked fife" and "wilderness of monkeys", to
Lorenzo's "young-ey'd cherubins" and Jessica's exquisite "I am never
merry when I hear sweet music". But the play, when Shylock is
absent from the stage, lacks flesh and blood. Antonio is a mere
melancholy wraith from whom the Jew might safely have cut his
pound of flesh without fear of sanguinary consequences. Portia,
although there is something superbly aristocratic about her, fails to
capture our sympathy, perhaps because she is herself never for one
moment in trouble—it is impossible that we should tremble all through

the speeches of Morocco and Arragon. While in the case of Bassanio, who is so emphatically likened by the servants to "a day in April", it is difficult to escape the feeling, try as we may, that he is anything more than a fortune-hunting sponger.

As a matter of fact, however, in writing *The Merchant of Venice*, Shakespeare did most handsomely by both Bassanio and Portia, for in the *Pecorone* of Ser Giovanni Fiorentino, the story on which the play is based, these lovers cut a very poor figure indeed. Portia is an unscrupulous money-grabber, who makes the most of her beauty by requiring all her suitors to go to bed with her, on the understanding that if they can enjoy her, they shall have her to wife, but if they fail, they shall hand over all the riches they have brought with them. As they are injudicious enough to accept the cup of wine she hands them before retiring, they fall into a deep slumber as soon as they lay head to pillow, and wake to find themselves impoverished.

As for Bassanio, in an attempt to win Portia, he three times induces Antonio to fit him out a ship laden with merchandise, under the pretext of trading abroad and bringing back a handsome return, but secretly in order that he may slip into Belmont and try his luck with the lady. Thus, it is really Portia who is responsible, through her grasping ways, for the unpleasant predicament in which Antonio finds himself with Shylock, and it is only right and proper that she should be the one to get him out of it. But this situation was devitalized by Shakespeare who, catering for the ethical North, could not contemplate the idea of a heroine who made a habit of doping her lovers in the bedroom, or of a hero who made a habit of borrowing money from his best friend under false pretences. He proceeded, therefore, to whitewash them as thoroughly as he was able, with the consequence that he left their characters, once engrossingly spotted, a rather uninteresting blank.

Nevertheless, Portia has her definite points. A great lady, of the noblest condition, finely bred, highly cultivated, distinguished in every action, the best educated of all Shakespeare's heroines, she is unusually witty and she is unusually managing. Miss Edith Evans, embarking on an adventure as brave as any in the theatre, did well to emphasize both these characteristics. Her Portia was always sure of herself—and how sure of herself Portia always was! "I pray thee over-name them, and as thou namest them, I will describe them".

Portia knew that she could bring off a brilliant sally on demand. She knew, too, before she entered the court, that she would emerge victorious. In this court scene Miss Evans assumed direction from the start and never relaxed her hold. I suggest to her, however, that after Shylock has turned a deaf ear to her plea for mercy, which is delivered as a test to find out whether this Jew has a spark of decency in him, she should exhibit signs of her supreme contempt for him. He has refused his chance. He is the scum of the earth. Very well, then: he shall have it hot and strong. I suggest again to Miss Evans that she should, in the earlier scenes, make more sparing use of her upper register, and that she should speak the lines beginning "How all the other passions fleet to air" a good deal less swooningly. The words themselves are so charged with emotion that it is enough for an actress merely, as it were, to speak them. The whole soul may safely be put into such simple phrases as "Know it then, and do't." But when the poet lets himself go, it is for the actress to rein herself in.

The great joy of Miss Evans's Portia, as of all her work, is that you understand everything she says. The meaning never becomes obscured. The sense never loses itself, as is so often the case with the utterance of blank verse, in an accursed cadence. It is difficult to believe that when Mr. Claude Ricks, for example, who plays the part of Lorenzo, gets going in the moonlight, he has any idea of what he is saying. He is just carried away by a hazy notion that beauty is very beautiful, and all this must be beauty, see-saw, Marjory Daw, look at the patines inlaid on the floor. Mr. John Garside's Young Lancelot is more intelligent, even if it is like the work of a fruity comedian without his fruitiness; but here again I cannot understand why such a quip as, "If you do, then it was not for nothing that my nose fell a-bleeding on Black-Monday last, at six o'clock i' the morning, falling out that year on Ash-Wednesday was four year in the afternoon", should be gabbled at such a rate that all you can hear is the gabbling.

Mr. Leigh, whose production is in the Atkins vein, should look to this. And if he is going to introduce traditional business for which there is no warrant in the text, I suggest that he might as well retain the business that is most effective. I hold no brief for Shylock, after Jessica has flitted, returning to knock on the door. Mr. Leigh may be commended on this omission. Yet there is, I feel, much more to be said for such an interpolation than for Shylock's return after Antonio has announced that "My ships come home a month before the day", merely in order that he may exhibit his already obvious antagonism to all Christians by expectorating on the stage.

Mr. Baliol Holloway's Shylock is, indeed, a Shylock that does not need to spit. It is a very straight and a very sound piece of work, in which, if there are few signs of genius, there is no sign of a flaw, Mr. Holloway is a workmanlike actor with a resounding method and no nonsense about him. The Old Vic is fortunate in his possession. His delivery of "Hath not a Jew eyes?" was magnificent: a blazing, indignant protestation. There was no sudden turning on of the tap of pathos. Mr. Holloway plays all his parts right through in one key, but it is always the right key. His Shylock is a bad man, as Shakespeare had to make him, but a human bad man, as Shakespeare had to make him, too.

GINGERING UP THE MERCHANT
(1932)

Mr. John Gielgud has fairly gingered up *The Merchant of Venice* at the Old Vic. During recent years unenterprising representations of this play have made it seem distinctly musty. But there is nothing musty about Mr. Gielgud's production. The hectic variety of costumes, inspired by many periods, turns Shakespeare's comedy into a sort of Three Arts Revel. Portia comes now as an eighteenth-century Arcadian shepherdess, now as a Victorian sylphide. Bassanio comes as a jockey. Salanio, dominating everything in bright magenta, might be a Hammersmith-Lyric Offenbach Pluto.

These costumes, delicious in themselves, cloy the true Shakespearean flavour. The damage they do is largely repaired by the strong speed with which the story is unfolded. A single nondescript set does duty for outdoors and indoors, Venice and Belmont alike. The play is thus disencumbered of those drawings and withdrawings of the curtain that cut Shakespeare up as badly as any blue pencil. This is what Shakespeare meant. And what Shakespeare meant is what matters.

Mr. Gielgud has done an important thing in finally proving the fallacy of the contention that Shakespeare without scenery becomes *ipso facto* dull. Nothing could be less dull than this production. It is, truth to tell, almost too lively. But it is continuously interesting. There are so many good ideas to praise and bad ones to condemn.

Here's a bad idea: Portia's Court openly mocks the Prince of Arragon—she never would have allowed it. Here's a good one: The caskets are distributed about the stage so that the long soliloquies are assisted by movement. Here's a bad one: When Portia tells Bassanio in a private heart-to-heart speech that her servants are his, they run and kneel before him in pretty subjection. Here's a good one: Old Gobbo's blindness is made comic from the word go, and the ensuing comedy is received without humanitarian qualms.

The words of the play are more intelligently spoken than usual. It was, however, unfortunate that on the first night Mr. Malcolm Keen should say, "If you tickle us, do we not bleed?" On his first night as Macbeth he said, "The time has been that when a man would die, the brains were out." These mistakes are radical rather than accidental. Mr. Keen acts out of a general feeling for his part rather than an observation of its particular requirements. Nevertheless, Mr. Keen's Shylock is the best thing he has done at the Old Vic. He is not a tremendous Shylock. To work up the cursing scene Macready used to have a super in the wings whom he shook and cursed before dashing on to bewail his daughter and his ducats. I'm sure Mr. Keen doesn't do that. But he is passionate and impressive and keeps his place in the scheme.

Miss Peggy Ashcroft's Portia is weak work: a nice girl at a party rather than a great lady and a challenging, self-confident wit. Top marks to Mr. Morland Graham as Old Gobbo. Here is a jolly old buffer who is so fond of fun that he would rather be made a fool of than not, and who probably, in his youth, made much better jokes than Young Gobbo.

IS SHYLOCK A BORE?
(1938)

For some years it has been the fashion to decry *The Merchant of Venice*, critics roundly declaring that here is a bad play better left unacted. This rash attitude has been engendered partly by the fact that *The Merchant* is so much more frequently presented than other Shakespeare plays of greater excellence, and partly by the fact that, being under the necessity of praising Shakespeare so often, critics feel that it restores their self-respect to give him a good drubbing now and then. See me slate Shakespeare! Yet the same critics who complain of this play have no hesitation in praising to the sky others of infinitely inferior quality. Glance at the list of current attractions. Can any playgoer with any pretence to taste and judgment seriously maintain that *George and Margaret* at Wyndham's is a patch on *The Merchant* at the Queen's? Or that *Idiot's Delight*, admirable though it is, stands the ghost of a chance of being revived three hundred years hence?

The truth of the matter is that, when you get a man of Shakespeare's quality writing a play, that play cannot avoid abounding in miracles. So, in *The Merchant*, you find Shylock, you find Portia's love-speeches to Bassanio, you find the loveliest last act ever written for any comedy, you find the wilderness of monkeys, and tell me where is fancy bred, and the marriage to a sponge, and the quality of mercy (whether you learned it at school or not), and marvel after marvel in every scene. And so we are grateful to Mr. John Gielgud for choosing this maligned but incontrovertible masterpiece with which to conclude his stimulating season in Shaftesbury Avenue.

There is nothing musty about this play, and there is nothing musty about this production. The Motleys seem to have set out with the express purpose of recapturing deserters who have seen the piece too often. These deserters will no doubt be allured, if not recalled to fundamentals, by the light, airy, candent peepshow to which they are invited to apply an eye. Something too much of a peepshow it may be, with trap-windows and portals and steps and bridges waiting, as it were, to reveal their function around a central light-weight pavilion with slender columns. A penny in the slot, and the charming motion is set a-going. The figures appear. And such is the power of acting that we forget the picture in the subject. Mr. Gielgud's Shylock strikes me as the finest thing he has done since his Old Vic days, making no bid for sympathy, as Irving did, but achieving it naturally through force of circumstance, just as Shakespeare, probably without preliminary intention, came to it in writing the play. Miss Peggy Ashcroft's Portia is lovely in love—Juliet all over again—which was, one suspects, Miss Ashcroft all over again—and therefore not characteristically Portia. One feels her father to be still alive and in control of the Belmont ménage. She obeys more naturally than she commands. Nevertheless, when in the throes that level us all, most deeply moving.

And is not Miss Angela Baddeley's Nerissa a true soubrette without one spark of false vivacity, the most engaging and amusing Nerissa of our time? Miss Baddeley is now an all-round actress. She can be charming, she can be funny, she can be tiresome and unattractive. Of how many other actresses could one say this?

THE MERCHANT OF VENICE
(1943)

It is, upon the whole, easier to sympathize with Shylock than to condemn him. This is no doubt partly due to the fact that he is defeated in the end: victory is always rather vulgar. But it is also partly due to the fact that the evil Shylock would do to others (the pound of flesh) is too extravagant to be easily credible; whereas the evil others do to Shylock (the theft of his daughter, the sale of his ring, the confiscation of his property, the conversion of his faith), might not inconceivably happen to us. Whether Shakespeare meant playgoers to be sorry for Shylock or not, he could not resist making out a case for him. In the original story on which the play was based, it was sufficient that a Jew should be a Jew to be a villain; Shakespeare it was who devised the extenuating circumstances, who made Antonio not only lend out money gratis (which no Usurers' Trade Union would permit), but call Shylock opprobrious names in public and spit on him into the bargain; above all, Shakespeare it was who arranged Jessica's elopement with a Christian—the last straw. Until this happens, there is nothing in the text to confirm the possibly unjust suspicion that Shylock meant to have his pound of flesh from the start.

Mr. Frederick Valk's Shylock at the New Theatre plays neither for sympathy nor for antipathy, admirably refraining from taking sides but losing no strength through lack of partisanship. If his performance is never exciting, it is always commanding, completely unfussed, and the size of big acting without acting big. Acting big is, no doubt, a fault on the right side when it comes to Shakespeare, but it is a pity that nearly all our actors should have to do it to get level with the poet. Mr. Valk is refreshingly equal to his task and does not need to emphasize any one aspect of Shylock's character—to be abnormally Hebraic or overwhelmingly venomous, or shatteringly paternal, or unprecedentedly stricken—in order to cover up an all-round insufficiency.

This is acting worthy of the ancient and honourable name of the Old Vic and of the modern and auspicious initials of C.E.M.A. Of nothing else in the production, which is a most lamentable affair, can the same be said, the general impression received being that it has been cast by Mr. Bevin, who might well be invited to sit through it and think again. And why not a couple of seats, too, for Mr. George Black, who might discover just the thing for his next beauty parade in Portia and the ladies of her court. Is this, indeed, the court of Portia, or can it be that the premises have been taken over for the term of the war by an evacuated and rather expensive finishing school? Whatever Bassanio may say, Miss Kay Bannerman's Portia is certainly something undervalued to Cato's Portia. It is a Portia for the films, posturing girlishly in what looks like a Hollywood nightdress, untouched by culture, incapable of wit, seeming neither master of her servants nor queen o'er herself, and attended by three casket-bearers who might at other times make up a very nice girls' four.

For the rest, whether we consider the depressant sets, the haphazard groupings, the lurchings of Gratiano in his untextual cups, the breakneck convenient speed of the peekaboo infant Balthazar, the philanderings of Arragon with one of the maids, the curiously detached bepuzzlement of Antonio over his own melancholy, or almost everything else, we can only wonder whether, granting the difficulties of the time, it is worth while putting on Shakespeare if the effect is likely to be putting off the public. But perhaps the public won't mind. After all, Mr. Valk is a tower of excellence. And the play is a good play, however much impetuous critics, who praise the performance, may asperse it.

AS YOU LIKE IT

MISS EVANS AS ROSALIND
(1926)

GIVE me a play like *As You Like It*. Among the intellectuals this has, perhaps, been one of the most underrated of all Shakespeare's comedies ever since Mr. Bernard Shaw wrote that it passed his understanding how anybody over the age of seven could "take any interest in a literary toy so silly in its conceit and common in its ideas as the 'Seven Ages of Man'", and declared that "an Eskimo would demand his money back if a modern author offered him such fare" as Touchstone's jest about the knight and the pancake. For my own part, I don't believe that an Eskimo would demand his money back even after hearing Ftatateeta mispronounced Teetatota, Totateeta, Tfatafeeta, and so on. While as for the "Seven Ages of Man" speech, it is only because it has been so consistently and so foolishly lifted out of its context and quoted out of character that it is taken as an attempt on Shakespeare's part at profound philosophical statement. In reality, it is the sour utterance of a crabbed fellow who delights to view the world through lemon-coloured spectacles: the infant mewls and pukes, the schoolboy whines and creeps unwillingly to school, the silly lover sighs like a furnace and makes ballads to his mistress' eyebrow, the soldier ridiculously risks his life for the bubble reputation, the justice moralizes (and well he may!) on a full stomach, the pantaloon shambles ineffectively in clothes a size too large for him, the toothless, sightless, tasteless, everythingless dotard might just as well be dead.

Of all Shakespeare' scharacters, is there any more fashionably modern than this Melancholy Jaques? He is the complete up-to-date intellectual, a crystallization of all the highbrows. His declaration that "the city woman bears the cost of princes on unworthy shoulders" and that one man's "bravery" (finery) means another man's "cost", suggests Socialistic inclinations. His statement that the banished lords are "mere usurpers, tyrants, and what's worse, To fright the animals, and to kill them up", indicates the humanitarian vegetarian. His disparagement of all the benefits of his own country is pure Bloomsbury. His "lisp" is the equivalent of the famous King's College falsetto.

The "strange suits" he wore are on all fours with Jaegerism and Café-Royalism. In argument he is always on the other side. He speaks to surprise. The only cause he really has at heart is the cause of his own intellectuality. He loves no man but himself. Thus, he does not side with the Banished Duke for love of the Duke, but for love of the banishment. And as soon as the Banished Duke is restored to his own, and the Usurping Duke goes into voluntary exile, he hurries off (a wonderfully shrewd touch) to join his former enemy. The pride of minorities is highly developed in him. Fighting on his own ground, he scintillates wit and, not infrequently, wisdom. Fighting on anybody else's, he becomes impotent, so that with Rosalind and Orlando, who will not come half-way to meet him, his satire degenerates into flat rudeness.

Mr. Baliol Holloway at the Old Vic misses the acidity of all this, giving the "Seven Ages" speech as though it were fit food for copybooks. But that is by far the most serious flaw in an otherwise excellent performance. As for the Rosalind of Miss Edith Evans, here is one of the divinest pieces of comedy this astonishing actress has yet given us.

Has there, I wonder, ever been an actress more sunnily in love? What art there is in every fling of the head, in every luxuriating stretch of the arms! How irresistibly entranced is this Rosalind in the full flood of her exuberant assurance! It is one of the greatest charms of this play that it succeeds in making us feel that very rare thing, a love untouched by agony. Most love is purgatory, but Rosalind, devising sports, knows all the time that she has got Orlando safe as houses, and nothing less than a lioness can give her a moment's anxiety. When I saw Miss Phyllis Neilson-Terry in the part a dozen or so years ago, I felt, oh, to be loved by this Rosalind! When I see Miss Evans, I feel, oh, to love like this one! That is a very important distinction. One should not fall in love with Rosalind—but, with Rosalind, one should fall in love. And so, at the Old Vic, I fell in love, I suppose, with Orlando, who was handsomely played by Mr. Frank Vosper in the proper picture-book manner. Or I fell in love with the Forest of Arden, which is but a vowel sound away from the Forest of Eden, and is a haunt we should visit at least once every spring. For every time we go there we find old delights, and every time we go there we find some fresh treasure we have overlooked before, whether it be Rosalind's " 'Tis like the howling of Irish wolves against the moon", or Jaques's description of Touchstone:

> In his brain,
> Which is as dry as the remainder biscuit
> After a voyage: he hath strange places cramm'd
> With observation, the which he vents
> In mangled forms.

Truly, a marvellous brief summing-up!

THE TAMING OF THE SHREW

A TRIP TO NORWICH
(1922)

IT has been contended that whereas in the beginning the artist copies nature, in the end nature returns the compliment by copying the artist. For this paradoxical assertion there is a good deal to be said. Whether a tree exists apart from our concept of it we do not know; but we do know that our concept of it exists and that this concept is largely dependent upon such wayward influences as mood, hearsay and education. In the eyes of a hundred beholders one tree will assume a hundred variations; and of these hundred beholders many will view the tree through the spectacles of some poet or painter who, translating his own vision into terms of art, has recreated for mankind the animate and inanimate world. The skylark, for example, has acquired a new grace and a new beauty since Shelley taught it how to fly. Sunrises have stolen new colours from the palette of the magician Turner.

When Nevinson turned drillmaster, soldiers became more angular in their marching. And now—here is April once again, April of which Shakespeare was so lyrical, and which is now so lyrical of Shakespeare. Now comes in the sweet of the year, and the red blood reigns in the winter's pale. The violets dim are sweeter than the lids of Juno's eyes. By shallow rivers the melodious birds sing madri-

gals. It is Shakespeare's month. All nature quotes the comedies. At
any twist in the lane we may meet Autolycus. Holofernes chops logic
in every wooded park. The Thames sparkles in expectation of the
gigantic splash of the Falstaffian buck-basket. Petruchio cracks his
whip. Rosalind and Touchstone are for the forest fringe. Master
Bottom stretches after his long sleep—and we stretch with him. We
would exercise our legs. The wander-fever has us in thrall. Whither
away? The Birthday Festival beckons us to the blue-eyed Avon. In
the Memorial Theatre at Stratford we may see the plays. Or, if we
would approach a step nearer still to Shakespeare, we may roam in
Chalcote Park, where the red deer flee at our approach. Why not
a Spring pilgrimage? with the Complete Works accessibly in knap-
sack?

There is much virtue in a pilgrimage. Journeys end in lovers
meeting. And the more difficult the journey, the more exquisite the
joy of the encounter. We will compose no jeremiad on the inevitable march of science which has so successfully tempted us with
railway trains and tubes and motor-cars. But the blessings conferred
by these facilities are not unmixed. What was once a gleaming luxury
has now become a drab matter of course. Travel is cheap. In Paris we
shrug our shoulders. In Rome we yawn. And as for visiting the play
in London, this has become such child's play that we think nothing
of it. We just drop in—taking our pleasure not so much sadly as
automatically. Time was when we—or our ancestors—dreamt of the
delight for days beforehand. Now we forget it almost as soon as we
have finished supper. We fail of our enjoyment because enjoyment
is largely a matter of disposition, and familiarity with the theatre has
bred a disposition which erects no barriers against contempt.

There was *Sarah of Soho*, which ran for a mere handful of nights at
the Savoy Theatre. We were not amused. But if, as a preliminary to
seeing this comedy, it had been necessary to swim a couple of rivers,
cross a couple of mountains, and kill a couple of dragons, would not the
subsequent entertainment have been considerably enhanced? Is it not
possible that many of the captive princesses so jealously guarded by
giants in fairy tales possessed (if the truth were known) no uncommon
share of beauty, and that the sight of them would have deeply mortified
their adventurous liberators had not these gentlemen been dazzled
by their own success? It does not seem to have occurred to anyone
to suggest that what is wrong with the theatre is the taxicab. But
one thing is certain: that in the days gone by, when townsfolk had
to rely for clownish drama on intermittent visits from strolling players
of the meanest merit, there were fewer complaints over the poverty
of plays and the inefficiency of players.

There is, we repeat, much virtue in a pilgrimage. As a preparation,
it is more effective than an orchestral overture. It is inevitable that,
on a journey to Stratford to see Shakespeare's plays, to Bradfield to
see Greek plays, to Ober-Ammergau to see the Passion Play, to

Bayreuth to hear Wagner's operas, or to Glastonbury to participate
in the Arthurian dramatic festival, we should instinctively accumulate
a sympathy which is invaluable in appreciating any work of art.

A few weeks ago we made a pilgrimage to Norwich in order to
see a performance of *The Taming of the Shrew* given at the Maddermarket Theatre by Mr. Nugent Monck's valiant amateur company.
We were induced to make that pilgrimage by the fact that the Maddermarket Theatre, which opened six months ago, is the only theatre
at present existing in England which is constructed on the Elizabethan
plan, and by the conviction that Elizabethan plays must taste better
in Elizabethan than in modern theatres, just as wine tastes better out
of a wineglass than out of a tumbler. During the whole of that journey
we were, quite effortlessly, becoming more and more Elizabethan in
our composition, and if we do not remember setting our ruff to rights
before we left the train, doubtless it is because actions such as these,
being performed unconsciously, are always difficult to recall.

The state of mind into which we had thrown ourselves was in
no way disturbed by the hotel to which we then proceeded, even
though it had been built a century too early for Shakespeare. But
we confess to a shock at the discovery, proclaimed on all the plates
and dishes, that Queen Elizabeth had slept in one of the bedrooms.
Nothing is more destructive of what house-agents call "an old-world
atmosphere" than emphasis on the fact that the old world no longer
exists. Norwich was Elizabethan to us until Queen Elizabeth was flung
at our heads, just as Stratford would be the most Shakespearean town in
England if it did not contain so many mementoes of his past existence.

And now let us explain that our desire to see an Elizabethan play
performed in an Elizabethan theatre was stimulated by no mere
antiquarian enthusiasm. The case against modernized productions of
Shakespeare is a case not for antiquarians but for modern playgoers, to
whom Shakespeare brought up-to-date must inevitably become
largely incomprehensible. Something over a year ago there occurred
nightly in a production of *A Midsummer Night's Dream* at the Court
Theatre an incident which admirably crystallized the whole case against
modernization.

In one of the opening scenes there was a long passage, consisting
of some eighty lines, written entirely in rhymed couplets. Among
these couplets was the following, spoken by Lysander: "I will
my Hermia. Helena adieu, As you on him, Demetrius dote on
you." Unfortunately, the actor who played the part of Lysander at
the Court Theatre, or the producer who taught him to play it, thought
that he could improve on Shakespeare. He had been to school, he
knew the correct, if un-Elizabethan, way to pronounce the French
word *adieu*, and so he spoke it in the French fashion, thus making
poor Shakespeare ridiculous by completely ruining his rhyme. There
will be few people obstinate enough to deny that *adieu* should in this
passage—and, therefore, throughout Shakespeare—be pronounced

"ad'yoo". And once this point has been conceded, there is nothing for it but an Elizabethan theatre. If it makes Shakespeare ridiculous to modernize his pronunciation, it makes him no less ridiculous to modernize, say, his costumes. We may know perfectly well that Greek mechanics in the time of Theseus did not dress themselves up like Warwickshire yokels in the time of Elizabeth; but if Shakespeare visualized a Greek mechanic in the costume of a Warwickshire mechanic and called him by a most un-Greek name, then, in presenting him on the stage, we must keep to that un-Greek name and dress him up like a Warwickshire mechanic. We must preserve in our costumes the anachronisms which exist in the text and which existed in Shakespeare's mind. And unless the machinery of production throughout is the machinery employed in Shakespeare's day, again and again we shall find absurdities and irrelevancies creeping in. Either we must give Shakespeare according to his own lights, or we must re-write him altogether, turn Bardolph into a cockney, and set Juliet jazzing at the ball.

The Maddermarket Theatre in Norwich is a revelation. In the modern theatre we present a series of pictures within a frame called a proscenium, which we fill with a curtain while the scenes are being shifted. The Maddermarket Theatre has no proscenium and no curtain. Its stage is an unframed rostrum thrust boldly forth—though not boldly enough—into the auditorium. And on this rostrum the characters, liberated from the stifling restraint of the picture-frame, leap into being, emerge from their age-long artificiality into living realities, strut, slash and swear not like puppets but like men and women.

Nothing could seem less antiquarian. You do not look on at the feast through a crack in the wall. You are actually present at it. You come upon it as you might come upon a fight in the street. There is no pause in the action. As soon as one set of characters has disappeared, another takes its place. The absence of scenery and curtains and the system of exits and entrances peculiar to the Elizabethan stage make for absolute continuity. We do not say that the performance at the Maddermarket achieved perfection. The play was cut, because Norwich likes to be in bed by ten o'clock. The lighting of the front of the platform was unsatisfactory. The players quite often stressed wrong words. But here was perfection almost within grasp. Shakespeare was out of his coffin even if he was still rubbing his eyes at the unaccustomed light of the brave old world.

The zeal of these Norwich players, who perform under the dynamic direction of Mr. Nugent Monck, is not the least remarkable feature of this auspicious enterprise. They are all amateurs who give their services free. Every night, after their daily business is over and they have ensured to-morrow's bread and butter, they assemble in the Maddermarket Theatre, there either to perform or to rehearse. For three weeks they rehearse; for one they perform. Their names are not given on the programmes. They make their own dresses and properties.

Many of the local shops assist by charging the lowest possible prices. The theatre is their own freehold. Mr. Monck is the moving spirit, and it was he who discovered the delightful eighteenth-century building, with galleries, which has been converted, under the direction of Captain Noel Paul, into a rough working replica of the rebuilt Fortune Theatre. It is a thousand pities that Norwich cannot come to London, but that is impossible, for the Maddermarket Theatre cannot be transported, and, in this case, the theatre's the thing. But it is safe to predict that, before long, many Londoners will make the pilgrimage to Norwich, and that they will not return from it empty-minded.

SHREW OR HOYDEN?
(1922)

Quite apart from the ruthless context of this thwacking comedy, the title should be enough to point the way. There is nothing ironical in it. It tells us that there will be a shrew and that we shall see her tamed. And it is the business of the producer to show us these things. Unhappily, neither of these points emerged clearly in the Old Vic production. Miss Florence Buckton was not a shrew but a hoyden in a tantrum. She prepared the way for her conversion with little smirks, suggesting that she was perfectly capable of seeing the whole situation in perspective, that she was only playing a part in a kind of furious game, and that she could secretly enjoy Petruchio's persecutions, as the heroines of Miss Ethel M. Dell's novels secretly enjoy the malicious streaks in that authoress's flapper-subduing heroes.

Finally, in the post-prandial oration on the Whole Duty of Woman she endeavoured to suggest that her subjugation was only a seeming show: this was a bantering address to Petruchio rather than a round reproof to Bianca and Hortensio's Widow. Perhaps it is not easy for a twentieth-century mind to feel quite happy over Petruchio's methods and the complete success which attends them. But *The Taming of the Shrew* is not a twentieth-century play; it was written before, not after, Ibsen wrote *A Doll's House*; to attempt to give a little feminist twist to a stark anti-feminist play is simply to stab art in the back. As well might an actor playing Young King Hal in *Henry IV Part 2* seek to soften the snub administered to Falstaff by winking a knowing eye at the old rapscallion, as who should say, "I'm only snubbing you because, in my new position, I can't very well openly encourage you, but meet me to-night at the old time in the old place and we'll have another good old spree in the good old way." If any proof were needed to clinch the argument that the original intention of *The Taming of the Shrew* was to show a scold, subdued even to the very unpalatable quality of her lord, it would be enough to cite Fletcher's *A Woman's Prize, or The Tamer Tamed*. This was a sequel to *The Taming of the Shrew* in which Petruchio reappeared, married to a second wife and was as badly treated by her as Katherine was badly treated by him. Apparently even in Shakespeare's day the tone of *The Taming of the Shrew* aroused some indignation, though it was customary to pillory shrews in plays long before Shakespeare's day. Possibly these plays link up with the old religious drama, for the original Shrew (spelt with a capital S) was none other than Satan himself—hence the popular oath "Beshrew me!" So the taming of the Shrew is fundamentally the exorcization of a devil, something far more serious than a mere bit of sport.

In this Old Vic production Mr. Hay Petrie plays the Pedant and plays him tipsy. If the Pedant had been tipsy, Shakespeare would unquestionably have given his speeches a tipsy flavour; not less unquestionably, he would have refrained from requiring Baptista to say to him, "Your plainness and your shortness please me well." The audience laughed loudly at this quite innocently-written remark, for it immediately followed a speech by the Pedant which, owing to this intoxication, could by no stretch of Baptista's imagination have been considered plain or short; and little Mr. Petrie, as he stood swaying exquisitely on the stage, did in very fact look so plain and so short that the application of the words was promptly fastened on to his personal appearance. Quite apart from the question of Shakespeare's intention, the effect of seeing one and the same actor play two tipsy parts on the same night was not without its disadvantages. For Mr. Petrie also played Christopher Sly—another remarkably clever piece of work, less broadly-based and oleaginous than the late Charles Glenney's inimitable creation, but laughable in every accent and gesture.

Mr. Robert Atkins opens the banquet scene with a rendering of *Should She Upbraid*. It would have been wiser to have spared us this interpolation and to have made use of the time it took up by allowing Biondello to deliver his celebrated speech on the coming of Petruchio at a pace which did not render the words inaudible. Nor was anything gained by Katherine's endeavour to work up an exit by crying "I want my supper!" and then repeating it three more times. Comparatively judged, the Old Vic is accomplishing admirable work. Absolutely judged, its performances have not really more than a faint smell of the real Shakespeare.

LA MÉGÈRE APPRIVOISÉE
(1924)

It was very daring of Mlle. Sorel to open her season at the New Oxford with *La Mégère Apprivoisée*, a French version in four acts of *The Taming of the Shrew*. As soon as the curtain rose, it was plain that we were in for something not very different from the eighteenth-century adaptations of Ducis, who transformed Ophelia into a daughter of King Claudius, preserved Hamlet's life, provided Gertrude with a *confidante* called Elvire, who naïvely asked, in the true *confidante* spirit:

> *Avez-vous des secrets que je ne puisse entendre, madame?*

and opened the whole play with a duologue between Polonius and Claudius, in which Claudius began:

> *Oui, cher Polonius, tout mon parti n'aspire,*
> *En détrônant Hamlet, qu'à m'assurer l'empire.*

The opening of Paul Delair's version of *The Taming of the Shrew* the other night was scarcely less surprising. The curtain rose on Baptista, Bianca, and somebody called Cambio. Before a word had been uttered, there was a clatter off-stage, and Katherine burst on. As the play proceeded we, at the New Oxford, were well aware that this was not Shakespeare, or anything like him. But do they know in Paris? And if they do not, are they not astonished at the pride we take in our national poet?

La Mégère Apprivoisée is *The Taming of the Shrew* cut down to the bare bones of Katherine and Petruchio. It is also a translation of a boisterous farce into a rather saucy bedroom comedy. Mlle. Sorel stormed and snorted, but she was rather a tomboy than a shrew, and when she kicked it seemed to be less a kick of anger than a concession to Sir Toby Belch's "Wherefore are these things hid? Wherefore have these gifts a curtain before 'em?" Most of the characters were dressed in mediaeval costumes, but Mlle. Sorel preferred the fashion of the eighteenth century, and had the courage of her preference, while Baptista was mysteriously clad like a Chinaman. I have heard of a performance in Japan in which Hamlet appeared in cycling knickerbockers, and I have lately read of the production in India of an Urdu translation of *The Comedy of Errors* in which an attempt was made to satisfy native taste by the introduction of such popular music-hall songs as "In the Shade of the Old Apple-tree" and "It looks like a Big Night To-night". But the French version of *The Taming of the Shrew* is scarcely less astonishing. It was certainly a relief to see the same players tackling, later on, with real precision and formality, Molière's *Tartuffe*, and that exquisite trifle, *Les Précieuses Ridicules*.

PETRUCHIO AND KATHERINE
(1925)

The third production of the season at the Old Vic is *The Taming of the Shrew*, and since it is improbable that this comedy will be better acted in our time than it is now being acted in the Waterloo Road, and since it will be invisible in a fortnight, let there be no to-morrow and to-morrow and to-morrow to retard the progress of the intending visitor. It is difficult to conceive a better Katherine or a better

Petruchio—too difficult, assuredly, for me, and too difficult, I suspect,
even for Shakespeare. For here is the Shrew that Shakespeare drew,
and here her master. Here is a female fury, magnificent in her tantrums
and worth the taming not purely for the sadistic pleasure of it but for
the sake of the woman's underlying fascination. And here is a fortune-
hunter with a flick of April in his merciless whip—an appalling husband for any but Katherine, as Katherine would be an appalling wife
for any but Petruchio. Thank Heaven they met and paired off and lived
happily ever after with one another, for they could never have lived
happily ever after with anybody else.

The Taming of the Shrew is, not unnaturally, a red rag to feminists,
and I have seen feminist actresses play the part of Katherine with a
latent suggestion that she is only submitting pro tem. for purposes
best known to herself, and that she will get her own back as soon as
she wants to. This is not to be defended. A play that was written to
appeal to the taste of one public cannot be "rescued" by seasoning it
in such a way as to make it more palatable to a public differently
disposed. And The Taming of the Shrew, which is woman-baiting pure
and simple, was no doubt a useful card to play in the Elizabethan
playhouses because it drew the devotees of bear-baiting, which was
as serious a rival to the theatre then as dancing is to-day. "It is no bad
sport to see them fight," wrote Don Manriquez de Lara, the Spanish
nobleman, when he beheld the spectacle of a pony with an ape fastened
to its back at the Paris Garden, "To see the animal kicking amongst
the dogs, with the screams of the ape, beholding the curs hanging from
the ears and neck of the pony, is very laughable." We might not
enjoy such a show to-day, but to present it gutted of its brutality for
the edification of humanitarians would be absurd. Either we must
leave the thing alone, or we must exhibit it to the last squeal and the
last drop of blood. There is no middle course.

Miss Evans and Mr. Holloway handle their scenes with superb
antagonism and a sure understanding of what the psycho-analysts
call attraction-repulsion. They feel, clearly, that they have met their
match in a double sense. And Katherine, who loses, is proud to be
beaten by such a good side. She has been tamed, I think, only as a
wife. I suspect that it is still unsafe for any but a husband to enter the
cage, that the father and the sister had still better be careful how they
treat her, and that she thoroughly enjoyed the discomfiture of the other
ladies when she made them feel so small with her oration on the
whole duty of woman. She is, indeed, a sensationalist, and once she
has been subdued to the quality of her lord, she rather enjoys the
novelty of it all—perhaps she needed a god, for there is, after all,
nothing in her tantrums to suggest that she is an egomaniac. But
these are subtleties of minor importance. The great thing about the
show is that the Katherine of Miss Evans is a fine woman to beat
and the Petruchio of Mr. Holloway is a fine man to beat her. Whether,
in the Elizabethan theatre, they were so ignorant of Italian as not to

E

know how to pronounce Petruchio I question. Italy was very much the vogue. I question, again, whether the humorous description of the sleeves of the tailor's costume spoken by Petruchio would have been evoked by such a costume as is furnished at the Old Vic. When Petruchio condemns a hat for looking as though "moulded on a porringer", and a dress for being "carved like an apple-tart", with "snip, and nip, and cut, and slish and slash," why exhibit a hat and dress that make hash of these comparisons? But the play is well produced and, on the whole, well acted all round on, Monday, Wednesday and Friday evenings, and Thursday and Saturday afternoons.

PETRUCHIO IN CORSETS
(1939)

This is a lively rather than a sympathetic production. Mr. Tyrone Guthrie, faced by a Shakespearean comedy, seems always to be struck by the idea that it would be "great fun to produce it like a ballet". So, indeed, it may be. The trouble is that Shakespeare's comedies are not like ballets. One of the distinctive features of ballet is that it contains no words. One of the distinctive features of Shakespeare's comedies is that they contain, not merely lots and lots of words, but words ever so much better than those in any other comedies in the world. Even *The Taming of the Shrew* is full of them. They were written to be heard, not to be suppressed. And Mr. Guthrie, if he wishes to be regarded as a producer rather than a suppressor, should do his utmost to give every word full value, including Biondello's superb description of Petruchio's Rosinante, not one syllable of which gets across the footlights.

During the first part of the evening, so busy are the actors acting like actors acting before a drunken tinker (which method of attack would have been indicated in the text had it been intended) that the upshot is just a racket, with figures from the *commedia dell'arte* (Mr. Roger Furze has a fine fling) to divert the eye. The characters gabble their lines in between the seemingly more important operations of whacking each other and falling down. There being a limit to these humours, Petruchio appears at his wedding in corsets and then gets to work with the well-known Crazy-Gang-Christmas-Pantomime bowl of dough, slapping it on to the faces first of his servants and next of poor Katherine, what time Grumio skips through a rope of harlequinade sausages.

One gathers an impression that Mr. Guthrie does not really like this play. But to invent another play is indefensible unless you put your name on the programme as co-author with Shakespeare. Mr. Guthrie becomes co-author when he shows us Petruchio quaking with fear before he meets Katherine for the first time, since he must know that Shakespeare would have provided words to express this had it been in his mind. He becomes co-author again when Petruchio, calling for Katherine at the finish, betrays anxiety as to whether she will come. It is a blessing when, in the person of Miss Ursula Jeans, she does come, giving the last speech actually as though it had been written to be spoken and contorting nothing for the sake of anything else.

In such a production, the taming of the shrew necessarily takes rather a back seat. Miss Jeans and Mr. Livesey, nevertheless, acquit themselves admirably. It would be a pleasure to see their contest fought on a field more suitably chosen. The greatest pleasure of the evening is the appearance of Mr. Robert Helpmann as (*a*) Gremio, (*b*) Nicholas, and (*c*) the Tailor—in the first and second of these characters he is excellent, in the last supreme. There is little doubt in my mind that Mr. Helpmann is our coming actor. One is torn between the feeling that it would be a catastrophe for him to leave the Wells and a feeling that it's a catastrophe he doesn't. Meanwhile, it is pleasant to congratulate him on the certainty that he won't have to teach dancing, anyway.

ALL'S WELL THAT ENDS WELL

SHAKESPEARE ALL ALONE
(1940)

WHEN the war broke out and the shows shut up, I suggested to a friend that then, if ever, was the time to put on *King Henry VI Part 3*, since in normal circumstances how could it hope to stand against *Under Your Hat?*—but with all competitors out of the field, somebody might go. A similar thought seems to have struck Mr. Robert Atkins, the staunchest Shakespearean in our theatre. *All's Well that Ends Well* never has been and never is likely to be popular. But here it is, all alone (at the time of writing) in the Strand, all alone (so far as plays go) in the West End. And if there's only one play on, it is almost a matter of national credit that that play should be by Shakespeare.

Why isn't *All's Well* more popular? All the scenes in which Parolles, that hollow drum of a braggart, appears are rich in humour. Wise things are continually said and fine phrases continually coined throughout the piece. But Helena, the heroine, is difficult, and so is Bertram, the hero she pursues. Although he dislikes her, she insists on making him marry her as a reward for curing the King of a fistula. And as his conduct does not make him seem worth winning by any woman, their ultimate reconciliation leaves one cold. The means, too, by which this reconciliation is achieved are just hack-plot stuff. That old ring business has been worn threadbare. And isn't it always rather hard to swallow nights of joy passed in bed with one woman under the impression that she is another? At the Vaudeville it is certainly not easy to imagine that the substantial figure of Miss Patricia Tucker could ever be mistaken for the slim figure of Miss Catherine Lacey, who tries to make her part less merciless by playing it in a kind of neurotic daze. A difficult part indeed. Helena would have been better written by Shaw, who would have turned her into an exposition, or by Ibsen, who might have plumbed Hedda Gabler depths.

So our apprehensive senses are best fed by the Parolles of Mr. Esmé Percy, who gives us perhaps too much of the affectation at the expense of the swagger and fails to bring out the tremendous comeback of that immortal line, "Who cannot be crushed with a plot?" when he has been finally exposed—but who is nevertheless full of drive and provides good sport. Still better are they fed by Mr. Ernest Milton who, as the King, speaking beautifully, sheds his mannerisms and brings the whole to a most royal and gracious conclusion. Mr. Peter Glenville grapples valiantly with Bertram, and Mr. Jerry Verno as Lavache comes not too badly through the severe test of the "O Lord, sir" scene. I would set this as a *viva voce* examination passage for the resource of all Shakespeare clowns. Mr. Atkins himself handles Lafeu with ease, amiability and good understanding. His production, in the Elizabethan manner, is simple, swift and sure. If Shakespeare came back to life, it is certainly Mr. Atkins, more than anyone else in our island, who, ever faithful, should be elected to the honour of receiving him.

TWELFTH NIGHT

AT THE COURT
(1918)

NAPOLEON'S negative affirmation that it is the general who makes the fewest mistakes who wins the battle may well be applied to producers of Shakespeare; for the success of the Shakespearean producer depends not so much on what he does as on what he refrains from doing. If only he would let well alone! If only he would allow Nature to take her course! The failure nine times out of ten is due to the fact that the server-up cannot keep his finger out of the pie before it comes to table. Mr. Fagan, however, whose production of *Twelfth Night* was presented to an enthusiastic audience at the Court Theatre last week, exercised so much more self-restraint than is commonly found that we can look forward with pleasure to his promised revivals of *As You Like It* and *Much Ado*. It is true that those who have this comedy in their hearts will suffer many a twinge. Personally, we could have spared the get-a-good-curtain-at-any-price meandering and maundering at the close of the carousal scene. We could have spared Antonio crossing himself before the image of the Virgin. We could have spared Olivia's portly little page boy shoving Viola out of Court. We could have spared the young ladies dressed up as male attendants who made Viola's adoption of masculine attire appear less an adventure than a fashion. And we could have spared, and spared again, the acutely un-Elizabethan Roger Quilter settings of two of the loveliest lyrics in our language, with that heinous repetition, at the close of "O Mistress mine", of the opening line.

Nevertheless, taken comparatively and as a whole, this production is a good production, and Shakespeare, who must be tired to death of turning in his grave, may rest peacefully for once. The scenery provided by Victor Maclure, if it is no great shakes, attempts no great shocks and is a rough compromise between Barker and Benson, engaging you without challenging you and leaving both the conservative and the "neo" factions all square. For the acting there is a great deal to be said, especially of the comic characters.

Head and shoulders, arms, legs and feet above all the rest, stands Mr. Arthur Whitby, in whose Sir Toby Belch flow radical juices warmed by ineradicable humour. Those who saw Mr. Whitby in the same part with Mr. Barker at the Savoy will be gratified to find that not a jot of the old wit, of the old gusto, of the old briskness and spryness has been lost. This is no Sir Toby from the taproom of the White Hart but a true gentleman born, one who might gain admittance to and be helped out of the most expensive club. Most Sir Tobys extract their fun from the hiccoughs and let the lines go hang themselves in their own straps. Mr. Whitby remains highly intelligent at his most maudlin, so that when, having asked, "Shall we rouse the night-owl in a catch that will draw three souls out of one weaver?" he adds, all the zest suddenly departing in an access of obfuscation, "Shall we do that?" those four words, "Shall we do that?" discover a condition of mind by which all future Sir Tobys must, one feels, either stand or fall. Another entrancing performance is the Aguecheek of Mr. Miles Malleson. Here again we have a knight, however foolish, in place of the usual gibbering clown. In his opening scene and in the duello Mr. Malleson gives us comedy of the highest class. Mr. Herbert Waring is an excellent choice for Malvolio—very dry, very fantastical, and irresistible matter for a May morning. Mr. Waring does not play to the gallery, nor, after the fashion of Sir Herbert Tree, does he put his moustache in curl-papers.

Viola is a gift if you were born for the part, a millstone if you weren't. There is in this character a sweet gravity, a deep, still magic that partakes of the quality of twilight and welling tears, with emotions yearning on the verge of expression but never directly expressed. Is there a more moving moment in any comedy than the moment when Feste sings "Come away, death," and Viola gives Orsino all the devotion of her eyes? Miss Leah Bateman's performance lacks the ultimate thing, which is the first thing every performance of Viola demands. But she avoids many of the pitfalls of her predecessors. She does not make the mistake of overdoing the boyish—while

Rosalind's attire made her a little more of a man, and Portia's made her almost quite a man, Viola's made her more a woman than ever. Miss Bateman escapes, too, the trap for actresses lying in such lines as "I am all the daughters of my father's house, And all the brothers too", the last five words being usually blurted out as an anxious afterthought attempting to cover up a "bloomer". There is not, however, enough romance in this performance. On the other hand, there is too much romance in Miss Mary Grey's approach to Olivia and in Mr. Terence O'Brien's approach to Orsino. These two characters are in reality creations in the subtlest comic vein, the one in love with love, the other in love with grief, both figures of delicate mockery. If this were realized by the actors, the flexibility of their affections manifested in the final scene would not appear so improbable, and the love of Olivia for Viola-Cesario would stay within the bounds of comedy, instead of edging over the borderline into realms almost Sopho-clean.

Mr. Alfred Brydone, with a voice as leathery as his name, is a sound Antonio; and Mr. Moffat Johnston does unusually well both with the nondescript Fabian and with the Sea Captain.

AT THE OLD VIC
(1922)

During the past month the only performances of Shakespeare open to the public in London have been those of *Twelfth Night* at the Old Vic. This masterpiece of exquisite refinements is, perhaps, the most elegant of all Shakespeare's comedies; if its full flavour is to be extracted, it should be produced with precision and punctilio; not a weed grows in the garden of Olivia, where the box trees are clipped into flawless formalities. The performance at the Old Vic was jolly and buoyant; Mr. Robert Atkins has many good points, and not the least of them is his vim; he walks straight into every play he produces with confidence and zest; he does not dally in the byways. This was a vigorous *Twelfth Night*; but the outlines of the production were blurred, the conception was rather burly, there was a lack of style.

Take the presentation of the Belch-Aguecheek scenes. This was not merely broad; it bulged with business, some of which was funny enough, but most of which was mortal to the exquisite cut of the comedy. The drunken orgy was overbalanced by the prolonged panto-mime at its conclusion; the "Saturday, Sunday, Monday" catch—sufficiently authorized by Sir Toby's "Sneck up!"—dominated the passage with Malvolio; and Shakespeare was unjustifiably saddled with a pun on the words "night" and "knight", Mr. Atkins over-looking the fact that in Jacobethan days "knight" was pronounced with a hard k. Mr. Atkins as Sir Toby did well to remember his rank, but he was too lumbering to be very merry; Mr. Rupert Harvey as Feste seemed more like a footballer than a fool; but Mr. Andrew

Leigh's Sir Andrew was superb—a dolorously frisky dormouse knight, never to be forgotten.

I have yet to see Orsino and Olivia, who should be presented as pure fantastics, delicate creations in the comic vein. "Away before me, to sweet beds of flowers: Love-thoughts lie rich, when canopied with bowers." That is Orsino: an emotional sybarite who does not realize that Feste is pulling his leg when he cries, "Now the melancholy god protect thee!" As for Olivia, is she not, in memory of a dead brother, resolved to "water once a day her chamber round With eye-offending brine"? and must we not agree with Viola when she says to Olivia that "you do think you are not what you are"? We need Mrs. Patrick Campbell for Olivia. At the Old Vic Olivia was finikin rather than affected, and on too small a scale.

Malvolio, too, seemed undersized, and the repetitive "Pack of you, pack of you, pack of you," with which the actor sought to emphasize but in reality diminished the effect of his final exit, betrayed a failing only too common in these Old Vic productions. The exits are faulty. Either the characters draggle off, or they lose their heads over a rhymed couplet, or they repeat the "tag" in an attempt (usually successful) to get a round. When he played Iago, Mr. Rupert Harvey —who, by the way, speaks with what I suspect to be a real Eliza- bethan burr—was actually permitted to say "All things shall be well" twice, in order that he might convey its full sardonic flavour to the audience. Miss Florence Buckton never commits such faults as this. An examiner would award her high marks for her elocution. But she was not born to play Viola—and Violas are born, not made. Let it be understood that, compared with other productions of the same play elsewhere, *Twelfth Night* at the Old Vic was admirable. It is only compared with other productions at the Old Vic—and with an insatiable longing for perfection—that it disappointed.

IN THE OPEN AIR
(1933)

Congratulations to Mr. Sydney Carroll on the opening of his Open Air Theatre in Regent's Park. I know that London already has sixty important theatres. I also know that of these sixty important theatres twenty are closed. The fact remains that London has not enough *kinds* of theatre. We still need a Greek theatre for the presentation of Greek plays. We still need an Elizabethan theatre for the presentation of Elizabethan plays. But we no longer need an Open Air Theatre for the presentation of pastoral plays and masques written to be acted in natural surroundings. Mr. Carroll has now given us that.

The Open Air Theatre provides playgoers with a fresh and unaccustomed experience. It is not so much an alternative to other theatres as an alternative to an evening on the Thames. The trees and bushes make a lovely background, and when, day fading into night, they are brilliantly floodlit, the figures on the sward become prettier than ever. Orsino languishes, Sir Toby struts, the Clown warbles, the moon comes up, and Viola and Sir Andrew twitter in the breeze. "Charming, charming," you murmur as you wrap your new cloak around you—for even a warm night is a little less warm than your anticipation.

But neither *Twelfth Night* nor any other play by Shakespeare was written for production in such natural surroundings. The subtleties of acting melt into thin air. The characters seem more like puppets than people. Every word can be heard, thanks to efficient amplifiers, but, issuing from amplifiers, the words (unless you are close up) do not seem to be spoken by the actors, who merely appear to be accompanying them with pantomime. It is rather like seeing a play through the wrong end of the opera-glasses—an exquisite but superficial delight.

I suspect that in any play presented amid natural surroundings nature must become the star performer. It is too dominant to allow the imagination free play. Only when nature is parried (as by the structure of Greek and Elizabethan theatres) or when it sleeps (as in bed) can imagination get its chance. In a good play written to be acted in natural surroundings this fact will be recognized, so that the whole affair will become a kind of tribute to nature, a service, a pagan rite, a what-you-will—but not a *Twelfth Night*, in which the people are more important than any box hedge.

So in this Open Air Theatre I feel myself farther away from Shakespeare than I do indoors. It is suggested on the programme that because you can see the sky as groundlings could in the old Globe Theatre, the Open Air Theatre gets back to Shakespearean conditions. It does nothing of the kind. The sky is a minor point. The stage is the main thing, and the stage in the Open Air Theatre is so un-Shakespearean that the Malvolio prison scene has to be left out—which, of course, completely ruins Malvolio's outburst on his last appearance.

Having said so much, let me repeat that this *Twelfth Night* is charming, charming—a pretty twinkling carnival—a nice new way to spend an evening in a deck-chair. The acting does not come out strong, resolving itself into so much delightful foreground. The players are hard put to it—none harder, perhaps, than Mr. Laurier Lister who, playing Sebastian, must look like Miss Margaretta Scott and Miss Phyllis Neilson-Terry, the two Violas, on alternate nights!

Miss Scott's Viola (the one I saw) is excellent and surprisingly fiery. Would not Mr. Nigel Playfair (Malvolio) and Mr. Robert Atkins (Sir Toby Belch) do better in each other's parts? Miss Neilson-Terry's Olivia I can never forgive for singing "When that I was" at the end of the piece. I suppose she does the same as Viola and would do the same as Orsino. An infuriating blunder that made me pray for a sudden thunderstorm.

AT THE VIC
(1933)

The new season at the Old Vic has opened hopefully. The general level of acting in *Twelfth Night* is higher than in any Old Vic production I can remember. This despite the fact that Mr. Charles Laughton and Miss Flora Robson don't join the company till its second production. Faults there are. The depth of the comedy is lost in a sort of spick-and-span-ness. The permanent architectural unscenic stage, which would otherwise be excellent, is cluttered with steps. The characters can't take more than a few paces in any direction without going up or down. But this can and should be remedied.

The choice of Lopokova for Olivia is another mistake. Lopokova is delicious, she is graceful, she is intelligent, she would be exquisite in the right part. But that part is not Olivia. For Lopokova is no grand lady. Also her foreign accent makes her scenes sound like Chauve-Souris. And imagine Olivia scampering from Malvolio like a rabbit in a fright as she utters her dignified, "Let this fellow be looked to . . . I would not have him miscarry for the half of my dowry."

Who give the best performances? Miss Athene Seyler as Maria —quick as a needle, lively as mercury, broad-based, sharp-pointed— the most infectious Maria I have seen. Mr. Roger Livesey as Sir Toby —a fine blunt sot. Mr. Morland Graham as Feste (if only he could sing!)—a sweet, diffident fool, out of his guard unless you laugh and minister occasion to him, surprisingly but not unwarrantably old. And Mr. Leon Quartermaine as Malvolio—perfectly spoken and perfectly timed—even though we do feel he might see a joke, which is fundamentally wrong.

Miss Ursula Jeans as Viola has too much sex appeal. She does not exploit it, but there it is, upsetting the music of her scenes with Orsino. These scenes lack distinction in the playing. But you will enjoy *Twelfth Night*. This is the unfustiest production since Mr. Granville Barker's—so unfusty that I hope it is unnecessary to remind Mr. Tyrone Guthrie that Shakespeare needs no sprucing up. What he needs is disencrusting.

MR. OLIVIER AS SIR TOBY
(1937)

Mr. Laurence Olivier has come out surprisingly as Sir Toby Belch in *Twelfth Night* at the Old Vic. He gets his laughs more from business than words. If Sir Andrew thinks life consists of eating and drinking, Mr. Olivier's Sir Toby thinks it rather consists of falling down. His sword play in the duel scene is so comic that it should become traditional. But there is no core to this Sir Toby, nor is he master of the revels. Just a sodden butt and a bit of a puppet.

Immeasurably the best thing in this production is the Feste of Mr.
Marius Goring—a worn clown, stark, tragic, like a stab in the heart
of fun. Never have I seen the baiting of Malvolio in prison better or
more mercilessly done—and here Mr. John Abbott, not overweening
enough in Malvolio's overweening passages, begins a fine performance
that leaves a deep impression. Mr. Alec Guiness as Sir Andrew does
well, and Miss Ivy St. Helier plays Maria as though she had been
playing Shakespeare all her life. She may stay in "legitimate" for the
rest of her career if she chooses.

Miss Jessica Tandy must (as Miss Evans did) work hard at her
voice if she is to play Shakespeare. Apart from indistinctness (Mr.
Olivier is at fault here too), she lacks music. Moreover, her emotional
approach is too realistic, diminishing the romance. Doubling the
parts of Viola and Sebastian is never satisfactory. Two people behind
me who had never seen the play before just couldn't make out what on
earth was happening.

RANDOM NOTES
(1937)

In the Henry Irving edition of Shakespeare, published fifty years
ago, the famous actor-manager marked in all the plays those passages
which, in his opinion, might suitably be left out when the plays were
performed. Many of these cuts were made on the ground of propriety.
In Twelfth Night, an unusually "pure" play, sixteen offending passages,
now fearlessly spoken and unblushingly heard, were square-bracketed.
That, in the Victorian age, was only to be expected. Other excisions
are more difficult to account for. The first really startling cut comes
in the drinking scene, where the passage preceding, following, and
including the singing of "O mistress mine" is recommended for
omission. The second really startling cut is the passage preceding,
following, and including the singing of "Come away, come away,
death". Thus the leading Shakespearean manager of the 'eighties and
'nineties made his C's, his U's and his T's. Now, the melancholy god
protect him!

Playgoers have only to see the present production of Twelfth
Night at the Old Vic to appreciate the dramatic value of Feste's songs.
"O mistress mine," concentrating into a dozen lines of divine harmony
all the philosophy of Omar Khayyam, makes the moment it apostro-
phizes one with the eternity it is reluctant to contemplate. Sir Toby
and Sir Andrew, under the melting influence of music and canary,
become demi-gods (if rather obfuscated demi-gods!) as they listen.
Hearing the song, as we do, through their ears, how much lovelier
it becomes than when sung out of context, though even then it is
lovely enough. "Come away, come away, death," we hear again through
the ears of those on the stage. Orsino is the First Listener, for Olivia
becomes the "fair cruel maid" by whom he is "slain". Yet one hears

this song at second remove through the ears of Viola, the Second Listener, who does not receive the air directly, for Orsino is between her and it, and all through the singing she, whose emotions are realer and stronger than Orsino's, reacts to his reactions. This is a relationship not explicitly set down in the text but so inevitable that no actress playing the part of Viola ever misses it. As for "When that I was", here is surely the most perfect conclusion to any comedy ever devised, though the cuckoo song in *Love's Labour's Lost* runs it close. Even Henry Irving—a great actor but not a great Shakespearean—could not bring himself to blue-pencil this.

Augustin Daly, who was a far greater offender than Irving, did not cut out songs. He put them in. When he produced *Twelfth Night*, he began with a storm on the sea-shore, for the first scene of this amazing version was that between Antonio and Sebastian. Then, similarity to *The Tempest* having been established, on came a band of blithe seasiders, warbling "Come unto these yellow sands". A little later Viola sat up on a bench like patience on a monument while Orsino's minstrels serenaded Olivia with "Who's Olivia? What is she that all our swains commend her?" This put Mr. Daly in some perplexity when he came, later, to produce *The Two Gentlemen of Verona*. Beerbohm Tree's version was better, but so elaborate was the setting of Olivia's garden, with "real grass, real fountains, paths and descending steps," that it could not be shifted and had to be used for episodes that were quite out of place in it.

Shakespeare's plays are full of mysteries, and there is one mystery in *Twelfth Night* which has always perplexed me and which I have never seen discussed. When Maria forged her letter, why did she write "M, O, A, I," instead of "M, A, I, O"? As Malvolio says, M begins his name, but "A should follow . . . there is no consonancy in the sequel." Although the letter goes on, "If this fall into thy hand, revolve", this hardly dissipates the doubt which was the last thing Maria wanted to set up in Malvolio's mind. Why, then, did Shakespeare write "M, O, A, I"? Is there some latent sequential consonancy that was understood by the audience? If so, what was it? I should be glad to hear theories. So here, Baconians and Oxfordians, is your chance.

> If music be the food of luv, ply on,
> Give me excess of it; that soorfayting
> The appeteet my sicken and saw dee.
> That strine agen, it had a deeing fahl;
> Aw, it kime o'er mee air, leek the sweet soond
> That braythes upon a bank of veeolets,
> Stayling, and giving odour.

The above is a very rough transcription of the opening lines of *Twelfth Night* as they would have sounded, according to professors of phonetics, if you had attended a performance of the play in Shakespeare's day. So the strange symphony would have continued. You would have heard Viola declaring that her father's daughter "never tawld her luv" (north country) but "sat leek Pytience on a monument smeeling at grief." You would have heard the Clown sounding his k's in "knave" and "knight"—"Ee shall be constrined to cahl thee k-nive, k-neecht." And the proceedings would have concluded with the cockney lament that "The rine it rineth every dye."

For the Old Vic to plunge back to Elizabethan pronunciation would be disastrous, but in the case of words used for rhyming purposes, as "adieu" rhyming with "you", should not the pronunciation be consistently Elizabethan throughout? And should not the same principle be applied to words used for punning purposes, since modern pronunciation sometimes makes the sense of Shakespeare's puns unintelligible? Take this passage in *Twelfth Night*:

> SIR ANDREW. I would I had bestowed that time in the tongues, that I
> have in fencing, dancing and bear-baiting. O, had I but followed
> the arts!
> SIR TOBY. Then hadst thou had an excellent head of hair.
> SIR ANDREW. Why, would that have mended my hair?
> SIR TOBY. Past question, for thou seest it will not curl by nature.

Sir Toby's explanation leaves modern audiences completely fogged. Shakespeare's pronunciation clears the matter up, for in his day "tongues" and "tongs" were pronounced alike.

Who is Fabian? What is he? Where does he spring from? Why is he introduced into the play at all? Here is a Shakespearean mystery that has been left unexplored. Is there any other character in Shakespeare with so many words to say who remains so completely characterless? Sometimes he is played young, sometimes middle-aged, sometimes bearded, sometimes clean-shaven, sometimes well-born, sometimes plebeian: a jack-of-all-types. Nearly all the lines that Fabian speaks could be spoken equally well by some other character on the stage. It is almost as though Shakespeare had dodged up an extra part at the last moment to give a player a job.

The English climate was as damp in Elizabeth's day as it is now. The groundlings must often have stood in the rain (being as enthusiastic as football crowds) during open-air performances. If 1601 was a wet summer, what an apt song for an auditorium open to the sky must have been the Clown's "With hey, ho, the wind and the rain!" Can't you see the groundlings, as they join in the chorus, drawing their old cloaks around them?

THE WINTER'S TALE

ANTIGONUS AND THE BEAR
(1925)

I KNOW of no scene in any play that gives or communicates more freshly and absolutely the sensation produced by sunshine after rain than the scene in *The Winter's Tale* where the Old Shepherd finds his fairy gold. It is a real gem—and very well done in the new revival at the Old Vic. I was, however, sorry that Mr. Robert Atkins omitted the bear. "*Exit, pursued by a Beare*", says the First Folio stage direction at the close of Antigonus's monologue. As there was no bear to be seen, his last words—"This is the chase, I am gone for ever"—were unintelligible to anybody not already conversant with the play. I suspect that in Shakespeare's day they had a real bear—a public so accustomed to bear-baiting would scarcely stand anything else. Antigonus, by the way, seems to have been a man of great presence of mind. The bear got him, and the Clown describes how, even as the brute was busy on his shoulderbone, "he cried to me for help, and said his name was Antigonus, a nobleman." In the teeth of a savage beast I, too, would cry for help, but I should be too much put about to think of adding, "My name is Herbert Farjeon, a dramatic critic. . . ."

Mr. Ernest Milton has returned to the Old Vic for this production to play Leontes. Of Shakespeare's three great studies in jealousy, Leontes is the most realistic. Ford, in the *Merry Wives*, is comic; Othello, smothering Desdemona for "the cause", is out of the general run. But every word of Leontes, every hug he gives his son when he is in the throes of the yellow monster, must go home to all who have experienced the most degrading of all the emotions. Mr. Milton, in these early scenes, is electrifying, but before he gets to the end of them he has spent himself; he is inclined to use himself up improvidently. The exquisite sheep-shearing scene comes out for once rather commonplace—it is hampered by a Hollywood Perdita and a Florizel who looks like a villain trying to be blithe in fancy dress. But it's a beautiful play. Altogether, the answer is in the affirmative.

AN HONEST AUTOLYCUS
(1933)

In making plans for next season I hope the Old Vic will try to secure Miss Veronica Turleigh, who has temporarily joined the company for *The Winter's Tale*. Her Hermione speaks well, moves excellently, and is never at fault. It possesses a Madonna-like beauty perfectly responding to the requirements of the part.

This lovely play goes well at the start and at the finish, but the middle sheep-shearing scene is ruined by a toy setting and ill-considered romps. What incredible business producers insist on introducing into Shakespeare! Imagine Perdita, after making the loveliest speech in the language about flowers, flinging them all over the stage, to be trampled underfoot by all the bumpkins of the countryside. And imagine Autolycus biting the coins he has come by and, on finding a bad one, throwing it away! If Autolycus couldn't and wouldn't, palm off a bad coin, who could or would?

SHAKESPEARE BOTTICELLIED
(1936)

Mention of the Old Vic brings me to the revival there of *The Winter's Tale*. This has been produced by Mr. Michael MacOwen in settings which begin by reminding one of Bellini and go on by reminding one of Botticelli. In the sheep-shearing scene the village maids are so refined they might all be daughters of kings and queens, which comes rather hard on Perdita. Mr. Morland Graham's Shepherd and Mr. Andrew Leigh's Clown are authentically Shakespearean, but the Autolycus of Mr. Alec Clunes, surprisingly young and personable, might easily be mistaken for Douglas Fairbanks in fancy dress.

Miss Vivienne Bennett's Hermione is the loveliest thing in this production. Although I have seen many actresses who act Shakespeare better than Miss Bennett, I have seen few who speak Shakespeare anything like so well. Her delivery of the speech at the trial is one of the most moving pieces of declamation within my memory—here, too, every gesture is good. If Miss Bennett will come and read Shakespeare aloud to me when I am too old to read him to myself, then, perhaps, the best of life is yet to be.

One can't help wondering what Hermione did with herself during those sixteen years when the managing Paulina kept her boxed up somewhere out of human sight. One can't help thinking that she might with safety have made her come-back a good deal sooner. It's a queer story all through. But what great stuff there is being spoken all the time! The pastoral passages exceed anything in their kind ever written before or since. The final scenes drag—Paulina is always a bore. But how staggering in its truth to nature is the jealousy of Leontes, and how well it is done at the Old Vic by Mr. William Devlin! How well—and yet, how not well enough! We are still waiting for an electric spark to light up Mr. Devlin's solid worth.

HISTORIES

KING JOHN

A KING'S A KING
(1931)

I HAVE enjoyed nothing more this autumn than *King John* at the Old Vic. To hear a good line by Shakespeare well delivered is a pleasure not to be matched. Mr. Ralph Richardson's Faulconbridge gives perfect satisfaction. He is a manly actor with fibre in his pathos and a core to his comedy. Perhaps no actor has ever failed in Faulconbridge; but few can have succeeded better than Mr. Richardson.

Also it is a pleasure to find in Mr. George Zucco a Hubert who does not bellow like the Bull of Bashan. Mr. Robert Speaight as John pays insufficient attention to the feeling of individual words, nor is he any inch a king—and in Shakespeare's plays a king's a king for a' that. Nevertheless, he creates a good slinky-minded impression in his plotting scene. What, by the way, was the point of putting out little Arthur's eyes when the royal object was to get rid of him altogether?

On a first showing the women at the Old Vic this year are weak. The female parts in *King John* are comparatively unimportant, but they are all under-played. I would exhort Miss Baylis to hitch her Old Victorian wagon to a real feminine star without delay. Shakespeare demands a large manner and the public knows it.

KING RICHARD THE SECOND

A LOOKING-GLASS FOR RICHARD
(1925)

THE performances which are now being given at the Old Vic of Shakespeare's *Life and Death of King Richard the Second* should be seen by all who are interested in this magnificent play because, from first to last, Mr. George Hayes reveals scarcely a single flash of directly experienced emotion in his acting of the title-part, and because only by some such rendering can the character be soundly defended from the charge of inconsistency which has so often been brought against it. Richard II is one of the most fascinating of all Shakespeare's problem characters—and the name of these problem-characters, as all attentive readers of the plays must know, is legion. Sometimes the difficulties which they present are dismissed with easy confidence as just so many final proofs of Shakespeare's profound knowledge of human nature: if the ways of this character or that are inscrutable, so, says the bardolater, is human nature: the less we understand them, the stronger the suggestion that they must be true to the unfathomable complexities

F

of life. But while Shakespeare clearly knew a thing or two more than most of us, it is dangerous to take him on faith. In small matters he was notoriously careless. Moreover, many of the problems raised by his characters are due, not to superlative insight, but to the fact that a number of the plays to which his name is attached are the work of more than one hand, and that episodes in the old plays on which he based his new ones often hung round his neck like millstones.

Shakespeare could not help humanizing, but he had to pay the penalty of his daring. While again and again he breathed life into the puppets invented by his predecessors, the necessity for retaining traditional incidents beloved of the public not infrequently caused his creations to fall short of flawlessness. Not Hamlet, not Shylock, not Othello will sustain without damage the relentless attacks of hair-splitting psychologists and factists, who impugn Iago (to give but a single example) for the multiplicity and insufficiency of his motives, of which they persistently demand a reasonable and comprehensive explanation. But any painstaking Tom, Dick, or Harry could, if he chose, have supplied Iago with a single question-killing motive, and the fact that Shakespeare was negligent in this matter does not make Iago one whit less real or living. The truth of the matter is that Shakespeare was faulty only in detail. He saw so steadily and so whole that, like many great portrait painters, he could not be bothered to spend himself on comparative trifles. In the broad sweep of his most elaborate characters there is nothing amiss. And while we may admit that he was full of faults, we must view with suspicion critical declarations to the effect that the Richard II of the early scenes of the play bearing his name is quite a different person from the Richard of the later scenes.

"It appears to me", writes Mr. Frank Harris, whose view in this case may be taken as fairly typical, " that Shakespeare began the play intending to present the vile and cruel Richard of tradition. But midway in the play he saw that there was no emotion, no pathos, to be got out of the traditional view. If Richard were a vile, scheming, heartless murderer, the loss of his crown and life would merely satisfy our sense of justice; but this outcome did not satisfy Shakespeare's desire for emotion, and particularly his desire for pathos, and accordingly he veers round, says nothing more of Richard's vileness, lays stress upon his weakness and sufferings, discovers, too, all manner of amiable qualities in him, and so draws pity from us for his dethronement and murder."

This Richard, however, draws no pity from me in his dethronement and murder; if he is pitiable, it is for the incorrigibly theatrical frame of mind which continually prevents him from feeling anything directly; he is a poet, an aesthetic egomaniac, dominated to such an extent by his imagination as to be next-door to a play-actor. All through the play he is an artificial, vain, self-sentimental poseur, playing the part suggested to him by the situation or by the last speaker, instinc-

tively recognizing states of mind and then flowing on the tide of them
with scarcely a pang, as pleased with himself in defeat as he is in victory, never unpacking his heart with words but always packing it
up with them. In action and feeling alike he is lamentably weak, for
all his fine apostrophic flights.

This weakness may be seen no less in his easy yielding of the crown
than in the way he depends, or pretends to depend, in moments of
crisis, on the intervention of supernatural powers. He falls back on
the magic of his kingship, in aid of which the very nettles shall sting
his enemies. "This earth", he cries, "shall have a feeling, and these
stones Prove armed soldiers, ere her native King Shall falter under
foul rebellious arms." Two minutes later he is, quaking with fear and
asking, "Have I not reason to look pale and dead?" because he has
learned of the secession of twelve thousand fighting men—whom
his theatrical imagination promptly increases to twenty thousand.
He has an insatiable passion for extremes. First it is: "I am unassail-
able." Next: "I am dead." Then Aumerle says: "Comfort my Liege,
remember who you are!", and, instantly taking his cue, Richard
cries, "Am I not King?" and vaunts again with Falstaffian mathematics
that his name is good for forty thousand.

Then Scroope comes in, preluding more bad news with the pious
aspiration: "More health and happiness betide my Liege, Than can
my care-tun'd tongue deliver him." It is enough. The greater "health
and happiness" are promptly Richard's. His kingdom, he cries, was
his care. "And what loss is it to be rid of care?" Then he hears that his
old friends, Bushy, Bagot, and Green, have "made peace" with Bolingbroke, and he falls wildly cursing them, calling on hell to "make
war upon their spotted souls." Next, the word "where" in Aumerle's
"Where is the Duke my father with his power?" echoes in Richard's
mind (like Northumberland's "down" in the succeeding scene), and
he wails "No matter where", suggesting that they shall talk of "worms
and graves and epitaphs," and sit upon the ground and "tell sad
stories of the death of Kings." Who can pity a persistent decadent
talking in this strain? Aumerle utters a word of cheer again, and quick
as lightning Richard responds, "An easy task it is to win our own."
Scroope says something gloomy, and Richard, down again, cries,
"What comfort have we now? By Heaven I'll hate him everlastingly,
That bids me be of comfort any more."

It is a wonderful scene; but any actor who tries to put real feeling
into all these whirlwind and ridiculous changes is doomed, for of
such whirlwind and ridiculous changes no man is humanly capable.
He would die straightway of sensitiveness. This Richard can only live,
I repeat, as a poetical play-actor. He is forever performing before an
audience, even if that audience is only himself. What could be more
theatrical than his carefully-timed pronouncement of banishment on
Norfolk and Bolingbroke at the very moment when they are about to
engage their lances? What could be more theatrical than his "Now,

mark me how I will undo myself"—mark how he insists on being marked—and his posturing with his property crown and his property looking-glass? What could be more theatrical than his request, on taking his last leave of his wife, that, when she is in France sitting by the fire on winter nights with good old folks, she should narrate the story of his "lamentable" fall and "send the hearers weeping to their beds"? Only when he is alone in prison do we get a flash of true self-perception. Then, and only then, does he realize that he has been playing "many people, And none contented." Then, and only then, does he bring himself to utter the words "While I stand fooling here."

Thus the Richard of the opening and the Richard of the closing scenes are reconciled by the play-actor. To Mr. Hayes we owe a debt of gratitude for presenting the character actorishly, yet never over-actorishly, in all its consistency. His performance, as I said in the beginning, should not be missed. It is worthy of the admirable production contrived, without fuss or flourish, by Mr. Robert Atkins. It is worthy of Shakespeare's superb, overwhelming play. It is a sound looking-glass for Richard.

RICHARD II—JOHN GIELGUD
(1929)

The Old Vic is now presenting *Richard II*, which, of all Shakespeare's plays, was the one most disliked by Queen Elizabeth. It was the best scene in the play she hated most—the scene in which Richard gives up his crown to Henry—and she actually had this scene censored, because she took it as a hit at her own position. In the early editions of the play this scene is omitted. Not until James came to the throne did it get into print. The fate of Richard II always haunted Elizabeth and she did not like to be reminded of it. "I am Richard II," she is reported to have said, "know ye not that?"

That the association did not exist only in the mind of Elizabeth herself is clear from the fact that on the very day preceding the Essex rising, the rebel leaders paid Augustine Phillips, a leading member of Shakespeare's company, forty shillings to revive *Richard II* at the Globe Theatre. Whether Elizabeth was exaggerating when, a few months later, she complained that the piece had been played at the time of the rebellion "forty times in the open streets and houses" with seditious interest, can only be conjectured.

There is marvellous poetry in *Richard II*, some of which is, I regret to say, murdered at the Old Vic by Mr. Brember Wills as John of Gaunt. This clever eccentric actor makes too many soda-siphon noises to be at his best in poetical utterance. But Mr. John Gielgud does well as Richard. If he never electrifies (and one does rather ask to be electrified by actors in Shakespeare), he very ably suggests the temperamental weakness and harsh cowardice that so often lurks in poetic souls. And Shakespeare's Richard was a poetic soul besides being a bit of a posturer.

CENSORED SHAKESPEARE
(1934)

The Shakespeare Company at the Old Vic has followed *Antony and Cleopatra* with a workmanlike if uninspired production of *Richard II*, which was last seen in London five years ago. This is not one of the most popular even of the comparatively unpopular historical cycle. It has suffered heavily in the classroom from the grim anxiety of school-teachers (lured on, no doubt, by John of Gaunt) to kill two birds with one stone. It has suffered no less heavily on the stage from the custom of regarding it as an independent and self-supporting play, instead of as the first part of a tetralogy, designed to be given in conjunction with *Henry IV Part 1*, *Henry IV Part 2 and Henry V*.

Each of these plays taken by itself is but the gigantic fragment of a magnificent dramatic structure which we are never likely to see until a National Theatre comes along to do for poor Shakespeare what is annually done at Covent Garden for lucky Wagner. But perhaps *Richard II* suffers most of all from a grave internal trouble, which develops alarmingly at a most critical moment just before the finish, when the playwright has us completely under his spell, when the piece is marching swiftly and surely to its catastrophe, and when we sit enthralled to learn what will become of Richard next. At this moment we are abruptly and astonishingly confronted by the diversion of Aumerle's implication in the plot to assassinate Bolingbroke—a diversion so irrelevant, so untimely, and so ill-composed that it might almost be regarded as a wanton act of aesthetic masochism. We can hardly believe our ears when, on the heels of Richard's superb outpourings, the Duchess of York falls to spouting her doggerel couplets;

> For ever will I walk upon my knees,
> And never see day, that the happy sees,
> Till thou give joy: until thou bid me joy,
> By pardoning Rutland, my transgressing boy.

Almost all the critics agree in regarding this intrusive episode as "not by Shakespeare"; even the Old Vic audience laughs at it. As soon as it is over, the play picks up again, but the damage inflicted is irreparable, our exaltation has been dispersed, and we leave the theatre much as we entered it.

The heart, then, of Miss Lilian Baylis may well be in her mouth when the time comes for Richard to undo himself once more. It is, however, possible, that she might materially assist her box office if she were to indulge in a little catchpenny advertising and if, since nothing is more attractive than forbidden fruit, she were boldly to announce *Richard II* as "Shakespeare's Censored Play". Not that *Richard II* was the only play in which Shakespeare had to submit to the blue pencil of the Master of the Revels. Again and again the words he wrote were scored through by the authorities, because they were held to be libellous, or profane, or offensive to foreign nations. But however galling the changes required in many of the plays may have been—for example, the changing of "God give thee the spirit of understanding" to "May'st thou have the spirit of understanding" —they were easily made. It was only when a whole scene was sumarily suppressed, and that scene *the* scene of the play, that something drastic had to be substituted. What must have been Shakespeare's feelings when, probably on the eve of production, he was informed that the deposition of Richard, looking-glass and all, must be cut out of his tragedy, because the fate of Richard had long haunted Queen Elizabeth, and the last thing she wanted was that her subjects should be reminded of the possibility of such occurrences.

Here, then, were 165 lines clean gone, and not merely 165 lines, but the very crest of the drama. It is easy to imagine the excitement in the theatre on receipt of this news, the hurryings and scurryings, the curses and consultations. Nor does it require much straining of the ear to catch an echo across the centuries of the inevitable question on the lips of all concerned: "Well, what are we going to do about it?" For something about it most assuredly had to be done. And here, I suggest, may be found a satisfactory explanation of the artistically indefensible Aumerle episode. Another dramatic incident of some kind was required to fill the gap, to shore up the tottering fabric. The original play on Richard II, which Shakespeare had improved beyond recognition, was scanned for assistance. The episode (laughed at again by the Old Vic audience) in which Bagot charges Aumerle with being an accessory in Gloucester's death was bundled in to prepare the way for the new-old episode of the "transgressing boy". And so the censorship, which has never been a respecter of artists, handed down to us, via Heminge and Condell, the present version, in which the censored scene and the substitution persist side by side.

Perhaps, however, the unpopularity of *Richard II* is due most of all to the inhospitability of Richard's character which, placed in circumstances which clamour for sympathy, is for ever making that sympathy impossible. If Richard is pitiable, he is pitable less for his misfortunes than for the incorrigibly theatrical frame of mind which prevents him from experiencing clean, direct emotion. He is always thinking about thinking and feeling about feeling, and it is this removal from reality that makes it possible for him to pass too easily from despair to hope, from cruelty to lenity, from rebellion to submission, from extreme to extreme of every sort. It may be said that he wears his emotions rather than experiences them, and that being a butterfly artist he delights in nothing more than in quick changes of fashion. How can we be sorry for him when he is so obviously enjoying such a thoroughly good time with his grief? And, consequently, what normal audience, by which I mean an audience that takes its heart to the theatre rather than its head, would wish to see Mr. Maurice

Evans's most admirably composed, if slightly undersized, performance of the part twice over? There is something lacking in this play, as there is something lacking in a prologue, and it would be unreasonable to ask more; for Richard II in Shakespeare's dramatic scheme was, after all, only the king who was deposed by the father of Henry V, and if we do not see right through his looking-glass, if we sit upon the ground with him to tell sad stories of the death of kings (whereupon, by the way, the characters do all sit on the ground at the Old Vic!), this epic of hero-worship will falter on its way. It is imperative that we should side with Bolingbroke, and this is fortunately made easy for us not only by the irresponsibility with which Mr. Evans displays Richard's weakness but also by the tact with which Mr. Abraham Sofaer tempers Bolingbroke's strength. We only regret that we shall not be permitted to watch his development through the two succeeding and most glorious plays which are devoted to the events of his reign. Unhappily, it is likely to be a long time before this is possible, since the two parts of *Henry IV* are even less popular than the one part of *Richard II*, so that the magnificent wit of Falstaff, who has had the misfortune to get mixed up in English history, remains almost unknown to the public.

RICHARD II—MAURICE EVANS
(1934)

Mr. Maurice Evans, who began his career as a Dorchester Player, is now the darling of the Old Vic. It was for him they shouted after *Antony and Cleopatra*, although he only played the subsidiary Caesar. As for the ovation he got when he had done acting Richard II on Monday night, it was uproarious even for the Waterloo Road. And a very creditable performance he gave. If it lacked the impetus and miasmic passion of John Gielgud's Richard, it was true to character— a confirmed and brilliant attitudinizer, unable to escape the toils of habit when confronted by stark and shattering realities.

Mr. Evans speaks his verse well. Having weighed his words— having tasted them and smelt them and felt them all over—he brings out the quality of the epithet. When he talks of "my unstooping firmness" he emphasizes the adjective, which is right, rather than the noun, which is what most actors, who only believe in nouns, would do. To act in Shakespeare must be one of the supreme excitements. Imagine *being* Hamlet, Othello, Macbeth, Lear, Thersites! So great is the temptation that the worst actors will surely be forgiven, if not in the Press, at least in Heaven.

After the Richard of Mr. Evans, I thought Mr. Abraham Sofaer's Bolingbroke the most effective piece of work—here was a man who could do the king business without turning it into a royal exhibition. The production by Mr. Henry Cass is serviceable but betrays considerable reluctance in getting off the mark each time a new scene begins.

Instead of plunging straight into the dialogue, preliminary business is introduced, as the lighting of candles, or a Grand Parade of Old Vic Students. This tendency should be curbed at once. It leads inevitably to cuts. And not for twice the number of candles or half the number of Old Vic students is a line of Shakespeare worth sacrificing.

SHAKESPEARE ON THE INSTALMENT SYSTEM
(1937)

Mr. John Gielgud has opened his well-planned repertory season at the Queen's Theatre with a revival of *Richard II*. His version mercifully omits the un-Shakespearean rhymed doggerel of the Aumerle anti-climax, which was probably only pressed into service in Shakespeare's day to compensate for the loss of the great Deposition scene. This Deposition scene came too near home for Elizabeth and was banned, as *King Lear* was banned in the later days of dotty old George III. In which connection it is interesting to read that over in New York, where Maurice Evans is playing *Richard II* to packed houses, lines and situations are now being associated not with Queen Elizabeth, but with ex-King Edward VIII.

All Shakespeare's plays need speed, but especially the histories, which do not set out to tell stories, and so create little tension as to what will happen next. In the case of *Romeo and Juliet* or *Macbeth*, although any pause for scene-shifting is deplorable, interest survives, as in the case of an exciting feuilleton *"To be continued in our next."* But where there is no narrative tension, it is all the more important that the panorama of events should pass swiftly before our eyes. The curtain comes down far too often in this production of *Richard II*, which yearns for a permanent set. The orchestra, beating drums, blowing trumpets, and generally suggesting thrills to come, does its best to keep us up to scratch. But this musical equivalent of *"Another powerful instalment to-morrow"* merely augments the trouble, for when the curtain goes up again, the promise of the orchestra is belied. Here are great poetry and superb psychology, but that is all.

To this general atmosphere of flatness the Motley décor unexpectedly contributes. The scene in the lists at Coventry is pictorially engaging. But a growing tendency towards the merely ingenious and dodgy has been allowed so much play that the stage often seems littered with bits and pieces, and rather drab at that. This drabness may be due to a desire not to repeat the Aucassinery-and-Nicolettery of *Richard of Bordeaux*. But the fact remains that Motley have, for once, failed to excel themselves.

What, however, one does get in this, as in all productions of Shakespeare by Mr. Gielgud, is poetry well and intelligently spoken. Particularly good are the mounting Bolingbroke of Mr. Michael Redgrave and the humorous old Duke of York of Mr. George Howe, to whose admirable discretion one could safely entrust all the dullest barons and bishops in Shakespeare. Mr. Leon Quartermaine's John of Gaunt is less happy casting, for Mr. Quartermaine never has been and never will be venerable, and the venerability of John of Gaunt stands second only to that of the Venerable Bede himself. Miss Peggy Ashcroft does not try to make the most of Richard's Queen, and is the more appealing for it. As for Miss Dorothy Green's Duchess of Gloucester, it is as safe as the Rock of Gibraltar, which may not be quite as safe as we thought it.

Remains Mr. Gielgud's Richard. This is a fine composition—a subtle blend of the affecting and the affected, of poetry and posture. Most of the scenes are an echo of Mr. Gielgud's masterly performance at the Old Vic some years ago, but it is an excellent echo, and in the final soliloquy he is at the very top of his form. This should be recorded. Why not, in fact, a Shakespeare Society to record Shakespeare's masterpieces as the Mozart Society records Mozart's?

KING HENRY THE FOURTH—PART I

CUE FROM A QUARTO
(1922)

IT has been well remarked that the producer who desires to recapture Shakespeare's original intentions may glean much from the title-pages of the Quartos; for the Quartos are the nearest things we possess to the acting versions of Shakespeare's time, and their title-pages often indicate the incidents which presumably were emphasized in the original productions. The First Quarto of *King Henry IV Part* 1 is prefaced by this announcement: "The History of Henrie the Fourth, with the battell at Shrewsburie, betweene the King and Lord Henry Percy, surnamed Henrie Hotspur of the North. With the humorous conceits of Sir John Falstaffe." This announcement strongly suggests that the "battell at Shrewsburie" was one of the star features of the performance.

The fighting scenes in Shakespeare's plays—the battle of Shrewsbury, the battle of Bosworth Field, the combats in *Macbeth* and *Julius Caesar*, the fencing match in *Hamlet*—were probably anticipated with the keenest relish by the playgoers and executed in first-class, professional style by the players: for foils were all the fashion, while the art of the sword and buckler had not become such an obsolete antiquity as it is to-day. It is improbable that Shakespeare would have dared to present so many fights had he not known that they would be carried through with the greatest skill and conviction; and the reason that they are so ineffective to-day is simply that they are so inefficiently and half-heartedly tackled. Drama in these scenes gives place for the time being to sport, just as it did in many plays during the late war, when drill parades were frequently held on the stage and roused in audiences an enthusiasm which would have been turned to derision had the players bungled their job. Should any of these war plays be revived three hundred years from now, and should their producers neglect to reproduce the smartness and accuracy which is essential to a proper representation of the drill-parade and trench-sniping scenes, the gallery will titter as it tittered at the Battle of Shrewsbury in the production of *Henry IV Part* 1 at the Old Vic.

Nevertheless, if the execution of these scenes at the Old Vic was ragged and unferocious, Mr. Robert Atkins did not try to minimize their importance, and that is greatly to his credit. He had the courage of his defects and made the most of a bad job, which is better than making the least of a good one. And on the whole he put up a very presentable entertainment. The Falstaff scenes (especially the robbery) were well played with genuine understanding and Mr. Wilfrid Walter made for the right points, if he did not always succeed in making them. Falstaff is really a dancer: an elephantine frame, pirouetting, with all the exquisite grace of a Genée, on the tip-toe of the mind. His wit is part of Shakespeare's attempt to whitewash young Prince Hal. Who would not be tempted into "low company" under such leadership? Shakespeare tried to bridge the gulf of the historians, who presented Prince Hal as all dissipation and King Henry V as all dazzle. But Prince Hal, explaining his recklessness as a device whereby he may appear so much the more dazzling when he shows himself in his true colours, does not escape the charge of sophistry.

By far the best thing at the Old Vic just at present is Mr. Hay Petrie, who has followed up his Sir Hugh in *The Merry Wives of Windsor* with three more performances which reveal him as a comedian of the very highest merit. His execution is flawless. He never intrudes, and yet he is so irresistibly comic that it is almost impossible to take one's eyes off him when he is on the stage. His failing is the licence which he permits himself not in execution, but in interpretation. In the present production he played Francis and played him Welsh. Had Francis been Welsh, Shakespeare would undoubtedly have given his speeches a Welsh flavour; not less undoubtedly, he would have called the potboy by some less un-Welsh name than Francis. But Mr. Petrie had made such a hit as the Welsh Sir Hugh that he was tempted, and, though he fell beautifully, he fell.

The Old Vic scores again with this production but leaves me with a feeling that there should be a special school for instruction in the art of speaking blank verse. How strange that young actors should begin in Shakespeare, the most difficult of all playwrights, and so progress, when they have become proficient, to (say) Sutro and comparatively elementary work of that order. As well start children on Homer or Egyptian hieroglyphics in order that they may tearlessly read in their maturity that "The cat is on the mat." A point which must not be passed over without comment is the growing tendency observable in Mr. Robert Atkins to introduce songs and dialogue unwarranted by the text. Bardolph did not sing "Pastime with good company" to Falstaff in the Boar's Head Tavern. Which is a very good reason why he should not.

HOTSPUR ON TOP
(1930)

Mr. John Gielgud's hit in *Hamlet* will do the Old Vic a lot of good this season. For playgoers follow a star. They will now go to see him as well as Shakespeare. If they are disappointed in his Harry Hotspur, then *Henry IV Part* 1 is not a superb play.

This Hotspur is a real thrill. Fuseli said that Michael Angelo could stamp sublimity on the hump of a dwarf. And though Hotspur can think of nothing but honour and renown, though he is like a boy gone cricket-mad, though he is grotesque in his passion for "bloody noses and crack'd crowns", Mr. Gielgud, without a spot of whitewash, makes him the one character in the production we can really admire. Here is a hero, if a hero in fantastic excess.

In Shakespeare's day *Henry IV Part* 1 was one of the most popular of all his plays, running, like *Richard III*, into six editions when published. But it needs a good Falstaff to bring out the salt—and Mr. Henry Wolston's Falstaff at the Old Vic is mere beefsteak, taking no pleasure in its own wit. Nevertheless, a production not to be missed. It goes with a swing. There are few traps in this play for producers, and Mr. Harcourt Williams avoids most of them.

OXFORD TRIUMPHANT
(1930)

At the Old Vic, in one of the intervals of *King Henry the Fourth, Part I*, I was addressed by a learned gentleman who subscribes to the belief that Shakespeare's plays were written by Edward de Vere, Seventeenth Earl of Oxford.

"Of course," he said (much virtue in "of course"), "the Gadshill robbery scene is autobiographical. This is conclusively proved by the remark made by Prince Hal that the affair will be 'a good jest for ever,' —that is, of course, 'a good jest for E. Vere.' This pun, of course, occurs in the plays again and again."

And really, though you may hesitate to believe it, what my learned friend said is quite true. I have just been glancing through the plays, and what do I find in five brief minutes? Perpend!

Wilt thou, E. Vere, be a foul-mouthed and calumnious knave?—
All's Well.
If E. Vere he have child, abortive be it!—*Richard III.*
You have been a boggler E. Vere!—*Antony and Cleopatra.*

And so on *ad infinitum*. Not to mention "A thing of beauty is a joy for E. Vere"—or was that Keats—or wasn't it?

MR. ROBEY'S FALSTAFF
(1935)

Mr. George Robey's Falstaff is a success—if not a completely accomplished success, a thing of gargantuan promise. On the first night at His Majesty's he may not (as he confessed) have known some of his words or understood them all. Nevertheless, he proved himself not only the best Falstaff of our time, but our coming Shakespearean actor. Having shown all he has to show on the halls, he may now launch into a new career. Bottom, Touchstone, Sir Toby Belch await him. Possibly he's the only actor alive who could make Launcelot Gobbo really funny.

Once Mr. Robey is at home in Shakespeare (he isn't yet), he will be magnificent. Already in the soliloquies, where he is rightly on single-turn terms with the audience, he is superb. His delivery of the speech gets the utmost out of the lines, letting nothing slip. Most Falstaffs on honour is a masterpiece. All through, if he misses the rhythm, he waste nine-tenths of the wit in abortive characterization. Mr. Robey has too much comic sense to throw away the grand laughs Shakespeare offers him.

He lets the characterization more or less take care of itself. It takes care of itself quite nicely, but this is one of the faults he may amend when he has gained more experience and ease in his new medium. For example, he gives the impression that Falstaff is slow-witted (though well-witted) instead of quick-witted. Falstaff flashed. Robey churns. But what the churning produces is of the first quality. It is not the usual unmarketable mess.

We learn from Mr. Robey's Falstaff many things. One of them is that it is a tremendous advantage to have Shakespeare's clowns (even though Falstaff isn't strictly a clown-part) played by men who are funny *before they begin*. That wins half the battle, not only because they *are* funny, but because the audience is *accustomed to laugh at them*. Shakespeare's audience, we may be sure, laughed at Will Kemp before he opened his mouth. He put them in a receptive humour. Mr. Robey does the same.

Mr. Sydney Carroll's brilliant casting of Falstaff should put an end to the long line of dreary legitimate actors who have made soggy hay of Shakespeare's comics. It paves the way for and should give courage to Leslie Hensons and such. That's not modernizing Shakespeare. It's re-Elizabethanizing him.

For the rest, this production of *Henry IV Part* 1 should be played about twice as fast as it is. The ghastly anti-Shakespearean traditions of His Majesty's Theatre drag the pace from the moment Mr. John Drinkwater as King Henry starts reciting the first line. For vigour and speed, Mr. John Laurie's Douglas is a model to imitate. If this epic play runs fast, it will run long. After which, we *must* see Mr. Robey in *Henry IV Part* 2.

KING HENRY THE FOURTH—PART II

WHAT'S IN A TITLE
(1922)

FOR this season's concentration on the Chronicle Plays the Old Vic deserves the warmest thanks of all Shakespeareans; for Comedy and Tragedy are always more popular than History, and although Shakespeare's historical plays abound in comedy and tragedy, their labels have in the past exercised rather a soporific effect on box-offices. If *King Henry IV Part 2* had been entitled *Falstaff*, the revivals would probably have been doubled in number, audiences being undeterred by bitter memories of grappling with genealogical claims to the throne in the class-room. But such a title would have been a betrayal of Shakespeare's own vision in penning the plays in question. Probably that vision has never been realized: a playwright who writes a cycle of plays, inter-connected and leading up to a brilliant climax, must in his mind's eye picture them as being one day acted sequentially and in order, just as he pictures the scenes in a single play being performed in the order in which he has set them down. The time may yet arrive when the Histories will receive the treatment they demand.

Meanwhile Miss Lilian Baylis and Mr. Robert Atkins may be congratulated on the work of popularization which they have undertaken. *King Henry IV Part 2* was the best of the performances given by the Old Vic company this season, as it was the best of the plays. Two scenes in particular live in the memory. The first of these is the Tavern scene in Eastcheap, not one jot of the gargantuan coarseness of which was bated. It is very difficult in this scene to strike precisely the right note.

On the one hand, there is the twentieth-century tendency to barley-water the bewildering strength of the Falstaffian sack; on the other hand, there is a tendency to react from this tendency into an over-zestful, flushed and hectic realism which is one step farther still from the spirit of the original. A first-class producer of Shakespeare is not, in his inspired moments, conscious of Elizabethanism: he simply becomes Elizabethan. And this tavern scene "went", as they say, because it betrayed no sign of affectation, no sign of forethought, no sign of afterthought. The second scene in this production which lives in the memory is the last scene in the garden of Shallow's house—perhaps the finest pippin in all Shakespeare. And here it was really the sweet sibilant singing of Mr. Hay Petrie's Silence, his thin and ancient and melancholy piping merriment that furnished the chief delight, seeming, as it did, to reveal the very core of country life in the days before daisies pied had been plucked by centuries of over-conscious poets and before pottle-pots had been vulgarized by apostles of the Chesterton and Belloc school who are more concerned with the abstract splendour of drinking than with the concrete satisfaction of drink. Mr. John Garside's Shallow, too, was a fine, mellow piece of work, while Mr. Wilfrid Walter had his moments as Falstaff—notably in his delivery of the soliloquy on sherris-sack. But Mr. Walter's was a curiously unequal performance, now up, now down—a performance which might have been quite brilliant had it not lacked the all-important quality of jollity. That Mr. Walter is not a pure Elizabethan was driven home by his delivery of the line, "I am glad to see your lordship abroad", in which he laid his emphasis on the word "am". One of the achievements of the evening was Miss Jane Bacon's delivery of the long Lady Percy speech. This was incomparably the best modulated piece of blank verse speaking heard at the Old Vic during the present season. The audience laughed uproariously and for the most part intelligently at the comic scenes, but there were times when one could not help feeling that they laid themselves open to grave suspicion. Falstaff's "If I do, fillip me with a three-man beetle" was received with an outburst of hilarity. It may be that the audience was an audience of scholars. Yet one could not help wondering just how many of them could have explained the meaning of "three-man beetle" had they been directly taxed.

A SHALLOW FOR LAMB
(1935)

To the Old Vic to see *Henry IV Part 2*—a superb play which should be visited the night after you've seen *Henry IV Part 1* at His Majesty's. But a dull, undistinguished production, with nasty little pictorial backcloths, and all the important affairs of England conducted in the dark, so different from the comic ones, conducted in the light. If only producers would stop having I'll-tell-you-what-we'll-do-this-time ideas and would concentrate on the I'll-tell-you-what-must-be-done-every-time essentials.

Falstaff not funny. Too chuckleheaded and no sap. But Mr. George Merritt had bad luck coming after Mr. George Robey. What *was* good? Well, Miss Vivienne Bennett, who, having spoken the prologue with sense, colour and gusto, maudled and vituperated with a good slash as Doll Tearsheet. And Mr. Morland Graham—next-door to perfect as Shallow—an exquisite Morland country piece—so foolish, so tender, so human, so silly-sweet. What an actor! I'm still longing to take Sterne and Lamb to see him.

RANDOM NOTES
(1935)

Mr. Bernard Shaw, who is a firm believer in progress, once said that he had the advantage of standing on Shakespeare's shoulders, and whether you agree or whether you don't, you must admit that he has had the advantage of Shakespeare in some respects. Take for example the five parts of *Back to Methuselah*. In spite of the tremendous practical difficulties of presenting them consecutively, the thing has happened. Both in Birmingham and in London Shaw's *maximum opus* has been played right through as he designed, and Shavians have rejoiced accordingly. But the four parts of *Henry V* have never been treated with equal reverence. Sometimes we get a chance to see *Henry V* or *Richard II*. Less often we get a chance to see *Henry IV Part 1* or *Henry IV Part 2*. But never in the history of the theatre have these four plays been presented consecutively as the Shakespearean plan demands. The first manager to do this will deserve a knighthood or a dameship. But of course he or she won't get it, the constitutional view of Prime Ministers being that beer is better for you than blank verse.

. . . . . .

This, however, is not the moment to complain. With *Henry IV Part 1* at His Majesty's and *Henry IV Part 2* at the Old Vic, these two plays may now, possibly for the first time, be seen on successive nights. Even though the different companies and different methods of presentation may offer some obstruction to the view, here is a chance not to be missed, for it is seldom enough that we see either of these plays even separately. Although Falstaff is probably the greatest comic creation in literature, ninety-nine playgoers out of a hundred are familiar with him only in *The Merry Wives of Windsor*, where his fun is but hot ashes after the flaming wit of the histories. Now he may be seen and heard at the very top of his form, a mind of mercury in a body of lead. Listen to his soliloquy on the two-fold operations of a good sherris-sack or to his comments on the semblable coherence between Justice Shallow and his servingmen, and marvel that the mind of man could have conceived in mere thought and executed in mere words such miraculously subtle and searching reflections.

. . . . . .

It is impossible not to like Falstaff because it is impossible not to like the most amusing fellow in the world. Yet, if we exclude his wit, has he a single good quality? He is a swindler, he is a lecher, he is a coward, he is a thief, he is a compound of such villainous qualities that his original name, Sir John Oldcastle, was objected to by the descendants of that famous knight, with the result that the Elizabethan Censor (being more humane to descendants than the Censor who permits old Moulton-Barrett in *The Barretts of Wimpole Street*) made Shakespeare re-christen Oldcastle Falstaff. Yet we are far fonder of Falstaff than we are of Prince Hal, who acquires, if he does not begin with, all the virtues; for in addition to his magnificent companion-ability, Falstaff is created in the enormous round, a complete human being viewed from all sides, whereas Prince Hal is made to measure and is hard to forgive for some of the very acts introduced to keep his honour bright—as the soliloquy in *Part* 1 where he excuses his roystering in low company on the ground that it will make him seem all the more splendid by contrast when he reforms, or his dropping of Falstaff like a hot brick in *Part* 2 the moment he becomes king.

.   .   .   .   .

Some of *Henry IV Part* 2 is difficult to understand if you have not studied it closely—and Shakespeare repays study provided that you appreciate him before your studies begin. You cannot fully appreciate the character of Pistol unless you realize that his passion for robustious fustian is a hit at the old school of drama which was being presented by a rival company at the Rose under Edward Alleyn, with whom Shakespeare gained his first theatrical experience and from whom he inevitably seceded. It is not improbable that the original actor of Pistol enlivened his performances by burlesquing Alleyn's cat-tearing histrionics, and that when he cried "Feed, and be fat, my fair Calipolis," a travesty of a line in Peele's *Battle of Alcazar* which was thundered by Alleyn with a piece of raw meat on the end of his sword, the groundlings at the Globe rioted with joy at the sally.

Again, the Hogarthian scenes with Doll Tearsheet and the Hostess are full of obscure words and references which are really worth understanding, as it is worth understanding French when you go to see a French play. It does help to know just what Doll Tearsheet means when she calls Pistol a "basket-hilt stale juggler" or when she calls Falstaff a "whoreson little tidy Bartholomew boar-pig."

By far the loveliest scenes in *Henry IV Part* 2 are those in Gloucestershire, where Shallow babbles of his glorified youth and Silence pipes a shrill treble in his cups and Davy-Davy-Davy strives to get his master to concentrate on the necessity for supplying a new link to the bucket or of paying the smith's note for shoeing and plough-irons.

Here we reach the very heart of English country life in Shakespeare's time, here we taste the very centre of the kernel of the sweetest nut ever picked in the western counties. As Hazlitt says: "The true spirit of humanity, the thorough knowledge of the stuff we are made of, the practical wisdom with the seeming fooleries in the whole of the garden-scene at Shallow's country-seat, and just before in the exquisite dialogue between him and Silence on the death of old Double, have no parallel anywhere else. In one point of view, they are laughable in the extreme; in another they are equally affecting, if it is affecting to shew what a little thing is human life, what a poor forked creature man is!" But enough of writing. The actors are the men. Now you shall see Shallow's orchard, where, in an arbour, you shall eat a last-year's pippin of his own graffing, with a dish of caraways and so forth; come, cousin; and then to bed.

KING HENRY THE FIFTH

OLD VIC PRODUCTION
(1937)

RE-ENTER Henry V. This is the Old Vic's Coronation production, heraldically given against a background of banners, now gay, now tattered, representing the fortunes of the day. A satisfactory performance of a magnificent play, with Mr. Laurence Olivier (wearing a fair wig) at his very finest in the soliloquy on ceremony and the prayer that follows it. Mr. Olivier is a reflective Henry V. His martial speeches, though ringingly delivered, lack the expected fire.

Watch Mr. Marius Goring. He follows up his Feste with some superb word-handling as the Chorus. Miss Jessica Tandy's French princess is delicious, but one could spare the interpolated song sung to her by her ladies in favour of some of the cut lines. The Motley costumes maintain a remarkably high standard—one wonders how long they can keep up their present pace. The secret of their continued success is that they don't delegate.

EYE VERSUS EAR
(1938)

At Drury Lane Mr. Ivor Novello seems to me more like Prince Hal than Henry V, which monarch he is now playing with plenty of grace but insufficient strength. *Henry V* would really be best presented twice a week in conjunction with the two parts of *Henry IV*, of which it is structurally the climax. It would also be best presented in a theatre of dimensions far less vast than those of Drury Lane, where it is assumed that the size calls for a pageantry at loggerheads with the protestations of the Chorus, and where the intimacy of many of the scenes is inevitably lost. It should never be forgotten that Shakespeare wrote with the advantages and limitations of a small theatre continually in mind. The size of the Globe theatre south of the Thames, auditorium and stage included, was no bigger than that of a lawn tennis court.

A spectacular production this, with armies and processions masterfully handled by Mr. Lewis Casson. But the eye and the ear are not co-operative organs. The more you see, the less you hear. The more you hear, the less you see. If Shakespeare wrote, say, eighty per cent for the ear and twenty per cent for the eye, then anything over twenty per cent that challenges the eye will either be wasted or detrimental to the intended effect.

What I liked best at Drury Lane was the performance of Princess Katherine given by Miss Dorothy Dickson, who would now be one of our leading legitimate ladies had she never been able to dance.

G

Every year she takes a step not back, but forward. Miss Joan Swinstead's Alice and Mr. Frederick Bennett's Fluellen might well be borne in mind the next time *Henry V* is revived. As the Chorus, Miss Gwen Ffrangçon-Davies, though she speaks with fine vigour, is too plainly under the necessity of playing a part as well as declaiming her lines. If the Chorus is to be a man, why not engage a man? If it is to be a woman, why not dress it as such?

KING RICHARD THE THIRD

RICHARD AND MARGARET
(1925)

I HAVE sometimes heard it said, and I have sometimes even seen it written, that Miss Edith Evans, who is now admitted on all hands to be a supreme comic actress, cannot play tragedy. I do not know whether the people who say and write these things have ever seen Miss Evans in tragedy. It is hard to believe that they would have committed themselves to such a rash and ill-advised opinion had they witnessed her performances in *I Serve*[1] or *The Witch of Edmonton*.[2] Nor is it easy to believe that, if they trouble to go down to the Old Vic, where Miss Evans may now be seen as Queen Margaret in *Richard III*, they will ever commit themselves to such a rash and ill-advised opinion again, for Miss Evans as Queen Margaret is like a figure from the grand old past of Shakespearean acting, the grand old past which may exist, for all we know, only in our imagination, but which is now confirmed by Miss Evans as at least a possibility.

Here is a gigantically-hewn fragment of acting on the epic scale. Here is a titanic emotional achievement, not pitched in the key of realism, which is comparatively easy, but in the key of heroism, which is so much more difficult and so much more exhilarating. This imprecating figure of an old queen, stirring up civil strife even in her senility, invoking the wrath of heaven on those who have dispossessed her, may rank with the biggest triumphs Miss Evans has yet won. Her towering passions have a sublime sculptural quality. As she advances on Richard, you could swear that she holds a thunderbolt in her upraised cursing arm. Ye gods and little Westenders! what dramatic history is now unfolding itself in the Waterloo Road!

Emotional acting in these days is too often narrowed to the limits

[1] *I Serve*. Miss Evans came out in this play in September, 1922. On the morning of its production the *Daily Herald* printed a special leader-page article which I sent in under the title "Our Greatest Actress." When, however, the article appeared, the title had been changed to "Our Leading Actress?" I have seldom felt more mortified but the editor defended the note of interrogation on the ground that it was best to be on the safe side.

[2] *The Witch of Edmonton*. This refers to the performance given by Miss Evans as Ann Ratcliffe at the Lyric Theatre, Hammersmith in 1921, not to her performance as Mother Sawyer at the Old Vic in 1936.

of the performer's personal experience. Miss Fay Compton, for example, whose performances are almost uniformly good, and whom I would not cite if I did not cherish an admiration for her work, never seems to me to accomplish or to be capable of accomplishing anything on a grand scale because her power of observation is so immensely superior to her power of imagination and because, in tackling a part, she seems always to ask herself the question, "How would (or did) I feel in similar circumstances?" The consequence is that, being an artist of considerable intelligence and sensibility, she never does anything incredible, appearing, in modern realistic plays, as large as life and twice as natural. But in heroic plays this method breaks down, because in heroic plays it is of no avail to appear as large as life and twice as natural; the aim of the player here should be a creation twice as large as life and half as natural. Nothing seems to me less likely to produce results of the first quality than the course advocated by the late Louis Calvert, himself an excellent actor, who suggests that a player studying the part of Shylock should call himself "Stingy" Smith, "the tightest man in town", and, having rechristened Bassanio Brown, should proceed to pluck the heart out of the dialogue by paraphrasing it after this fashion:

"STINGY" SMITH: So you want me to lend you three thousand?
BROWN: Yes, for ninety days or so.
"STINGY" SMITH (*repeating, that there may be no mistake*): Three months?
BROWN: Robinson will go security for me. (*The name Robinson fills Smith with hate, but he checks himself.*)
"STINGY" SMITH (*calmly*): Robinson, eh? So Robinson will back your bill?
BROWN: Right. What do you say?
"STINGY" SMITH (*with a tinge of sarcasm*): Hm. Your friend Robinson is a good man.
BROWN: He certainly is. Do you know anything against him?
"STINGY" SMITH (*hastily*): Oh no, no, no. Lord no, not in the least! I simply meant that his credit is good. I meant his name to a bill should satisfy anyone. But I'm a cautious man. I go slow. Robinson is a shipper, and all he's got is his ships. They're likely to be wrecked, of course. Still, I think I'll take a chance.

This Barry Jacksonian method may assist toward a capable naturalistic performance of the part of Shylock, but it beats me to guess how Mr. Calvert would paraphrase the pound of flesh. It is an unsound method because it leaves out of account the important fact that, while the same idea may be expressed in two different ways, a speaker chooses one way rather than another because it more faithfully reflects his emotional attitude toward that idea. As soon as you begin to paraphrase the words, you begin to paraphrase the emotions behind them You cannot separate the two. And in the same way, as soon as a player begins to paraphrase a character in terms of his own personality, all hope in the way of a memorable performance may be abandoned.

Miss Evans stands out above her fellow players because she works with her imagination and not with her experience. She does not assume that human nature is the same all the world over and that Portia and Margaret are therefore both Miss Evans. She leaves herself out of account, realizing that the art of the playwright thrives, and thrives rightly, not on the similarities but on the differences between his *dramatis personae*. She does not absorb her part, she becomes absorbed in it: absorbed, where Margaret is concerned, in the aloofness, the bitterness, the violence, the superiority, *and* the blankverseness. She plunges into blank-verse emotions inspired by the understanding that if they were the same as prose emotions, there would be no place in the English language for blank-verse. Here is an amazing old woman, fierce in her dispossession, intolerant of the woes of the younger generation which cannot match "the high perfection of her grief." And here is an actress who can teach all our other actresses not only how to be witty, but how to curse and weep.

It cannot be too strongly emphasized that the productions at the Old Vic this year excel its previous productions in this: that both the leading lady and the leading gentleman are players distinctly above the common run of leading ladies and gentlemen. Mr. Baliol Holloway's Richard is wonderfully well done, notable for its grace in the earlier scenes—and nothing but grace can possibly redeem that coffin-courtship from utter incredibility—and for its grim cynicism and power all through.

This is something more than a man with a limp and a wry mouth and a black heart. It is a human being with a zest for overcoming obstacles and nothing but scars to show for it when he has overcome them all. There are moments when Mr. Holloway seems to be acting even with his fingernails. I thought he was particularly good in the throne scene where he is insolently fobbing off Buckingham's petition with requests to be told the time. He marked, too, very clearly the difference between the gaiety of the arriving Richard, with everything to win, and the care of Richard arrived, with everything to lose. This is essentially a "show" part. I am not certain that Mr. Holloway, for all the touches with which he embellishes it, might not with advantage play it just a shade more showily. But I should certainly stop short of this recommendation were I not opposed to the old saw that it is best to let well alone. To say that Mr. Holloway might be finer is not to suggest that he is not, as he stands and speaks and moves, very fine indeed.

Altogether, this piece is better acted than was *The Merchant of Venice*. True, Richmond smacks of the village green, Dorset of the football field, Elizabeth of the boarding-house. But many of the smaller parts are very soundly done, while Mr. Andrew Leigh's production marches swiftly and keeps to the point. I cannot, however, approve of the orchestral stepdance introduced for some of Richard's leg-dragging exits. This sort of thing may be all very well for Dubosc in *The Lyons Mail*. Richard's music is in his own couplets.

RICHARD AS PERVERT
(1937)

Mr. Emlyn Williams as Richard III at the Old Vic makes sense of every word. His delivery of the opening soliloquy is masterly. In the whirl of passion the content of his lines never loses its equilibrium as so often happens with Shakespearean actors.

His reading of Richard's character is less satisfactory. The Richard of the play is objective and sardonic, not, as Mr. Williams suggests, a sensuous pervert whose senses faint with ecstasy over the contemplation and performance of each fresh crime. Such a Richard would insist on doing the murders himself instead of getting them done for him.

The production at the Old Vic suffers from costumes which might do for a masque but fail to drive home romping drama with conviction.

RANDOM NOTES
(1936)

"What in hell would your Richard be without my spangles?" This remark, which was made in a fury by Andrew Jackson, proprietor of a patent for ornamenting leather with gold and silver, to Edwin Forrest, a famous American Richard III, has always struck me as worth preserving; for though it may seem to underrate the value of acting, spangles are certainly more appropriate to a performer of Richard III than to one of, say, Mark Antony or Macbeth. The part is essentially a gaudy part, demanding an actor of melodramatic genius rather than one versed in subtleties and fine shades. Although it was created by Burbage, it might fittingly have been written for Alleyn, from whose blood-and-thunder company Shakespeare had just seceded. "I am determined", says Richard in his opening soliloquy, "to prove a villain." And an out-and-out villain, worthy of his deformities and free from any redeeming qualities, he proves. Possibly he is the greatest monster in dramatic literature. Whether Marlowe, who served Alleyn so well, did or didn't have a hand in *Richard III*, his influence is everywhere apparent.

.   .   .   .   .   .

Edmund Kean was probably the greatest Richard III the theatre has yet produced. He started rehearsing the part when he was 13 and made his historic success in it at Drury Lane when he was 26. Between those ages this Richard weathered some stormy passages. Once,

Guernsey, when Kean appeared in the part, he was greeted with hisses and derision. For a time he endured the hubbub, until, reaching the line, "Unmannered dog, stand thou when I command", he strode down to the footlights, glared at the audience, and put the line in the plural. An uproar followed, with demands for an apology. "Apology!" cried the little man, "Take it from this remark: The only proof of intelligence you have yet given is the proper application of the words I have just uttered." Whereupon he was bundled off the stage, and another actor enlisted to continue the part.

.   .   .   .   .

One of the oddest performances of *Richard III* ever given was in Dundee in the middle of last century. Much interest has been aroused at the New Theatre lately by the exchange of parts between Mr. Gielgud and Mr. Olivier in *Romeo and Juliet*. But what is this compared to a performance of *Richard III* in which a different actor plays Richard in each of the five acts? Langley took the first act, Coleman the second, Murray the third, Ellenden the fourth, and Tom Powrie the fifth. The no-star system with a vengeance!

.   .   .   .   .

There is in *Richard III* a clear echo of Shakespeare's association with Alleyn, whom he had lately seen and with whom he had possibly acted in Peele's *Battle of Alcazar*. This was the play in which Alleyn as the Moor made the eyes of the groundlings start out of their heads, one of his big scenes occurring in the last act, when the Moor is routed by the enemy. The Moor is on the stage, alone with his Boy. "Villain, a horse!" he cries. A moment later he repeats, "Villain, I say, give me a horse to fly!" And then, a third time, "A horse, a horse, villain, a horse!" Shakespeare certainly bettered this when he made Richard III, alone on the stage with Catesby, twice cry, "A horse, a horse, my kingdom for a horse!" That line quickly became the vogue. Peele, on hearing it, may well have made a wry mouth and gulped a cup of sack to the memory of Greene.

.   .   .   .   .

Ars longa, vita brevis. And so we are unlikely ever to see *Richard III* given, as it should be given, on a fourth night, the first three having been devoted to the three parts of *Henry VI*. It stands in relation to these plays as *Henry V* stands in relation to *Richard II* and the two parts of *Henry IV*. As a culmination, it gains enormously in significance. Moreover, the character of Margaret cannot be fully appreciated if her past history is not fresh in the mind of the audience. But the general opinion of schoolboys grown to man's estate is that a little of the Wars of the Roses, which were so confusing that armies sometimes had to fight two battles in the same place, goes a long way. The tetralogy suffers in consequence.

KING HENRY THE EIGHTH

MISS THORNDIKE AS QUEEN KATHERINE
(1926)

THE audiences now crowding the Empire Theatre in Leicester Square to see the production there of *Henry the Eighth* suggest that, for all the jeremiads written and spoken on Shakespeare as a dividend-producing proposition, his name is, nevertheless, one of the biggest draws in the West End. It may be doubted whether there is anything that metropolitan playgoers want to see—or want to want to see—more than Shakespeare. The only obstacle in the way of their enjoyment is the fact that Shakespeare wrote Shakespeare's plays.

Like a popular actor in an unpopular role, poor Shakespeare has to struggle as best he can against *Macbeth*, *King Lear*, *The Tempest*, and the rest of his masterpieces. All things considered, he struggles very successfully. If you question this, suppose, for a moment, that Mr. Frederick Lonsdale had been the author of the *Hamlet* we saw the other day in modern costume at the Kingsway Theatre. Is it unreasonable to conjecture that the play would, in those circumstances, have been withdrawn, through lack of support, in a bare fortnight? Suppose, on the other hand, that Shakespeare had written *Spring Cleaning*. Is it unreasonable to conjecture that *Spring Cleaning* would still be playing to packed houses?

It is now generally agreed that Shakespeare had only a finger in the pie of *Henry the Eighth*, while by some he is denied even that. But what if, greatly daring, the management at the Empire had announced this play, not as by William Shakespeare, but as by John Fletcher, whom the experts now generally recognize as author of the greater part of it. Would there not, on the night of my attendance, have been a few empty seats visible in that vast auditorium, despite the magnetic name of Sybil Thorndike, despite the seasonal boom of the Christmas holidays, despite the fact that the wives of Bluff King Hal were more numerous even than the husbands of Pauline Frederick? I think there would. For, truth to tell, *Henry the Eighth* is not only a bitter disappointment to any devotee of the *News of the World*, but, quite apart from that, is a dull play insufficiently relieved by one or two fine scenes. There hangs over it a certain restraint, a certain uneasy circumspection, suggesting that the author, or authors, may have been a little afraid to let themselves go, owing to the recency of the events dramatically chronicled.

An historical play written about people who were alive only yesterday may be far more interesting to-day than an historical play written about people who lived three hundred years ago, but in three hundred years it is likely to become inferior to its rival in interest. To-day we applaud *Abraham Lincoln*, but it will not be surprising if

our descendants find themselves not a little bored by the flat sobriety
imposed on the treatment of the theme by propinquity. No doubt,
the exhibition of the Infant Elizabeth at the close of *Henry the Eighth*
was calculated to create a great sensation in the Jacobean theatre,
comparable to the sensation which would be created by the exhibition
in our present-day theatre of a Baby Edward the Seventh. But if we
except a magnificent speech here and there, the loss of topical interest
leaves *Henry the Eighth* barren and tedious. There is no central point
on which to fix one's interest, no comic relief to speak of, for Bardolphs
and Doll Tearsheets can scarcely be admitted into a play called—as this
play was originally called—*All is True*. There is plenty of information in
it for the young. Schoolmasters may rejoice, on behalf of their pupils,
in such guide-bookish passages as Griffith's summing up of Wolsey:

> He was a scholar, and a ripe and good one,
> Exceeding wise, fair spoken and persuading,
> Lofty and sour to them that loved him not,
> But, to those men that sought him, sweet as summer.
> And though he were unsatisfied in getting,
> (Which was a sin) yet in bestowing, madam,
> He was most princely: ever witness for him
> Those twins of learning that he raised in you,
> Ipswich and Oxford—one of which fell with him,
> Unwilling to outlive the good that did it,
> The other (though unfinished) yet so famous,
> So excellent in art, and still so rising,
> That Christendom. . . .

This Baedeker oration may be avidly consumed by visiting Americans.
But it is dull poetry and anti-dramatic. And, quite obviously, not
Shakespeare.

That reference to visiting Americans is not inappropriate to the
whole play, for *Henry the Eighth* is a show play, and seeing it is rather
like seeing the sights. Mr. Lewis Casson has, in these circumstances,
done well to give it a display production—a production at once
dignified, heraldic and a little pompous. The decoration furnished
by Mr. Charles Ricketts, in his best *Saint Joan* vein, is rich and subdued. If it is a little too College-of-Arms, stained-glass and university-
townish to allow full scope for the type of acting best suited to the
play, it is well conceived. I do not know whether it was the idea of
Mr. Ricketts that the ladies of the company should all, with the
exception of Anne Bullen, refrain from putting any colour on their
faces: from Miss Thorndike downwards, they seem to have stepped
straight from the walls of a gallery of contemporary portraits, with
a most pleasing, austere effect. Nevertheless, this, again, imposes a
queer restraint on the acting, like the restraint imposed on acting in
Egyptian pieces in which the ladies are required to walk about with
their hands and arms in angular positions, simply because they are so
shown in the pictures of the time. One day, in the distant future,

some producer, endeavouring to revivify the Society life of our own time, may turn to Sargent, present twentieth-century peers with their wives and daughters after the manner of this artist, and be applauded for it. But that will make it additionally difficult for the players to get any real flesh and blood into their performances.

Nevertheless, *Henry the Eighth* at the Empire is, on the whole, well produced and well acted. Miss Thorndike's Katherine is admirably done, with something of the strength of a Genevieve Ward in the trial scene, and with beautiful restraint at the end. Although Miss Thorndike is famous for grand outbursts of emotion, she is really at her best when she is holding herself in. Her Katherine never sacrifices breeding to pyrotechnics.

Mr. Norman V. Norman's Henry VIII is a striking old boy and will bring much grist to the Empire box-office, but it is pitched in rather a low-comedy key—there were moments when he might have been mistaken for Mr. Robert Hale trying to curb his extravagance. Mr. Norman looks his part to perfection, and if he suggests that Henry was more accustomed to sitting on a three-legged stool than on a throne, his performance has the merit of great vitality and a highly accomplished technique. It is infinitely superior to the lugubrious fog-horn Wolsey of Mr. Lyall Swete, which lacks power and descends almost to bathos in the great "Farewell" scene. Mr. Swete delivers these memorable speeches in the kind of voice affected by music-hall comedians when they set out to burlesque clergymen. One feels that he would be more at ease if he could only add "my brethren" at the end of each sentence. Still worse is his trick of suiting the intonation to the simile—as when (to give but one example) he speaks the lines:

> I have ventured
> Like little wanton boys that swim on bladders.

Here he most excruciatingly mollifies his voice to convey the charm of the "little wanton boys", completely losing his emotional bearings in the poetry. Surely, a simile that revolutionizes one's frame of mind must be a very false simile indeed!

Some of the smaller parts are excellently played. There is the Old Lady of Miss Ada King, Tudor to the very tip of her nose; the grave and exquisitely spoken Cardinal Campeius of Mr. H. R. Hignett; the florid Third Gentleman of Mr. Bruce Winston, who is an actor born, if ever there was one. Mr. Arthur Wontner's Buckingham is less satisfactory. His elocution is indistinct. Although I heard every word, I had, very definitely, to prick up my ears in order to do so. Miss Angela Baddeley's Anne Bullen, on the other hand, is a little too piping—but, apart from this, and from a faint tendency in the direction of "Oh-No-John" League-of-Arts artificiality, her performance is charmingly contrived and, in its silences, unexceptionable. And she is so fair to look at that I suspect a good many hearts of beating a little faster while she is on the stage.

MR. LAUGHTON AS HENRY VIII
(1933)

Mr. Charles Laughton's performance as Henry VIII at Sadler's Wells has been under-praised. Perhaps critics thought Henry would dominate the play from first to last as he dominates the film. Perhaps they were disappointed when they found he didn't. Perhaps they failed to realize that he shouldn't because the play doesn't ask for it. Truth to tell, it is a poor, patchy play, made poorer and patchier at Sadler's Wells by cutting. The fact that Shakespeare didn't write most of it makes the cutting none the more excusable. Nor does the fact that the cut bits are bits that give chances to non-star actors.

Mr. Laughton's Henry is royal, robust and vivid. It is impetuously restless, which is right. It has a heart, which is right. It is overweeningly selfish, which is right again. Granted that it errs seriously on the side of comedy, which is untrue to the play. But almost every word leaps to life. Here beyond question is an actor to whom truth and emotion spring as convincingly from verse as they do to most actors from prose.

Most Shakespearean actors, having decided on the sense to be conveyed and the words to be emphasized, are so overcome by the cadence (which is important) that they merely flounder in a sea of hope. To Mr. Laughton the words are as factual when he speaks them as they were to the author when he wrote them down, one by one, on his paper. Mr. Laughton could not, one feels, be overborne by the most hackneyed quotation in Shakespeare, because it does mean something, and he chafes to be kindled, and only the meaning can kindle him.

The mounting at Sadler's Wells is rightly dignified and heraldic. After Mr. Laughton's Henry, the most notable moments are provided by Miss Flora Robson's finely-spoken and finely-felt Katherine of Aragon, Miss Athene Seyler's masterly Tudor beldame, and Miss Elsa Lanchester's rendering of *Orpheus and his lute*, which she sings with the moving impersonality of a boy. Mr. Robert Farquharson's Wolsey rasps its way monotonously through long speeches, like sawing a log you wish you'd never started on.

By going to the play as well as to the film you may see all six wives, which, I suppose, is what most people really want.

MIDSUMMER MADNESS
(1936)

How pleasant it is on hot summer nights to sit in the Open Air Theatre, watching the birds fly overhead and listening to the drowsy hum of London, while actors lard the greensward with their sweat in this play or in that—just what play hardly seems to matter, for the

trees and the breeze have a way of levelling art, and all actors, too,
seem about equal in the sight of Nature. I can't conceive a *great*
performance getting across as great in Regent's Park. Even Edmund
Kean as Richard III would, I feel sure, seem just rather charming.

Take, for example, *Henry VIII*, with which the now-happily-saved
Open Air Theatre reopened last Monday. Here, one thought, was
a most unsuitable play for outdoor representation. Of the seventeen
scenes in the original version, fourteen take place indoors, two in
London streets, and the remaining one in a palace yard. But having,
like *As You Like It*, been written for quite a different kind of theatre,
it seemed just about as suitable. If you ask why choose *Henry VIII*,
you may also ask why, to open the Open Air Theatre, choose Miss
Frances Day, who is not associated in our minds with either Shakespeare or the open air? And the answer is why not? Very pretty she
looked in her floating flounces on the lawn, with Mr. Sydney Carroll
kissing her hand in his most courtly style.

How pleasant, I repeat, it is to sit in one's deck chair and idly
watch this gentle midsummer madness. Here Baliol Holloway, sinister
in scarlet, emerges as Wolsey from the bushes. Here Bluff Lyn Harding
treads a measure on the grass with sweet-eyed Vivien Leigh, a fair
neck for a headsman. Here Phyllis Neilson-Terry, majestic under a
sickle moon, pours forth the woes of Katherine, while hordes of
beefeaters (surely a record number?) lurk in the brake for their next
well-trumpeted entrance. If it's not something specially written, like
the incomparable *Comus*, for the open air, I frankly don't much worry
what they play. So the weather be warm and the birds in tune, let
them give *Mrs. Warren's Profession* and I'll not complain.

RANDOM NOTES
(1933)

There are many mysteries surrounding the play of *Henry VIII*,
not the least being the mystery of its authorship. Was it by Shakespeare?
Or had Shakespeare only a finger in the pie? Scholars and poets now
generally agree that Fletcher wrote most of it. But no management
has yet had the literary courage or the commercial foolhardiness to
announce: "*Henry VIII*, by John Fletcher." For this admirers of the
piece, who like to see it attracting full houses, may be grateful. What
a pity that certain other excellent Elizabethan plays—in which Shakespeare had no hand at all—were not included in the First Folio! If
they had been, we should then see them on the stage at regular intervals
instead of allowing them to lie buried in classical oblivion. Much
virtue in a name.

Here is another mystery connected with *Henry VIII*. Was it the
play which was being acted by Burbage's company on June 29th,
1613, when the Globe Playhouse was burnt down to the ground?
Contemporary accounts tell us that the play was "a new play called

All is True, representing some principal pieces in the reign of Henry VIII", and that "King Henry making a masque at the Cardinal Wolsey's house, and certain chambers being shot off at his entry, some of the paper, or other stuff, wherewith one of them was stopped, did light upon the thatch." Fortunately there were no casualties— "only one man had his breeches set on fire, that would perhaps have broiled him, if he had not by the benefit of a provident wit put it out with bottle ale." But it may be that valuable manuscripts were not similarly extinguished. If our *Henry VIII* be not the same play as *All is True*, it may have been written to supply the loss.

There is, however, a more interesting theory as to the genesis of *Henry VIII*. The first time this monarch was put on the stage was in a highly popular play by Samuel Rowley, written between 1603 and 1605 and entitled *When You See Me, You Know Me*. Here Henry was represented as a bluff dotard in a comic light which can hardly have been pleasing to James I, with his zealous championship of the divine right of kings. He would naturally, as Mr. William Poel has pointed out, be gratified to see Henry depicted as rather less than a buffoon. Moreover, in 1606 an Act was passed forbidding profanity on the stage. In *When You See Me, You Know Me*, Henry can hardly open his mouth without invoking the Trinity. He used the expression "Mother of God" alone no less than twenty times. After the passing of the Act all existing plays (including Shakespeare's) were overhauled and profanities were liberally removed. But to deprive Henry VIII of his profanities in *When You See Me, You Know Me* would have been to take half the stuffing out of the character. For contemporary stage purposes, the play must have been killed as dead as a doornail. All of which may account for the far more restrained and dignified portrait given of the monarch in *Henry VIII*.

The exhibition of the Infant Elizabeth in the last scene of *Henry VIII* was a semi-topical touch. Nevertheless, this was not Elizabeth's first appearance on the boards. Only two years after her death, Thomas Heywood produced a play entitled *If You Know Not Me, You Know Nobody*, in which Good Queen Bess was the principal character. And there was a Censor then as there is to-day!

TRAGEDIES

CORIOLANUS

SHAKESPEARE ON LABOUR LEADERS
(1924)

IF Julius Caesar had never landed on the shores of Britain, and so had never gained his remarkable ascendancy over the minds of British schoolmasters and British schoolboys, the play named after him by that astute man of business, William Shakespeare, would probably have been far less popular.

Theatregoers are attracted by *Julius Caesar* as they are attracted by *Cinderella*: because they have grown up with these people in the nursery. They are not attracted by *Coriolanus* because Coriolanus never frightened their forefathers. This is unfortunate, for *Coriolanus* is a titanic play—a masterpiece of psychological sculpture, hewn out of the imperishable rock of human nature. Its application is so enduring that it would, to-day, quite comfortably carry the title of *Strife* or *Loyalties*. Its contempt of the "beastly plebeians" and its affection for the godlike patricians is expressed in terms so magnificent that it would be difficult for the extremest Bolshevik to withhold his admiration or to grudge the aristocratic classes their colossal luck in possessing such a champion.

Whether Mr. Robert Atkins is a Bolshevik I do not know: but it is pretty safe to conjecture that, as director of a People's Theatre, he does not find the lower classes all foul breath and grease: and he is therefore to be congratulated on underlining the spirit of the play so emphatically in his revival at the Old Vic by shrewd touches of Elizabethan realism. To give but one example, he has presented Sicinius Velutus and Junius Brutus, the People's Tribunes, as a couple of outrageous Hebraic scarecrows, fit for bonfires. And he has done well, again, to underline the nobility of the nobility.

Nowhere, indeed, is Mr. Atkins more at home than among the stern masculinities of the Shakespearean histories, Greek, Roman, English. To the exquisite elegances of such a comedy as *Twelfth Night* he is temperamentally less attuned. But it is the triumph of Shakespeare rather than the disgrace of Mr. Atkins that the variety and range of mind exhibited in all these plays should make it impossible to find any producer capable of producing them all satisfactorily. For the same man to stage sensitively and effectively *Coriolanus*, *The Merry Wives of Windsor*, and *Romeo and Juliet*, is even more difficult than for the same man to act sensitively and effectively Othello, Orsino and Bottom the Weaver. No theatre devoted to the production of Shakespeare's plays would really be complete without at least three different producers.

Excellent as is the production of *Coriolanus* at the Old Vic in many respects, it would be idle to pretend that more than about one-fiftieth of the play "gets through". This is mainly due to the acting of the two all-important parts, Volumnia and Coriolanus himself. There are not, of course, many players on our stage to-day equal to the part of Volumnia, though Miss Sybil Thorndike would be good, and Mr. Norman McKinnel even better: but there must be any number of players equal to a correct conception of the character, and the astonishing thing about Miss Hutin Britton's performance was that it was primarily a failure, not of technique, but of mind.

Imagine, if you can, a Volumnia who is frivolous and feather-brained—a Volumnia (as one member of the audience aptly put it) resembling a burlesque of an old lady on a flag-day rather than the Olympus to which she is compared: and you have imagined what Miss Britton is like in the first half of the play. In the later passages she draws nearer to the spirit of the part, but she never achieves the massive domination or the intolerable drive by which Volumnia has made Coriolanus what he is. At her best, she is all effort and no strength.

Of Mr. Ion Swinley's Coriolanus it is more difficult to speak. It does not stand out head and shoulders, as it should, above the other patricians, it misses the flash of choler and the haughty swell of intolerant superiority. When he descends from the plinth, after exhibiting himself for the suffrage of the people, Mr. Swinley does not, in those three words, "Is this done?"—make more than a bread-and-butter business of his lacerated pride. True, he seems to be a brave fellow, and a man of action—but the tempestuous sweep of the part was appallingly impeded by the actor's unfamiliarity with his lines. It is not going too far to say that Mr. Swinley's bad memory, which has been troublesome in the past and which on Monday night compelled him to lapse into a repetition of his part, line by line, after the prompter, ruined all possibility of illusion. And it must frankly be stated that, owing to this defect, Mr. Swinley is not wisely cast for long parts.

Some of the trouble might be avoided if the Old Vic (and every theatre in London) would adopt the sensible Continental method of a prompter's box in the middle of the stage, which renders the small, still voice of the man with the book practically inaudible. But that does not alter the fact that it is the first business of actors to know their lines. How they do manage to know them will be to me a never-ceasing miracle; but obviously it can be done.

It was, nevertheless, a fitting comment on the character of Coriolanus that he had to be prompted to say good-bye to poor Virgilia, his wife—an extraordinarily moving character whose tragedy lies in the fact that she has practically nothing to say. Another small part beautifully drawn by Shakespeare is Valeria who, with her chitter-chatter, is like a lyric from Theocritus. Immeasurably the best performance in the play was Mr. Hay Petrie's Roman Citizen, every word being delivered not merely as though it meant "something", but as though it meant what it was meant to mean. Mr. Wilfrid Walter's Menenius was most intelligently done.

The fighting, as usual, was unconvincing. I am sure that Shakespeare would not have given his public so much of it had it not been popular with the Elizabethan groundlings. And I am sure that it would not have been popular with the Elizabethan groundlings if it had been as tamely done as it is in all modern productions. Until these encounters receive as much attention as an assault-at-arms at a modern Military Tournament, many of Shakespeare's plays will be doomed to end in disaster. Certainly, I felt at the Old Vic that Cominius was speaking the truth when he said to Coriolanus:

> If I should tell thee o'er this thy day's work,
> Thou't not believe thy deeds.

TITUS ANDRONICUS

STAGE FRIGHTFULNESS

(1923)

THE production of *Titus Andronicus* at the Old Vic this week may be regarded as an extravagance, committed not so much for the sheer Neronic delight of committing extravagances as for the steady satisfaction of piling up a new record. In no single theatre and under no single manager in the world have all the thirty-six plays attributed to Shakespeare by the editors of the First Folio yet succeeded in getting themselves produced; nearly everybody present at Monday night's performance must have been conscious of this soon-to-be-demolished fact; and it was probably this consciousness which enabled the audience to endure with such fortitude the spectacle of Miss Lilian Baylis doing, as it were, her thirty-fifth lap, like an untiring long-distance bicyclist whose last circuits arouse the spectators to their highest flights of enthusiasm. Certainly, it will be a remarkable record—a record so remarkable that, when it has been finally achieved, Miss Baylis and Mr. Robert Atkins may well find the prospect a little flat. They will want fresh fields—Shakespearean, of course—to conquer. And since (apart from the very doubtful plays) there are no fresh fields, I suggest to them that they might do worse than reconquer the old field in a new way. It has lately been discovered by many Old Victorians for the first time that the three parts of *Henry V* present, when played consecutively, a meaning which evaporates when one of them is wrenched, like a quotation, out of its context.

And just as the same discovery applies to the whole of the Chronicle Plays, so, in a slightly different but scarcely less fascinating sense, it applies to all the plays that Shakespeare ever wrote. Now suppose that Miss Baylis and Mr. Atkins were to treat the complete series as a series of chronicle plays, regarding the thing chronicled as the

H

development of a great artist and a human soul. Suppose they were to address themselves to the task of producing all the plays chronologically, in the order in which they are debatably believed to have been written. Not only would the public be afforded an exciting opportunity of following the development of Shakespeare's mind as it developed during his lifetime, but students of the theatre would be afforded an extraordinarily valuable opportunity of following the development of his stage-craft.

Those who agree with Mr. William Poel that the only reasonable way of producing Shakespeare's plays is the way in which Shakespeare himself meant them to be produced are a good deal confused by the fact that during the twenty-odd years of Shakespeare's career as a dramatic author the mechanism of the English theatre was changing at a tremendous rate. To declare arbitrarily that "Shakespeare" must have been produced in such-and-such a way is to neglect all that happened between the first performance of *Love's Labour's Lost* and the first performance of *The Tempest*; and the best way to find out just what did happen during that interval of time is by undertaking the practical experiment of production, step by step. The Old Vic is not, of course, an ideal medium for such an experiment.

It is one of our national disgraces that we do not possess a single theatre (not even the Maddermarket) which provides a platform on which Shakespeare can be acted in the real Shakespearean manner. But half a loaf is better than no bread, and a great deal might be learned if, the next time Miss Baylis "sees it through," she would begin at the beginning and place *Titus Andronicus* not thirty-fifth, but, say, first or second on her list.

Embarking on such a voyage of discovery, Mr. Atkins would have to abandon a good many of the effects employed in his present production. *Titus Andronicus* is one of the most Grand Guignolesque of all Elizabethan plays, a stark piece of stage frightfulness in which, to quote the expressive tautology of Smee, "horror piled on horror do horrify me most horribly." Its horribilism has got the old Blue Books on War Atrocities beaten hollow. On Shakespeare's stage its

> murders, rapes, and massacres,
> Acts of black night, abominable deeds,
> Complots of mischief, treason, villainies
> Ruthful to hear, yet piteously performed,

were presented in the plain, unwavering light of day (as Sir Henry Irving, in a moment of inspiration, suddenly decided to present the last scene of *The Lyons Mail*). But as though it is not enough that a ravished girl should be exhibited for the delectation of a sensation-swallowing audience with the hands cut off and the tongue cut out by her dual ravishers—as though it is not enough that a poisonous queen should have her two massacred sons served up to her for consumption in a pie—Mr. Atkins, endeavouring to emphasize the violence, degenerates into italics and bathes his stage in purple and crimson mists. This is on all fours with the rumblings of thunder introduced into the last scene of *Othello* by Sir Herbert Tree in an attempt to make the climax really impressive. The effect is rather to emasculate than to strengthen. The "goodness" goes into the shoots; the fruit fails to swell; and Tamora who, deprived of the protection of the "limes", would be driven to gobble up her sons with unction, pecks at them daintily, leaving the coloured electric lights to do the rest. True, I don't like being sickened in the theatre; but this is a sickening play, and if it does not sicken, it does not achieve its end.

Again, when Lavinia takes her father's chopped-off hand between her teeth, I feel that I am being cheated of my money's-worth if, in the performance of this nauseating business, she delicately turns her back upon me. It is a thoroughly satisfactory hand (by which I mean it is a thoroughly sickening hand), but the real object Titus had in view when he commanded Aaron to slash away, is, at the Old Vic, discreetly and ungratefully thwarted. Mr. Atkins may provide, in substitution, a ruddy tree marked (apparently) with broad arrows, as though to suggest that even Nature in such a play cannot escape the criminal taint. But the utmost achieved by this tree is to offend the aesthetic sense. It does not make you vomit in your stall—a liberty to which, as a sensitive product of the twentieth century, I, personally, feel myself entitled. *Titus Andronicus* is, in many respects, an admirably managed piece of work, but since, emphatically, I abominate it, when I see it on the stage I claim the right to be allowed to abominate it to the top of my bent.

Nevertheless, Mr. Atkins deserves much praise. He launches into the horrors and lunges through them far more courageously than nine modern producers out of ten would launch and lunge; and most of the members of his company thwack the empty casks which do duty for characters with good, resounding vigour (Tamora, Demetrius and Chiron, who disguise themselves as Revenge, Murder and Rape, are in reality only Revenge, Murder and Rape disguised as Tamora, Demetrius and Chiron). Mr. Ion Swinley (whose lapses of memory threw the prompter on the first night into such a state of nerves that in the end this gentleman fell to prompting the actors after they had spoken their lines), fills out, if he does not fill in, the saturnine Saturninus.

The same may be said of the Titus of Mr. Wilfrid Walter and the Tamora of Miss Florence Saunders. Mr. George Hayes gloats picturesquely over the inky Aaron, a very vivid devil; Miss Jane Bacon makes of Lavinia a very slaughterable lamb. Best of all (this now goes without saying at the Old Vic) is Mr. Hay Petrie, who plays the tiny part of the clown with such astonishing beauty, humour, truth to life, truth to the theatre, pathos, imagination, intelligence, instinct, depth, sharpness, and penetration, that every word he speaks and every movement he makes is a living, thrilling thing. Heaven will be incomplete without him.

ROMEO AND JULIET

A CASE FOR MALE JULIETS
(1923)

IN my opinion Shakespeare's plays should be presented as Shakespeare intended them to be—without cuts or alterations of any kind, without scenery or accessories, dressed in the costume of the 16th and 17th centuries, and with all the women's parts played by young men.—W. S. GILBERT.

Mr. Shaw, commenting on the fact that a number of those present had laughed at the suggestion in Mr. W. S. Gilbert's letter that Shakespeare's women should be played by boys, said that he judged from that that they had never seen women's parts played by boys. He used to see it at Westminster School, and some of the performances he had seen there by amateur schoolboys had been more effective than performances he had seen by clever actresses. If they had proposed to Shakespeare that he should have his female parts done by women, he would not only have been shocked at the idea, but he would probably also have declared that he could never get from women the force in acting that he could get from boys.—Report of a public discussion on the best method of presenting Shakespeare's plays.

Not the thing itself, but the idea of the thing evokes the idea . . . I had never seen Shakespeare acted, and I went to the Lyceum and there I saw that exquisite love-song—for Romeo and Juliet is no more than a love-song in dialogue. . . . The woman, too, I wished with my whole soul away, subtle and strange though she was; and I yearned for the youth as of old time in the part: a youth cunningly disguised, I said, would be a symbol; and my mind would be free to imagine the divine Juliet of the poet, whereas I can but dream of the bright eyes and delicate mien and motion of the woman who had thrust herself between me and it.—GEORGE MOORE.

The introduction of actresses upon the stage was scarce known before the Restoration, and it furnished the poets of the latter period with appropriate representatives for their female characters. This more happy degree of personification, as it greatly increased the perfection of the scene, must have animated, in proportion, the genius of the author. A marked improvement, therefore, may be traced in love scenes, and, indeed, in all those wherein female characters are introduced.—SIR WALTER SCOTT.

In the last of the four quotations given above it will have been observed that Sir Walter Scott ascribes to the introduction of actresses upon the stage an improvement in the delineation by dramatic authors of the feminine character. Whether such an improvement did or did not take place is a point outside the argumentative scope of this article. What is important and relevant is the fact that Sir Walter Scott marked, whether for better or for worse, a change. Just as the writer of the libretto of a Christmas pantomime will make some change in his portraiture of Aladdin if he knows that the part is to be played by a man, or of the Widow Twankey if he knows that the part is to be played by a woman, so the writer of a serious play presupposes a male or a female interpreter for his heroine and, in his character-conception and plot-manipulation, is affected by that presupposition. And there is valuable work ahead for the student who will apply himself to an analytical examination of the female characters in Elizabethan and Jacobean plays, and who will discover where the playwrights have been affected by the presupposition that these parts would be played by boys and men. It is, for example, pretty certain that Shakespeare's practice of getting his heroines into masculine attire whenever possible was due to the presence of the boy-actor. It is obvious, again, that he had a male actor in mind when he made Hamlet say:

What, my young lady and mistress! By'r lady your ladyship is nearer to heaven than when I saw you last, by the altitude of a chopine. Pray God your voice like a piece of uncurrent gold be not cracked within the ring.

Girls' voices do not "break"; and when (as is almost invariably the case) the part of this strolling player of female characters is given to a woman, the whole point of Hamlet's badinage is obscured.

Then there is the jest in Rosalind's epilogue to *As You Like It*:

If I were a woman, I would kiss as many of you as had beards that pleased me.

This was, of course, written for the mouth of a boy-actor; and many actresses must have felt, with Helen Faucit, "a kind of shrinking distaste" for the task of speaking it. Although "some of the words I omitted, and some I altered," the speaking of this epilogue, Miss Faucit confesses, "remained the one drawback to my pleasure."

I am aware that the three points just made in no way establish a case for male Juliets, but they do at least suggest that Shakespeare, in the course of composition, did not become entirely oblivious of the sex of his interpreters, and that a case may, therefore, be establishable. At first blush, ninety-nine playgoers out of a hundred would hold up their hands in horror at the male-Juliet suggestion. And yet they pass without comment the apparently growing custom of entrusting male Shakespearean parts to female performers—a far more horrifying proceeding, which is considered far less horrifying because, for some recondite reason, the girl as boy is accorded a welcome which is coldly withheld from the boy as girl. Whether Shakespeare would have delighted in a female Juliet remains a matter of speculation. But one may declare with some certainty that the spectacle of a young lady cutting capers as Falstaff's high-spirited Boy in *King Henry V* would have caused him a certain amount of consternation.

This was the treat to which Mr. Bridges Adams invited me one afternoon at the Garrick Theatre. Imagine my feelings when, on the evening of the same day, I went to see *The Merchant of Venice* at the Old Vic, and there, just after Portia had been ridiculing the idea of a woman turning "two mincing steps into a manly stride", I found the Venetian Court of Justice packed with feminine magnificoes in moustaches, all doing their best to illustrate the sense of Portia's remark. Indeed, the whole point of that scene—a girl dressed up as a man in the midst of men—was obscured by the fact that nearly all the other girls in the scene were dressed up as men too! This Christmas pantomime dressing up of women as men, which is a regular feature of almost all modern performances of Shakespeare, must be reformed altogether. Not only are the male "supers" feminized wholesale; the smaller male speaking parts are entrusted to actresses—on the assumption, I suppose, that the small parts don't really matter! Actresses are chosen to deliver prologues and to play Macbeth's Witches—who, if "sisters", were bearded and most unfeminine. The boyishness of Puck is utterly disregarded. Ariel has been given over so completely to the ladies that it is not at all uncommon for audiences to leave *The Tempest* under the impression that the tricksy spirit is supposed to be a girl. And even when Sarah Bernhardt masquerades as Hamlet or Sybil Thorndike announces her favourite part to be King Lear's Fool, the Hazlitts of our time find no difficulty in preserving their reckless gravity.

But suppose the situations were reversed. Suppose some producer, greatly daring, gave us not Sarah Bernhardt as Hamlet or Sybil Thorndike as King Lear's Fool, but Basil Rathbone as Desdemona or Bruce Winston as Mistress Quickly! What a hubbub of derision, what a storm of intolerance would be aroused! Yet Shakespeare did not write the part of Desdemona or the part of Mistress Quickly with a feminine interpreter in his mind's eye. He wrote them for men and boys to act. Up goes the old cry! "Ah, yes! but how glad he would be to-day to see his heroines played by women!" Realism, always realism. And here let me hasten to explain that I do not object to Sarah Bernhardt as Hamlet or to Sybil Thorndike as King Lear's Fool because I consider it absurd for a woman to play a man's part, but only because I consider it absurd for a woman to play a part which the author designed for masculine interpretation. Basil Rathbone as Desdemona, Bruce Winston as Mistress Quickly, would be carrying out the author's intention.

"But," reiterate the realists, "Shakespeare's plays are serious plays, they are not pantomimes, and it is intrinsically more effective in a serious play for feminine parts to be acted by feminine performers." Let them beware of the logical conclusion of this premiss. If the illusion of a play is more complete when a woman acts a woman than when a man acts a woman, then it must follow that the illusion will be more complete when an old woman acts an old woman than when a young woman acts an old woman. The time may come when the public will ridicule the idea of such an actress as Miss Athene Seyler playing the part of an ancient imbecile, because Miss Seyler is neither ancient nor imbecile. And so we shall demand that only lunatics shall play lunatics, duchesses duchesses, cockneys cockneys, crooks crooks, K.C.s K.C.s, and—witches witches! That is the logical conclusion of realism in casting; and if such a conclusion should ever obtain favour, what will be the effect on the playwrights? Faced by the problem of providing parts for people whose capacity for acting is limited in extent, they will inevitably be driven to writing plays in which very little acting is required, and the possibility of effective illusion will thus be maintained. But if, in those conjectural times, there should be a revival of *Hamlet* and the producer should attempt to satisfy the requirements of the play by securing a real queen for the part of Gertrude, a real Danish prince for the part of Hamlet, a real soldier for the part of Fortinbras, two real gravediggers for the parts of the gravediggers, and—no, the Ghost of Hamlet's father would have to be eliminated altogether—then the public would no doubt conclude that the play of *Hamlet* was not a very good play, and they would not go to see it, and the wiseacres would wonder why Shakespeare was no longer popular!

All of which touches, of course, only the fringe of the subject. A full dress debate on the Case for the Male Juliet might yield an interesting discussion.

JULIET AND HER ROMEO
(1924)

A few months ago a theatrical manager, on the eve of producing one of Shakespeare's plays, wrote me a letter in the course of which he said: "You are always clamouring for Shakespeare, but you never seem to like him when you get him."

This remark is not without foundation. The prospect of seeing a play by Shakespeare always excites me. But the actors are generally so far from realizing my dreams that, by the time the performance is half done, I find that I have ruled them out of court, that the enter-tainment has resolved itself into a combat between them and me. Determined to do my utmost to frustrate their knavish tricks, I strive, with eyes and ears half closed against the unwelcome sights and sounds that break upon them, to save what I can for myself from the wreck. Clearly, my answer to the theatrical manager must be that I am dissatisfied because, even when they play his plays in the theatre, I so very seldom do "get" Shakespeare.

The other night my heart certainly beat a little faster than usual when I went to the Regent Theatre to see *Romeo and Juliet*: for this is one of several plays that I cannot hear mentioned without promptly declaring it to be the best play in the world. The "balcony" scene was heavenly, the "Romeo banished" scene finely done. But when I left the Regent Theatre, I was a sadder and not a wiser man. Elysium had fallen a little flat. If a brow-beating counsel had required of me a plain answer, Yes or No, I should have been compelled to answer No—and to answer more in sorrow than in anger. For meeting soon afterwards a man of sensibility who had been swept off his feet by the performance, and who, finding that I was not equally overwhelmed, defended himself by explaining that (as a matter of fact) he had never seen the play before, and had not read it for some fifteen years, I was frankly glad, and wanted to congratulate him on the happiness that had come to him. And I wondered whether I, on my side, should not have been explaining in self-defence that I (as a matter of fact) had seen the play a score of times before, and that during the last fifteen years I had read it at least fifteen times.

When, not long ago, a play in the writing of which I had a hand was rehearsed and produced, I remember being astonished at the difference between my own conception of the parts and the actual interpretation given by the players. I realized for the first time the astonishing limitations imposed on actors by their personalities. Judged by ordinary standards, the play was well acted: all the critics were agreed on that. And I, astounded at first by their lack of perception, realized at last that whereas the performances of the actors seemed to me, in the capacity of author, just so many direct lies (admirably told lies, some of them), had I been a critic encountering the play for the first time, I should have agreed with the verdict of my colleagues.

If, as an author, or if, as a lover of Shakespeare, you have grown up with your characters, and so do really know what they are like, you will inevitably set up a more exacting standard. And since I know all the people in *Romeo and Juliet* as well as I know my brothers and my sister, I was disconcerted at the Regent Theatre, in spite of the admirable speed with which scene followed scene, to find a Juliet who was not Juliet, a Romeo who was not Romeo, a Capulet who was not Capulet, and a Nurse who certainly never nursed my favourite heroine. In Miss Barbara Gott's Nurse, indeed, were mirrored some of the cardinal faults of the production. She was a clean Nurse, an efficient Nurse, a Nurse the Norland Institute might be proud of. There was nothing touch-and-go about her, nothing to suggest an ancestry for Mrs. Gamp. And as the Nurse, so the production. There was nothing touch-and-go in the atmosphere conjured up for Verona, which seemed to be a model mediaeval city without a smell, instead of a smouldering bonfire, ready to leap into flame at a puff.

Fire is the element that quickens *Romeo and Juliet* to life. It has been well said that the purity of Juliet is not the purity of snow, but of fire. And this is where Miss Gwen Ffrangçon-Davies failed. She played the part in the wrong latitude. She was never of the south. Nor was she ever alight. She was intelligent, she was girlish, she spoke her verse with a sense of its sense and a feeling for its feeling, keeping time, distance and proportion. But she never swept the board—and was she not on the one hand just a little co-educated and on the other just a little arty, looking as though she had stepped out of Rossetti's *Ecce Ancilla Domini*, or like a cross between Botticelli and Faith Celli? The generous, lavish, warm, tumultuous, torrential, palpitating Juliet gave place to a Juliet who knew a thing or two, who would get her Romeo by hook or by crook—whereas the real Juliet would get him only by hook. Of all Shakespeare's heroines Juliet is the most dynamic, the most single-minded, the most unself-conscious, the most irresistible. From the moment she sets eyes on Romeo, Romeo is as doomed as John Tanner is doomed the moment he comes face to face with Ann Whitfield. Juliet did not belong to Romeo. Romeo belonged to Juliet.

> For never was a story of more woe,
> Than this of Juliet and *her* Romeo.

It is, perhaps, well that the violent delight of these immortal lovers should have reached, as Friar Laurence predicted, a violent end. Had a reconciliation between the two Houses been effected through some less catastrophic agency than death, marriage would surely have revealed the incompatibility of their temperaments. For Juliet was an objectivist, Romeo a subjectivist. Juliet wanted Romeo, Romeo wanted to want Juliet. And it is difficult to believe that Juliet's impetuous, unswerving determination to get what she wanted would not in the end have reduced Romeo to a state of desperate exhaustion, or that Romeo's eternal about-it-and-about would not have exacerbated Juliet past bearing-point.

It may be that I am not quite fair to Romeo. Possibly I have always been a little jealous of him. But, as a lover, was he not a very poor sort of a fish? When Juliet is pouring out the full flood of her hot virgin passion, by what lover's right is this Montague conscious of the fact that the moon is tipping the fruit-tree tops with silver? And when he murmurs

> How silver-sweet sound lovers' tongues by night

I could brain him with my opera-glasses. Why did he not take up with the lively Helena, or the lady-widow of Utruvio? They would have done just as well. "How silver-sweet sound lovers' tongues by night"! After that appalling confession that he had been listening as much to the sound of the words as to the words themselves, if it had rained on the way home from Juliet's balcony, I can believe that he might have exclaimed, "Oh, I am fortune's fool!" Rosaline, certainly, must have been a woman of some sense.

Mr. John Gielgud's Romeo leaves no very definite impression. He merges into the general mediocrity. And the "Oh, I am fortune's fool!" that Romeo really did utter—a tremendous climax—is almost inaudible. Mr. Scott Sunderland is a very square Mercutio; Mr. Campbell Gullan's Friar Laurence wavers between the comic and the sinister; Paris, as usual, looks like Miss Phyllis Monkman decked out for a Three Arts Ball. And so Miss Ffrangçon-Davies may be acclaimed by far the most distinguished performer. If she is no peach, she is lovely chilled asparagus.

A GOOD PRODUCTION
(1935)

Critics argue much over the way Shakespeare should be presented. What sort of scenery? What sort of costumes? What sort of stage? What sort of ghost, witch, fairy, fencing, music, interval, and so forth? But while all this is important, the root of the matter lies in the speaking and the acting. An ounce of passion is worth a pound of paint. And so *Romeo and Juliet* at the New deserves the success it will have because the Romeo is good, the Juliet is good, the Mercutio is good, the Nurse is good. The magic of the romance is in their flesh and blood.

I have never seen a better Romeo than Laurence Olivier. His fault is to accelerate the last half of a sentence as though it were less important than the first. But the excitement of his love, the violence of his grief, give the action a thrilling impetus. He is the only actor I have ever known to succeed in that diabolically difficult outburst with the Friar. His cry, "Thou canst not speak of that thou dost not feel!" is living anguish. Mr. Olivier comes through scene after scene with flying colours. A performance with fire in it. Unlike most Romeos, he really does seem to be in love.

I have never seen a better Nurse than Edith Evans. And I don't believe anyone ever has. This, to be plain, rises yards higher and spreads yards broader than Mr. Olivier's Romeo. Coarse, garrulous, wordy, dominant, massive with the accretions of an experience that has left her fundamentally shallow-pated, it is a mighty achievement in characterization never irritatingly elaborated, and in elocution governed continually by internal word-sense. "Our greatest Shakespearean actress", said John Gielgud on the first night. And there isn't a doubt about it. If only I were Miss Evans, I would read Shakespeare out loud to myself all day long.

I have seen better Mercutios than John Gielgud. His death scene is disappointing. Too much charm and not enough bitter physical pain. That "plague on both your houses" was surely no playful jest. But before this Mr. Gielgud is excellent, speaking beautifully (but not too beautifully) and lighting up like the flash of sunlight on the blade of a rapier. As the Prologue, which he also plays, Mr. Gielgud is invaluable. If only these small parts could all be taken by our best speakers! The more parts the best actors can double, the more the credit and not the less the dignity.

As for Peggy Ashcroft's Juliet, this is charming, sensitive, and most feelingly done. The balcony scene enchants—so do lots of things in this production, the first half of which moved me continuously. Miss Ashcroft has much to contend with. She is no controller of situations—and Juliet was. She does not naturally pour out her soul —and Juliet did. Nevertheless, Miss Ashcroft has gained in breadth, and really I can't think of a living actress I'd prefer in the part.

Good points are that this production moves ever so much more swiftly than *Hamlet* (than which it's twice as good). That the Pinturicchio-Carpaccio settings by Motley delight the eye. And that under Mr. Gielgud's fine direction the words are intelligibly spoken all through. The most serious blot is Frederick Lloyd's Capulet—a self-made, comic Capulet, with a slow instead of a quick and fidgety mind. Mr. Gielgud and Mr. Olivier are to exchange parts in a few weeks.

MR. GIELGUD AND MR. OLIVIER
(1935)

Mr. John Gielgud is now Romeo, Mr. Laurence Olivier Mercutio. And what, no doubt, you want to know is which (as they asked about Garrick and Barry) is better than which. Both are so good in both parts that one has no desire to make unavoidable comparisons. As Romeo Mr. Olivier was about twenty times as much in love with Juliet as Mr. Gielgud is. But Mr. Gielgud speaks most of the poetry far better than Mr. Olivier. We can understand this Romeo saying "How silver—sweet sound lovers' tongues by night" (instead of "sounds Juliet's tongue"). A fine piece of work. Yet—I must out with it—the fire of Mr. Olivier's passion carried the play along as Mr. Gielgud's doesn't quite.

As Mercutio Mr. Gielgud has it till the duel scene. Then Mr. Olivier's inflammability leaps to triumph. Already he is speaking verse better than six weeks ago. His banter is no match for Mr. Gielgud's. He lacks, perhaps, a sense of humour. But quick, quarrelsome, dangerous—yes. The death is very moving. Yet here *both* actors are far too nice over "I was hurt under your arm". There should be an insuppressible sting of reproach in these words, uttered, possibly, on a shoot of pain. For these are the words that precipitate Romeo inevitably into action.

Here, however, are two young actors of whom our stage may justly be most proud. With Miss Edith Evans and Miss Peggy Ashcroft they make *Romeo and Juliet* at the New a lovely, living thing. To see it again has been an intense and memorable pleasure. Let but the Page to Paris change parts in another six weeks with the Captain of the Watch, and how willingly we'll go again!

JULIET PLAYS TENNIS

If you want to see Shakespeare done in Shakespeare's way, which is the only right way, don't forget that Robert Atkins is starting business with his Bankside Players at the Blackfriars Ring next Sunday—*Henry V* the play. This is about fifty times as important as the launching of the *Romeo and Juliet* film—though I suppose it is tragically important that so many people should nowadays know Shakespeare only through the medium of the pictures.

Talking of the *Romeo and Juliet* film, may I call your attention to the most remarkable stage direction ever printed in any edition of Shakespeare? It occurs in the Motion Picture Version of *Romeo and Juliet*, price two dollars, published by Metro-Goldwyn-Mayer, and is to be found in the scene where Juliet is waiting impatiently for the Nurse's return from Romeo. Here Juliet says, "From nine to twelve Is three long hours; yet she is not come. Had she affections and warm youthful blood, She'd be as swift in motion as a ball." And then comes the Metro-Goldwyn-Mayer stage direction: "*She imitates the stroke of a racquet.*"

TIMON OF ATHENS

A TRAGEDY OF EXTREMES
(1922)

THE Old Vic concluded its memorable Shakespeare season with an excellent production of *Timon of Athens*: a vast, rough-hewn piece of dramatic sculpture, intrinsically a masterpiece of imperfection, extrinsically something of a curiosity, because it is so seldom exhibited to the public. Managers fight shyer of *Timon* than of many of the other plays because it concentrates on portraiture rather than on plot, and because few of the portraits are flattering to the sitters. Timon himself, like so many great tragic figures, would provide excellent food for comedy, and even in Shakespeare's play sometimes becomes bathetic. Regarded from the standpoint of a Molière, his violent prodigality is as ridiculous as his headlong reaction into misanthropy when he discovers that trencher-friends require a full trencher. "The middle of humanity thou never knewest, but the extremity of both ends." Shakespeare, however, tackled Timon in no holiday mood. If God created man in His own likeness, then there must be some share of godliness even in a born fool. Was Shakespeare attracted to the theme of Timon because he had himself suffered some similar emotional reverse through man's ingratitude? and while he half-condemned himself for his distemperature, did he still half-cling to his grievance? No writer is objective in his choice of subjects.

It is clear that in the portions of *Timon* written by Shakespeare, the poet let off a great deal of steam; and it is fascinating to speculate on the process by which that steam was generated.

Mr. Robert Atkins, who is an actor of size, rarely undertakes a part at the Old Vic—a wise abstention, for producers have enough to do without acting, and actor-management in nine cases out of ten means the doom of the actor. He nearly ruined the opening performance of *Timon* because he did not know his lines and was continually sawing the air for words. Apart from this, he was equal to, but not of the same nature as, his part. There was something too ponderous in his method. One looked for the flash of lightning in that "Methinks, I could deal kingdoms to my friends," and one heard only a distant rumble of thunder. His subsequent ravings in the wood were rather blunted than sharpened by his method of delivery. Yet his stature was sufficient, and he spanned the breadth if he did not pierce the depth of the part. Mr. Austin Trevor and Mr. Hay Petrie were first-rate as the Poet and the Fool, and Mr. Rupert Harvey, playing at the top of his form, did not abate a whit of the acidity of Apemantus. Some of the smaller parts were weakly acted, but poor performances at the Old Vic are usually due rather to incompetence than to perversity, and are the more easily excused on that account.

Once again, Mr. Atkins's production was admirably fearless and straightforward. The combination of curtains with scenic sets; the performance of the duties of male supernumeraries by females (soldiers are nearly always feminine at the Old Vic); the intermittent tableau tendency, which led to the introduction of an additional scene at the finish, undreamt of by Shakespeare or his collaborator, with soldiers and senators saluting Timon's grave—these were all blemishes. But Mr. Atkins nearly always grasps the essentials of a situation, and his direct, unhesitating, almost charge-of-the-light-brigadeish methods keep the tide in swift motion throughout.

POOR TIMON!
(1935)

An actor of Shakespeare's great parts may use the words as an accompaniment to the emotion or strike the emotion through the words. Mr. Ernest Milton in *Timon of Athens* at the Westminster chooses the former and far less satisfactory method. Having got into a state, he often speaks the words so fast and so erratically that they are hard to follow. The result is monotonous, because the things Timon feels are immeasurably less interesting and varied than the things he says.

It's a thousand pities this masterpiece, so seldom acted, should be as poorly done when it is acted as in this Westminster production. Not one part strikingly performed. A long, irrelevant street fight introduced that has nothing to do with the case. A ballet so protracted that Mr. Rupert Doone, the choreographist, has his name on the programme as big as Shakespeare. And what is the point of Elizabethan costumes if the ladies in farthingales are allowed bare arms?

So, exit Timon for another generation. It's tragic how tolerant critics can be over the sport of plucking feathers from the lovely live Swan and it's amazing that so many of them should, after seeing this production, have set *Timon* down as poor stuff. Can it be that they don't believe in reading a play before they see it? Well, they might do so now. There are several editions.

JULIUS CAESAR

CAESAR UNDER A CLOUD
(1932)

THE Old Vic company acted on Monday night much as though, just before the curtain rose, news had been brought of the sudden death of Lilian Baylis. Nearly all the players seemed stunned. They went through the piece in a daze. They fumbled for their words. They appeared to be completely unable to pull themselves together. And they were, generally speaking, much too small for their Roman boots.

Mr. Ralph Richardson's Brutus looked the idealist but was never the hero—and Shakespeare cast these men in an heroic mould. This was too much in the bread-and-butter vein. Mr. Robert Harris's Mark Antony might have had a couple of correspondence lessons in rhetoric. Mr. Richard Riddle, excellent as the Soothsayer, played Octavius as though you could have knocked him down with a feather and as though he would have liked it.

One superb piece of acting there was—the Cassius of Mr. Robert Speaight. What Mr. Speaight lacked in inches he made up for in passion. In his outburst in the quarrel scene his legs quivered with emotion. He showed from the first moment the agony with which his love for Brutus inspired his fury against him. Here, if ever, was a man doing violence to his feelings. Mr. Speaight improves. He could play Thersites. And couldn't Mr. John Gielgud play Troilus and Miss Edith Evans Cressida? and mightn't the piece, with the back-wash of the *réclame* of *Helen*, run a good fortnight?

The production of *Julius Caesar* at the Old Vic had many faults. The secretion of the rabble in the well of the orchestra during the Forum scene destroyed what effect Antony's oration might otherwise have produced. No good (if we except the music) ever comes out of the well of the orchestra at the Old Vic. Nevertheless, the evening *was* worth while. Shakespeare won through—and he doesn't always.

The general basis of the Harcourt Williams production gave him scope to enlarge himself. I can't condemn a production of *Julius Caesar* that makes me take out the play when I get home and read it again before I go to bed.

THE TREE TRADITION
(1932)

A massive company has been assembled at His Majesty's Theatre to restore what is called the Tree tradition with an overwhelming production of *Julius Caesar*—which, I need hardly tell those who know anything about the Tree tradition, means *Julius Caesar* with plenty of lictors and vestal virgins, or, to sum the matter up in the base vernacular, *Julius Caesar* with knobs on. It was, you may remember, the Tree tradition that gave us *A Midsummer Night's Dream* with real rabbits scuttling across the stage and a whole set of wings of different colours for Titania. It was the Tree tradition that arranged appropriate rumbles of thunder when Desdemona was smothered, in order to make the proceeding really impressive. In short, it was the Tree tradition that buried the light of Shakespeare under a bushel of spectacle—that stuck a feather in its hat and called it Swan of Avon.

This being so, the new production of *Julius Caesar* at His Majesty's Theatre may justly claim to have done what it set out to do. If it is not as lavish as the old Tree shows, the Alma Tadema set on which the curtain rises is a guarantee that it will proceed along Tree lines, while the lumbersome pace of the speakers, combined with a liberal introduction of business, assures us that some of the best scenes, including those stark, vivid moments with Cinna the poet, will have to be omitted.

In exchange for this, the female interest, so sadly deficient in the original play, is considerably enhanced. Miss Lily Brayton, returning to the stage to play the underwritten part of Calpurnia, is given an extra chance to move her audience by appearing at the end of the Senate scene to mourn over the body of her husband. Miss Dorothy Green, having had some of her few lines as Portia blue-pencilled because they do not fit in with the production, is permitted, after she has pleaded in vain with Brutus, to make the dramatic discovery of a document revealing the secret of the conspiracy. And so we go back to the good old days.

For this tribute to the memory of a dead manager rather than of a live playwright all the heavyweights in London, from Mr. Oscar Asche downwards, seem to have flocked together. With Messrs. Lyn Harding, Basil Gill, Godfrey Tearle and many other stalwarts of the buskin, the company is rather like a football team consisting entirely of full backs. The lines of blank verse succeed each other like bowls bowling down a bowling-alley. The actors, veterans of legitimate,

seem to be mesmerized by their own voices. The nimble flame of
Shakespeare is extinguished by the hooves of elephants. Here, once
again, is the awful Shakespeare we *ought* to like.

Individually, by far the best performance in the piece comes from
Mr. Tearle, whose elocution has more variety than that of his comrades
and whose Antony kindles into sensibility when he is orating over
Caesar's body. This is good, intelligent work. Mr. Gill's Brutus is
lourd and colourless. I think he is the handsomest man on the stage
to-day, but whether his face is his fortune, I am not so certain. Mr.
Harding's Caesar borders on the heavy villain, Mr. Holloway's Cassius
lacks the essential canker, Mr. Asche's Casca is too much in the
centre of the stage. As for the crowd, it is massive and vociferous
and suggestive in some of its elements of a sort of *Chu Chin
Caesar*.

Whether the super who shouted "Shut up!" during Antony's
funeral speech was told to, or whether he just lost his head, it was a
jolly moment. Even jollier, I thought, than the moment, or long series
of moments, when Casca and Cassius sheltered from the streaming
rain under a red lamp in what looked like the entrance to a real old
Roman night club.

INTERMITTENT SHAKESPEARE
(1935)

At the Old Vic, the story of a dictator. Mr. Henry Cass, the producer,
has told us that *Julius Caesar* is very modern in many of its political
implications. But Mr. Cecil Trouncer in the name-part seems hardly a
model for Mussolini. He is more like a very old actor returning to the
stage after twenty years' retirement, to show how he used to do it,
at some benefit matinée.

I thought this *Julius Caesar* a dull and stolid affair—about as
Roman as an old Royal Academy picture, about as Elizabethan as
Shakespeare's statue in Leicester Square, about as modern as 1910.
Cassius (William Devlin) unsubtle but strong. Antony (Ion Swinley)
vigorous but uncertain. Brutus (Leo Genn) a numskull. Good
speaking by Miss Vivienne Bennett as Portia and Mr. Alec Clunes as
Octavius.

As a matter of fact, the growing tendency at the Old Vic to do
plays not by Shakespeare, however imperative financially, breaks up
a continuity which has been invaluable in the past. The more plays
by other playwrights they give at this theatre, the less likely it is that
Shakespeare's will be understandingly acted and produced. It's grand
to have seen Ibsen last time and to be going to see Tchekov next
time. But we mustn't be surprised if the Shakespeare in between isn't
quite what it was.

MACBETH

MR. HACKETT AND HECATE
(1920)

I

THE "Tragedie of *Macbeth*" is now being given at the Aldwych Theatre. The "Tragedie of *Macbeth*"—or something like it. The moment the curtain rises on the Aldwych version, one hesitates to identify it with the version for the First Folio, for this is what immediately happens:

> *1st Witch*: Ha! ha! ha!
> *2nd Witch*: Ho! ho! ho!
> *3rd Witch*: Hee! hee! hee!

In support of which it may be claimed that if these words were not written by Shakespeare, then the less Shakespeare he. Certainly they are not to be found in the First Folio, nor are they to be found in any other folio on God's earth. The First Folio begins with "When shall we three meet again?" and ends, after a speech by Malcolm, with "*Flourish. Exeunt Omnes*." The Aldwych version, having begun as stated, ends, after the fashion of versions prepared by actor-managers, with the death of the actor-manager to a final triumphant farewell cackle of Witches, thus returning to the interpolated first *motif*.

The Weird Sisters begin and end the Aldwych *Macbeth*, and they are devilish busy, too, all through it. Not only on the stage but off. It is safe to estimate that they repeat, off stage, the chorus quoted above *at least* thirty times. Whenever any fresh crime is contemplated, whenever it is committed, whenever it is regretted, you hear the Weird Sisters crying fatefully in the wings, "Ha! ha! ha!" "Ho! ho! ho!" "Hee! hee! hee!" Which, you might think, would satisfy them for one evening. But no. Even when the curtain is down, even when the scenes are being shifted and the playgoer behind you is complaining that the play is "too heavy", or that Mr. Hackett, being only fifty years old, has no need yet to act a man of Macbeth's age (both of which complaints were uttered by the playgoer behind me)—even at these moments, bang in the middles of the long intervals, the myrmidons of Hecate persist in their resolve to wring our withers, ha-ha-ing, ho-ho-ing, and hee-hee-ing, while the band most assiduously plays.

The band at the Aldwych plays not only during the pauses between the scenes, but during the words between the commas as well. It plays, in fact, right through the piece, so that the general impression is that of an important new orchestral composition by Mr. Norman O'Neill, with words (some of them) especially written for the occasion by William Shakespeare. There are times when one feels the words,

I

however well-meant, to be a mistake, they do so distract one's attention from the music; but there are other moments when the dialogue unquestionably helps. Whenever, for example, the Witches cry "Ha-ho-hee!" the strings and the brass automatically rise to supreme emotional climaxes which it is impossible to ignore.

The music of Mr. O'Neill and the recurrent cachinnations of the Witches are the outcome of our modern realistic methods of production. The modern producer of Shakespeare gets so near to the bone of realism that at the last moment he takes fright over the absence of the atmosphere which he has so scrupulously eliminated and calls in a panic for music and screeches. *Macbeth* is not awful enough! How awful! It must be made awful! Wire for Mr. O'Neill! In other words, the realistic producer insists on getting in a real lily, and then proceeds to paint it white because it isn't white enough. And, of course, it isn't.

But this is not the only consequence of the application of realistic methods to the production of Elizabethan plays. Another consequence is that when Elizabethan plays, which were not intended to be produced realistically, make demands which cannot be realistically met, the realistic producer pretends, whenever he can, that the demands have not been made. Macbeth sups full with horrors, and the play was written expressly that the public might sup full with horrors in his company. But since it is not possible to stage the horrors of *Macbeth* realistically, as many of them as possible get left out.

So, at the Aldwych, the murder of Banquo is completely funked. The murder of Lady Macduff and her "poor prattler" is also funked (*i.e.*, cut). Lady Macduff, whose presence is necessary to the understanding of Lady Macbeth's character, never even appears. Young Siward is done delicately to death in the wings. What is the result? That when Macduff bemoans the loss of all his pretty chickens and their dam, our sympathy becomes an entirely abstract matter. And that when Macbeth groans, "I am in blood stept in so far", his hands do not seem half as bloody as they should. The stage should be strewn with the corpses of Macbeth's victims, but the only corpse we are allowed to see at the Aldwych is that of the victim Macbeth himself.

In the case of Banquo, not only the corpse but the ghost is funked. The stage directions in the First Folio for the Banquet Scene are, explicitly: "*Enter the Ghost of Banquo, and sits in Macbeth's place*", and again, "*Enter Ghost.*" At the Aldwych realism gives us—and what a *reductio ad absurdum* of realism!—no Ghost at all, but a spotlight on an empty chair. The producer jibs at the thought that the banqueters shouldn't see a ghost Macbeth sees. We must have our spookery logical! But really, is it less logical that they shouldn't see the spot-light?

Again, there is that moving Birnam Wood. "*Enter*", says Shakespeare, "*Malcolme, Seyward, Macduffe, and their Army, with Boughes.*" Army with boughs! A colossal job for a realistic producer! The cinema

might manage it. But the theatre! So cut it out! Cut out all the sport!
The realistically impossible sport!

Is Shakespeare dull? The modern public thinks he is. No wonder
the modern public thinks he is. The modern realistic producer daren't
let him be anything else. The modern realistic producer has knocked
him lifeless and is now busy belabouring the body. An unfair fight.
Never hit a man when he's dead.

II

Whichever way we turn in considering the problem of the stage
presentation of Elizabethan plays, we come back always to the
Elizabethan theatre. At the Aldwych *Macbeth* I was much unsettled
by the dilatory delivery of most of the actors. Mr. Hackett in his
beautiful rendering of the "To-morrow, and to-morrow, and
to-morrow" speech was as slow as a snail, reminding us of the old
saying that to-morrow never comes. "If only the actors would hurry
up," I chafed, "then it would not be necessary to make such liberal
and disconcerting cuts in the text." These cuts were, it is true, largely
due to the long intervals for scene-shifting—intervals unknown to
the Elizabethan theatre, which had no scenes to shift. But some of
the lost passages might have been saved if only the actors had
accelerated their pace.

All the same, *que diable allait Shakespeare faire dans cette galère*—the
modern theatre? We want the whole of the plays—no less. Suppose
the actors in a modern theatre spoke fast enough to give us the whole
of the plays in the time allotted? Shouldn't we complain? Unquestionably, we should, because we only want the whole of the play to be
spoken in order that the whole of the play may be heard, and in the
comparative vastness of the modern theatre, exacting a sonorous,
exaggerated, semi-elephantine delivery, a quickfire *Hamlet* or *Othello*
or *Macbeth* would often be incomprehensible. But in the Elizabethan
theatre, which was so constructed that no spectator was more than a
dozen yards or so from the front of the stage, it was possible for the
actors to take things at a fairly human rate and for the blank verse to
be spoken trippingly on the tongue. And so, when we critics go to
Macbeth and criticize production and the acting, only too often what
we should be criticizing is the theatre.

Nevertheless, if one has acquired the gift of the blind eye and the
faculty of translating what one sees back into Elizabethan terms, a
good deal of profit may be extracted from most modern productions
of Shakespeare and a great deal from Mr. Hackett's *Macbeth*. For Mr.
Hackett is that very rare occurrence, a really good Macbeth. Whether
it was due to Mr. Hackett's interpretation I will not be certain, but it
seemed to me that, as the play proceeded, I understood the tragedy
of Macbeth as I had never quite understood it before: the tragedy of a
man who cannot make up his mind between predestination and free-
will—a tragedy of thoroughly bad thinking. Macbeth hears the

prophecies of the Witches. If he had dismissed them as stuff and nonsense, all might have been well. If he had accepted them as Gospel,
he could have left the rest to Fate. The trouble is that he both believes
and doesn't believe them. He strives to make assurance (because it
isn't assurance) double sure. He murders Duncan, he becomes king.
Just as the Witches said. But is this his doing or the doing of the
Witches? He can't decide. If he had made up his mind *one way or the
other*, he would never have proceeded to the murder of Banquo, which
he contrives because the Witches (in whom he believes, or doesn't he?)
have declared that Banquo shall beget kings. It is this mental muddle,
this running to and fro between the Witches and the castle to learn
his fate in order that he may upset its apple-cart, that drives Macbeth
into his amazing maunderings and deliberate recklessnesses.

At the outset Mr. Hackett's interpretation lacks what I can only
describe as "blur". It is too definite, too separated. "Why chance
may crown me" should be coloured by "as he purposes", and "as he
purposes" by "why chance may crown me". In Mr. Hackett's rendering
they are two distinct and unrelated *motifs*. But once he reaches the
effect of it all, the frenzies of reflection, the rigours of desperation, he
opens out on a grand scale, such as, I think, no living English actor
could achieve in the part. By the time he comes to the lines,

> Blow wind, come wrack,
> At least we'll die with harness on our back,

he has worked his dishevelled soul into such a state of abandoned
exaltation that he actually dances off the stage like a madman. It is in
no way belittling this Macbeth to say that its greatest achievement
is a *pas de seul* executed to a couplet.

Mrs. Patrick Campbell's Lady does not recall the original. There
is no animal magnetism in it. What is this queer matronly savour?
Surely the prayer of such a woman as Mrs. Patrick Campbell presents
should be "uncivilize" rather than "unsex" me? But possibly it is
unwise in these days to entrust this part to a leading lady of the first
magnitude, for it is radically ancillary. Legends of Mrs. Siddons have
led us to demand more than we are reasonably entitled to get. *Macbeth*,
after all, is the title of the play. One suspects that Shakespeare forgot
all about the Lady towards the finish and only polished her off when
it suddenly occurred to him that she was still hanging around somewhere.

HISTORIC NIGHTS
(1925)

How refreshing it is, after a long succession of devitalizing first
nights in that Mecca of fashionable imbecility, the West End, to get
back to the Old Vic on the south side of the river, where Shakespeare
is always ready to receive you in your oldest clothes! And what a mock-

ery the idea of putting on party dress for Shakespeare seems to be—
like scrambling into a stiff shirt before you feel yourself entitled to
open the window and listen to a nightingale, or putting on gold braid
to look at a sunset.

These but the trappings and the suits of homage. They may, perhaps,
help a lame musical comedy over a stile, but they never did *A Midsummer Night's Dream* a ha'porth of good. Perhaps the success of the
Old Vic is partly due to the fact that it assumes no essential relationship
between *The Tempest* and patent leather shoes, between *King Lear*
and lip-salve.

Mr. Robert Atkins's production of *Macbeth* is admirable. The
modern method is to treat the play as though it had been written, not
by Shakespeare, but by Maeterlinck. Mr. Atkins, digging out the
horror, escapes at once the pitfalls of Bloomsbury aestheticism and
Seven Dials sensationalism. His own performance of Macbeth is
rather ponderous and lacks variety of pace. But where will the Old
Vic find another producer such as Mr. Atkins?

Far too little fuss has been made over Mr. Atkins's imminent
departure from the scene of his triumphs. If there is to be no Royal
Commission to inquire into the cause, no general petition for a reversal
of the judgment, at least his services should be as publicly recognized
as those of a victorious general after a great war. For although Mr.
Atkins did not make the Old Vic, he made it worth while. Where we
had laughed at Macbeth and shuddered over Falstaff, he made us laugh
at Falstaff and shudder over Macbeth.

And Lady Macbeth. For last week's Lady Macbeth—Miss Olivia
Burleigh—was quite the best of the half-dozen I have seen. She was
always in command. She took the part easily in her stride. There was
no strenuous grunting and sweating to unsex herself—indeed, she
gave us for once no witch in plain clothes but the real Lady Macbeth,
as feminine as she was galvanic. A performance which, if given by one
of our fixed stars in Shaftesbury Avenue, would be making London
talk.

WAS SHAKESPEARE A MURDERER?
(1927)

In his time Shakespeare seems to have been and done most things
under the sun, or so those who deduce his biography from his plays
instruct us. He *must*, they say, have been to Italy, have been jealous,
have been an attorney's clerk, have been shipwrecked, *et cetera*. But
why stop there? Go to *Macbeth* at the Prince's Theatre. Mark that
marvellous line "Who would have thought the old man to have had
so much blood in him?" We have had Shakespeare as Botanist,
Scientist, Astronomer, Master Mariner—why not Shakespeare as
Murderer? Gallons of acrimonious ink might be shed in deciding just
what old man Shakespeare killed, and how.

If, however, Shakespeare *was* a murderer, he has paid the penalty by being murdered ever since he died. At the Prince's Theatre Mr. Charles Ricketts, being a real artist, murders him most beautifully with scenery that necessitates the lowering of the curtain twenty-one times before the play is over. Twenty-one times *Macbeth* is cut untimely off in the very thick of the action. Twenty-one times you sit in darkness twiddling your thumbs for the next Ricketts setting. And while, all things considered, the changes are made with some expedition, the effect is devastating. Instead of boarding an express, you board a stopping-train to Dunsinane. "Stop! stop! stop!" cries the devil-porter stage-hand. Here's a stopping indeed. Here you may roast your swan. Here is the Shakespearean producer's primrose way to the everlasting bonfire.

That many of the settings devised by Mr. Ricketts are spaciously beautiful and respectably barbaric is a matter of small moment. The vital point is that all this production impedes rather than assists the play, suggesting that Mr. Casson must be out to prove himself a twig of the old Tree. The bagpipes, too, liberally supplied by Mr. Granville Bantock, divert attention from the matter in hand, making one reflect too much on the geography of the play. The characters might almost as usefully be brought on eating shortbread. Mr. Casson is a workman-like producer for whom I have the very greatest respect, but it seems to me that he is in danger of being bitten by the serpent of the West End. The atmosphere of the play is in the words of the play, and, quite apart from the intelligent elocution of these words, if all the pains that are lavished on music and scenery were diverted to teaching the actors how to fight, the exchange would be well made.

This fighting in Shakespeare's plays is one of the worst-managed things on the English stage. Shakespeare repeatedly introduced it because the Elizabethans loved a good fight as much as we love a good fight to-day—but in modern crook plays, when the characters get to grips, we see that it really shall be a good fight. Dilute the stage fisticuffs of our time to the strength of the hacking and hewing with which the end of *Macbeth* or *Julius Caesar* is regularly rendered ridiculous and you will get a gallery hooting with merriment. I should, of course, be sorry to see Mr. Ainley or Mr. Basil Gill get a bash over the knuckles with the broadsword, but there is no good reason why a stage-actor should not be as ready to take risks as a film-actor. If stage-actors are not prepared to "go the whole hog" in every scene written by a play-wright, then it might be better to act the play with those scenes excised.

The weediest clerk sitting in the Prince's Theatre must feel that, if only he could leap on to the stage, he could give Macduff his quietus in two two's, untimely ripped or no. That "untimely ripped", by the way, always seems to me a very thin quibble. Had I been Macbeth, I should have redoubled my strokes, crying to Macduff that he was nevertheless incontrovertibly "of woman born", and that if he thought he could put it across me that way, he was very much mistaken.

The best performance in this production is the Lady Macbeth of Miss Sybil Thorndike, who, if she lacks subtlety, has size—and an actress of size is a very rare and salutary occurrence nowadays. Miss Thorndike's acting is restrained throughout, but there is great power behind it, and every word is articulated with one ear on the sense. I am glad, too, to record that there is not nearly so much prolongation of vowel sounds as in some of her past impersonations. Once or twice I thought I detected a modern intonation, as when she cried, "Why *did* you bring these daggers from the place?" This is by no means the first time that I have heard a Shakespearean player stress the auxiliary verbs "to do", "to be", and "to have", but I would ask Miss Thorndike to consider whether this is not really a rather slovenly, post-Shakespearean trick. Surely, in the passage in question, there would be much more dignity and force in emphasizing the "Why". Miss Thorndike looked magnificent, even in the parrot-house costume provided for her first entrance, and she moved majestically. A good Lady Macbeth, warranted to keep any irresolute husband up to the mark!

Mr. Ainley was much less satisfactory. He lacked sinews. He flabbed. He seldom gave the impression that he was really expressing thoughts when he spoke his words, and sometimes he gave the impression that he was merely trying to remember them. His elocution was a little less mellifluous than usual, which was all to the good, but the petulant jigging of the knee by means of which he repeatedly attempted to indicate the distraught state of Macbeth's mind became very irritating and reduced the stature of his emotions.

Mr. Basil Gill gave the public a good helping of Macduff. His lamentations over his "pretty chicks" were less moving than is usual, but he made the audience definitely aware of the presence and importance of Macduff before that scene, and here scored a point over most of his predecessors in the part. The Witches, who performed a protracted and entirely unnecessary dance, came through their ordeal well. They spared us the traditional gibbering yowls and spoke quite sensibly about pilots' thumbs without reducing their incantations to the level of a Red Indian war-whoop. Mr. Casson's Banquo suffered from a certain matter-of-factness in the utterance, and his prompt explanation, on the disappearance of the Witches into thin air, that "the earth hath bubbles as the water has", was tossed off rather like a scientific explanation with which any man of education like Macbeth would, no doubt, be already familiar. As producer, Mr. Casson did well to spare us nothing of the horror in the murder of Banquo and of Lady Macduff's son—what beautiful little boys Shakespeare drew! That dying cry, "He has killed me mother, run away I pray you!" is enough to move one to Coleridgean ecstasies. Indeed, it is almost as moving as little Arthur's immortal "O this will make my mother die of grief!"

MACBETH WITH TABS ON
(1928)

If the newspapers want a phrase for Sir Barry Jackson's latest Shakespeare production comparable to the famous "Hamlet in Plus Fours", I don't think they could do better than "Macbeth with Tabs On", which comes trippingly from the tongue and conveys the staff-officer atmosphere now surrounding the once-barbaric Thane of Cawdor. Machine-guns are the order of the night at the Court Theatre just now. They begin and they end the play, and in the middle of the play they interrupt the blank verse so effectively that the speakers are constrained to repeat their words, thus ruining the rhythm.

But there is little attempt at rhythm in this production, and the marvellous dirges of despair chanted by Macbeth himself are reduced to something not unlike the monotonous, jerky clatter of the Morse Code. The explosion of shells, the steadying of Scottish nerves with Scottish whisky—not too modern, let us hope—the substitution of a fine old crusted butler for the ancient porter, the lighting of cigarettes, the consumption by Lady Macbeth of drugs in order to screw her courage to the sticking-place, the murder of Lady Macduff over an elegant afternoon cup of China tea—these, and such as these, are the devices by means of which it is sought to prove, in the wildest orgy of bardolatry ever organized, that Shakespeare is as much at home to-day as he was in the sixteenth and seventeenth centuries. And no doubt many supporters of this method will ecstatically exclaim, "Bless thee, Macbeth, bless thee, thou art translated!"

Some of them, however, are not quite comfortable over the latest results. "Does", writes one, "the whole play in general respond to the modern dress treatment? Not like *Hamlet* did, and not like others might—*because it is a weaker play*." The italics are his. Dear, dear! *Macbeth* not good enough for modern dress. What a pity Shakespeare didn't make it a little better! And what a blow if we should discover that nearly all Shakespeare's plays, when put to the acid test, are pretty poor stuff after all!

"Bless thee, Macbeth, bless thee, thou art translated!" But the flaw in the translation is that it is not thorough enough. Those who support the modern-dress theory may point out with truth that Shakespeare's plays were acted in modern dress in his own time—modern Elizabethan dress; but they must not overlook the fact that this dress harmonized with the language spoken by the characters, which was essentially Elizabethan. If you do not bring the dialogue up-to-date with the costumes, you make the whole performance as ridiculously bewildering as would be a performance of, let us say, Mr. John Galsworthy's *Justice* in which the characters exclaimed "Marry!" and "Beshrew me!" and "God-a-mercy!" And while it is true that the Elizabethan stage was littered with anachronisms, the historical ignorance and simplicity

of the public made these anachronisms as effective as accuracy. Julius
Caesar may not have worn doublet and hose; but what is that compared with the anachronism of a Scottish general in the twentieth
century murdering right and left in order that he may become King
of Scotland, which, as far as the throne is concerned, apparently does
not stand where it did. How comes it that the producer has overlooked
the obvious necessity of making Duncan up like King George?

The plain truth of the matter is that translating Shakespeare into
twentieth century terms leads to a most misleading equation. Human
nature may remain constant, but manners and customs and habits
of thought change with history. No modern general believes in witches.
No modern general, when the opposing army advances under cover
of branches, imagines that supernatural powers have made a forest
march. If you have never read or seen *Macbeth* before, this production
will seem like nothing on earth. If you have read or seen it before, it
will seem like nothing in Shakespeare.

It must, however, be admitted that, if there is any virtue in the
new method, this virtue stands no more chance against the Macbeth
of Mr. Eric Maturin than it did when Hamlet was played by Mr.
Colin Keith Johnston. Never shall I forget how every line of Hamlet
was massacred by Mr. Keith Johnston's stertorous intake of breath,
which made him seem like an hereditary prince grappling with asthma.
Nor shall I ever forget how every other line of Macbeth is massacred
by Mr. Maturin's trick of intensifying his voice into a raucous whisper,
like a man in a passion trying to shout with a sore throat. This vocal
failure was accompanied by an emotional failure no less marked. Mr.
Maturin did not exhibit the effect of Macbeth's experiences upon his
soul. The ancient despair of the great general dwindled into a staff
officer with the fidgets. This was the nearest thing to "a Scottish
gentleman in considerable difficulties" I ever hope to see.

But after these expressions of discontent, it is pleasant to approach
the Lady Macbeth of Miss Mary Merrall, an actress who has not hitherto
occupied the place on the English stage which she deserves, and who
is possessed not merely of intelligence, but of a technique at once
broad and subtle and finely controlled. Miss Merrall acts all through
in the large manner that needs no rattling of beads to suggest barbaric
instincts. Her reading of the letter is punctuated by perfect pauses,
in every one of which she lays bare her mind. Her handling of the
supper scene is masterful; the bitter intensity with which she speaks
the simple words "My worthy lord, your noble friends do *lack* you",
will, I am sure, revert to my memory every time I hear them spoken
by any other actress. And after the guests have gone, what could be
more expressive or more evocative of human compassion than the
restlessness of her eyes, never overdone, the despairing resignation of
her voice, when she applies herself again to the never-ending task of
nursing Macbeth. What a world of weariness she puts into the line
"Almost at odds with morning, which is which".

Here is a performance to see. And here is a performance we may hope to see again in circumstances something more propitious.

MR. LAUGHTON'S MACBETH
(1934)

The Old Vic is concluding its notable season with *Macbeth*. This is Mr. Charles Laughton's biggest Shakespearean effort. There are flashes of tremendous agony in his acting, as when he recoils from the ghost of Banquo or speaks of the terrible dreams that shake him nightly. But between these flashes the performance sags. He has thought it all out, but has he felt it all in? And when, in the difficult later scenes, Shakespeare rises to the peaks of poetry at the expense of realistic feeling, does not Mr. Laughton refuse to follow his playwright, failing to understand that heroes and heroines who speak blank verse are bigger than life-size?

Never is Miss Flora Robson's Lady Macbeth as thrilling as Mr. Laughton's Macbeth at its best. But it is more consistently satisfactory, and in the sleepwalking scene grips us completely. The production is swift but cowardly, boggling at ghosts and apparitions expressly demanded in Shakespeare's stage directions. The ghost of Banquo may only have existed in Macbeth's mind, but if that is so, the same applies to his soliloquies. It is hopeless to be more reasonable than your playwright. That way madness lies.

MINUS THE THRILLS
(1935)

Macbeth at the Old Vic is one of Shakespeare's thrillers. Or should be. But Mr. Cass, the producer, flies in the face of the text to keep the thrills at bay. When the text says *Enter Ghost*, no ghost enters. When the text says we are to see an armed head, a bloody child, and a crowned child with a tree in his hand, these are not shown. When the text says there is to be a procession of eight corpse kings, what we get is just eight points of light. When the text says *Enter Murderers*, they don't, but speak inaudibly offstage, Lady Macbeth and her boy (who has been rocking a superfluous cradle) rushing into the wings to be invisibly slaughtered. When the text says an army shall enter *with boughs*, there are no boughs, yet Malcolm still says "Your leavy screens throw down." When the Witches say that hand-in-hand they "Thus do go about, about", they sit stock-still. And the Porter *runs* on to be slow about opening the gate!

But—when Macbeth says "Hang out our banners on the outward walls", miserable flags are clumsily run up to distract attention from his marvellous maunderings. *And*—lest this should fail to engross us—clouds then proceed to move across the backcloth. Macbeth! Macbeth! Macbeth! The acting is humdrum. Miss Vivienne Bennett begins well, but does not stay the course. Mr. Ion Swinley lacks colour and character and looks like a nice old bishop. And what's this new convention, begotten of Broadcasting House, that where there are two murderers, one shall be rough and shaggy, and the other just down from Oxford?

HAMLET

MR. FORBES-ROBERTSON'S FAREWELL
(1913)

WHEN Juliet called parting a sweet sorrow, she knew that she was going to see Romeo again in a short while. If it had been *adieu* instead of *au revoir*, she would have found no sweetness, only a bitter anguish. And because it is *adieu* we are wishing now to Mr. Forbes-Robertson there can be only anguish in the hearts of all those who, appreciating the noble quality of his work, witness his farewell performances.

Mr. Forbes-Robertson is one of the Olympians. He is always on the heights. The sublimity of his elocution falls like a note from a mightier age. He is our greatest classical actor. And I fear that, with the termination of his season at Drury Lane, we shall find we have said good-bye not only to Mr. Forbes-Robertson, but to all classical acting in this country. It is strange that this great actor, who is so pre-eminently fitted for the Greek drama, should, during his career, have been so little connected with it. But he has achieved inspired work in many other branches, and his Hamlet—which everybody should be compelled to see by Act of Parliament—will take its place as one of the loftiest performances in the history of the stage. It matters nothing to me that he fails to accord with my own conception of the character. Hamlet is, to me, a romantic, not a classical figure. He is a reality, not a symbol. His destiny is in his own hands, he is not in the hands of Destiny. His intellect thwarts his action, but he does not *stand for* action thwarted by intellect.

Reverse these considerations and you have the classical idea as represented by Mr. Forbes-Robertson. Whether you agree with his reading or not, you must admit that this Hamlet is a grand abstraction, full of poetry and dignity, and magnificently free from the "strutting and fretting" that is creeping into modern "realistic" interpretations of Shakespeare. Of Hamlet's many qualities, he lays the strongest accent on that of speculative student. He brings out very strongly, too, Hamlet's extraordinary gentleness and breeding—his "And look you mock him not" is a lesson in courtesy to the most considerate. Perhaps the highest note he touches is in the little scene with Horatio (played in a wood) that precedes the final catastrophe, worthy to rank with Irving's performance of a somewhat similar scene in *Becket*. I do not know whether readers of *The World* are ever sent to or kept from the theatre by my notices, but I am willing to stake my reputation with them on the beauty of Mr. Forbes-Robertson's Hamlet. And if, having taken my advice, anybody can say that he has not found the performance elevating, and can prove that he is an intelligent, sensitive lover of Shakespeare, I readily offer to give him his money back.

HAMLET IN FRENCH
(1922)

The presentation of two scenes from *Hamlet* by the *Comédie Française* at the Coliseum was deplorable; for the patrons of this variety theatre consist largely of people who imagine that Shakespeare is above their heads and whose delusion is not likely to be dissipated by listening to a hacked-off piece of a tragedy spoken in a language they do not understand and sandwiched between an up-to-date China-town ragtime song and an expert comedy juggler. M. de Max's Hamlet, as revealed in the King's prayer scene and the scene in the Queen's chamber, was formal, theatrical, and in the alexandrine tradition. His elocution was well chiselled; his wiping of his hand after touching the medallion worn round the Queen's neck was just cheap thinking. But it is really a mistake to criticize the acting of M. de Max when what should be criticized is the *Comédie Française*, for tottering into variety, and the Coliseum for aspiring to rise in the aesthetic scale. The ladies in my immediate neighbourhood frankly stated that they were "bored stiff" and resorted to captious comments on the "storm without", by which these scenes were liberally accompanied. Apparently French producers, like English, find it difficult to conceive of tragedy without thunder and lightning.

THE OXFORD HAMLET
(1924)

I have seen it suggested that, in choosing *Hamlet* as the play for production in 1924, the Oxford University Dramatic Society displayed more audacity than wisdom. That a company of young men, all in the early twenties and none with half-an-hour's professional experience, should attempt to tackle what is generally allowed to be the greatest tragedy in the English language may, on the face of it, seem like an invitation to disaster. But if the O.U.D.S. had resolved to play for safety rather than for glory, they really could not have made a more fortunate choice.

What amateur societies generally do not appear to realize is that a play with no life in it is much more difficult to present entertainingly than a play that is vital in every syllable. All over the country in every season of the year amateurs are misled by their own modesty into attempting creaky comedies and incredible little sketches about burglars in drawing-rooms that would tax the technique of the most accomplished professionals, and even so keep the public at bay. Bad plays, if they are to be converted into good entertainments, require practised players. *Diplomacy* has long been recognized by West End managers as a drama for an all-star cast.

But the better the play, the more safely it may be handed over to the tender mercies of the amateur. *King Lear* and *The Trojan Women* have so much to lose that they can lose much and still be numbered among the wealthy. If a good burglar be considered preferable to a bad Lear—if amateur societies are more concerned to conceal their shortcomings than to amuse their audiences—they might as well make a bold bid for perfection by taking the local town hall and announcing a public recitation of the alphabet. Which, however immaculate the execution, would unquestionably make a dull evening's entertainment.

So much, then, for the O.U.D.S. choice of *Hamlet*. Now for the presentation. And here I must begin by finding fault. Instead of keeping the performance pure in its amateurism, the parts of Gertrude and Ophelia were handed over to two professional actresses—Miss Florence Glossop-Harris and Miss Lila Maravan; while the services of a professional producer—Mr. J. B. Fagan—were also enlisted. As regards the appearance of the professional actresses, I know that this has become an established custom with the O.U.D.S., and I am not going to pretend that either Miss Glossop-Harris or Miss Maravan seriously upset the equilibrium of the performance. What I deplore is in the fact that such an excellent opportunity should be missed for restoring Shakespeare's female characters to the care of the male actors for whom they were originally written and by whom they always should be played.

The objection that in Shakespeare's day the boy-heroines were specially trained might carry some weight in the case of professional performances; but in the case of the O.U.D.S., where not even the boy-heroes are the product of special training, the balance would not be impaired. Certainly, one of the most satisfactory performances in the O.U.D.S. production was that given by Mr. A. Ker (New College) as the Player Queen. A public that refuses to accept a man in the role of a girl, because it cannot forget that the girl is really a man, will end one day by refusing to accept an actress born in London as the Queen of Denmark, because it cannot forget that the Queen of Denmark is really a Londoner.

The invitation to Mr. Fagan was, perhaps, a still greater mistake —and I say this in no disparagement of Mr. Fagan's parts as a producer. True, I was not happy over all his "cuts". The stage, too, was often so dark that it was impossible to see the faces of the actors— and if lighting is to be so realistic that you can't see the faces for the night, why should not speech be so realistic that you can't hear the words for the gabble? There were also unpardonable minor flaws, as the distraction of Laertes pulling on his gloves while Polonius delivered himself of his now platitudinous advice. On the other hand, the setting was simple and agreeable, the pace was swift, and for the

first time in my experience the King made a fight—or, rather, a flight
—for his life in the last scene, running upstairs and downstairs, with
Hamlet hot at heel: an exciting moment, none the less Elizabethan
for its reminiscence of *Scheherazade*.

But the qualities and defects of Mr. Fagan are beside the point I
wish to make. Here are a lot of enthusiastic young men who have
studied *Hamlet* for themselves; who are untouched—shall we say
unsullied?—by the traditions of the professional stage; and who, by
the freshness of their attack, might teach us something if only they
would shoulder the whole of the burden. Shakespearean production
stands in need of this freshness of vision before everything else.
Given a working knowledge of the principles of the stage for which
Shakespeare wrote, we want producers who will take up the plays as
zestfully and irreverently as the Brothers Melville take up a modern
melodrama. It is true that, unaided by Mr. Fagan, the O.U.D.S.
might have committed a thousand blunders. But these might have been
forgiven them for striking a few new sparks—or for leaving a few
old sparks unstruck!

For if amateurs have more to learn than professionals, they have
less to forget; not in what they do but in what they leave undone lies
their chief merit; and it was on this account that I found many of the
actors in the O.U.D.S. *Hamlet* so refreshing. They were content—
perhaps it would be fairer to say that they were driven by lack of
technique—to leave well alone, to observe that policy of neutrality
which comes, when a play is worth hearing, as such a merciful dis-
pensation to sensitive audiences. I liked the O.U.D.S. *Hamlet* because
it escaped from the professional clichés of gesture and inflexion. The
actors were not out for rounds of applause and higher salaries. They
had something of the earnestness and sincerity of the Primitives.
Even in the inefficiency of the least efficient there was a charm. At
least they did not suffer from the hopeless competence that nothing
can redeem.

Of only one actor can it be said that he showed a real talent for the
stage. That actor was Mr. G. Isham (Magd.), who, if he did not
reveal Hamlet, revealed a presence, a voice, a grace, a fire, and a
confident sense of power over his audience. In so far as it was a
glowering, sleepless Hamlet, Mr. Isham's performance was in the
spirit of the part. In so far as it was a mannerless, humourless Hamlet,
it fell short. His attitude towards Polonius was not so much that of a
young wit amusing himself at the expense of a despised old fool as
of a lout kicking a football. At the end of it all I could no more tell
what Mr. Isham thought about Hamlet than I could have told
twenty years ago, when he was in swaddling-clothes. Nevertheless,
the Hamlet of an actor. And perhaps, in another twenty years, a
Hamlet worth recalling.

A NEW LIGHT ON HAMLET
(1924)

There is so much to be said on the production of *Fratricide Punished*, which was given by Mr. William Poel at the Oxford Playhouse last Monday, that I really do not know quite where to begin. A whole article might be devoted to a narration of the events included in this bald, straightforward, fascinating version of the Hamlet myth; a second article might be written on the relation of this version to Shakespeare's famous play; a third article might deal with the translation employed by Mr. Poel; a fourth with his production at Oxford; and then there would still remain the temptation to write an article on Mr. Poel himself, not only congratulating him on his latest effort, but extolling him (for I am nothing if not a Poelite) as the most important Shakespearean since Shakespeare.

Ever since Shakespeare's death, actors, producers and editors have taken part in a conspiracy to "improve" Shakespeare's work. Heminge and Condell set the ball rolling with the First Folio, when they bowed to the classical convention which had been re-introduced by Ben Jonson, and cut Shakespeare's plays up into acts and scenes. But by far the most serious blow Shakespeare has ever suffered was the adaptation of his plays to the requirements of the picture stage which came in with the Restoration. There is no question but that many of the adapters did their work, considering the circumstances, exceedingly well, just as a writer of film scenarii might—from the standpoint of the films if not from the standpoint of Shakespeare—turn out an excellent film version of *Macbeth*. But if the flesh-and-blood theatre were to disappear altogether, and if we were left in consequence with nothing but film versions of Shakespeare's plays, it would scarcely be unreasonable for anybody who understood Shakespeare to rise up in arms and to protest that the public was not really seeing Shakespeare at all.

And this is exactly what Mr. Poel did when he found Shakespeare, who wrote for a platform stage, suffering from the mutilations that are inevitable in picture theatres. It is common knowledge that Mr. Poel was labelled a pedant for his pains, just as one might be labelled a pedant for preferring an oil-painting by an Old Master to a living-picture representation of it on the stage of a variety theatre. But it is also common knowledge that he has exercised a tremendous influence over Shakespearean production, which is now tending steadily in the direction he has always so staunchly advocated.

It was, perhaps, Mr. Poel's interest in essentials and his realization of the paramount importance of structure that led him to concentrate his attention a short while ago on a translation of the old play called *Der Bestrafte Brüdermord oder: Prinz Hamlet aus Dännemark*, which was given by English players in Germany during Shakespeare's lifetime, and "probably," according to Mr. Poel, "at the very time when Shakespeare's *Hamlet* was being acted by his own Company at the Globe Playhouse in London." *Der Bestrafte Brudermord*, or *Fratricide Punished*, is the bare bones of Shakespeare's *Hamlet*—whether the bones or the body came first is a matter still under dispute. But by one thing nobody who attended the performance at the Oxford Playhouse could fail to be impressed, and that was the remarkable resemblance between the two.

The plot of *Fratricide Punished* closely follows the plot of Shakespeare's play, incident by incident, omitting the soliloquies and the graveyard scene—which are in no way essential to the action—but showing Hamlet on English soil and introducing a harlequinade in which Ophelia becomes mysteriously transmogrified into Columbine. The German play abounds in other quaint differences. Rosencrantz and Guildenstern do not appear, their place being supplied by two banditti, who accompany Hamlet to England to shoot him by the King's orders, but who, standing one on each side of their intended victim, shoot one another instead. The resemblances are, however, much greater than the differences, and it is not only the course of the story, but the words used that often bring Shakespeare's play to mind.

These resemblances were even greater than many of the audience imagined, for it had not been clearly explained that what they were witnessing was a translation from a German translation of an English play, with the consequence that the lines were taken rather at their face than at their translation value. Thus, when Polonius said, "He keeps bringing in my daughter", it was not realized that the words originally spoken by the English actor in Germany were probably Shakespeare's own "Still harping on my daughter!" And there were several more instances of the same kind. It would be a mistake to argue from this that *Fratricide Punished* was, therefore, post-Shakespearean. It might have been a version of the play on which Shakespeare based his own, keeping in the best bits—for he was a master of this art, as of many others.

It is amusing to find Shakespeare praised again and again for the extensiveness of his knowledge, and then to find the passage on which that knowledge was based almost word for word in some other book, out of which he had inspirationally "cribbed" it. One of the supreme examples occurs in *Venus and Adonis*, lines 295-300, where he gives a description of Adonis's horse:

> Round-hoof'd, short-jointed, fetlocks shag, and long,
> Broad breast, full eye, small head, and nostril wide,
> High crest, short ears, straight legs, and passing strong,
> Thin mane, thick tail, broad buttock, tender hide:
>   Look what a horse should have, he did not lack,
>   Save a proud rider on so proud a back.

What a remarkable knowledge of horsemanship had the Bard, exclaims the reader, little witting that in *The Fowre Chiefest Offices belong yng to Horsemanshippe*, translated by Sir Thomas Blundeville in 1565, the most important "points" to look for in a horse are thus described:

"Round hooves, short pasterns with long fewter locks, broade breast, great eies, short and slender head, wide nostrils, the creast rising, short ears, strong legs, crispe mane, long and bushy tail, great round buttocks."

It does not follow, then, that *Fratricide Punished* is post-Shakespeare because we find the King's first speech to begin: "*Obschon unsers Herrn Bruders Tod noch in frischem Gedächtniss bey jedermann ist, und uns gebietet, alle Solennitäten einzustellen, werden wir doch anjetzo genöthiget, unsere schwarze Trauerkleider in Cormosin, Purpur und Scharlach zu verländern.*" Cf. "Though yet of Hamlet our dear brother's death", etc.

In view of the fact that many of the audience were not aware, as I have said, that they were listening to a translation, it was particularly unfortunate that the translation employed should have been in some respects so bad. "Don't be frightened" might, much more appropriately, have been rendered "Be not affrighted." But this was mild compared with Polonius's announcement, after the play scene, that "The actors *have* made a mess of it!" No wonder the audience laughed—and no wonder it laughed again when Hamlet, having tricked his would-be assassins into shooting each other, cried "Almighty Providence, thanks be to Thee for this angelic idea!" And no wonder, again, Mr. Esmé Percy, lured into burlesque, thereupon exclaimed: "These rascals I will ther-row into the water!" Mr. Poel himself seems to have been betrayed occasionally into laughing at the puerilities of *Fratricide Punished*—a point of view for which, bad translation or no bad translation, I can see no excuse. There were moments when his production was wonderfully impressive—under no other producer have I ever heard Miss Florence Saunders, who delivered the prologue as Night, speak half so beautifully. But there were other moments when he seemed to suspend all effort. The harlequinade was certainly a difficult problem, but I was astonished to find Columbine in a Victorian ballet-skirt, with a flautist playing—however reticently—Schumann's *Carnaval*.

It was not an actors' afternoon, but a word should be given to Mr. Percy's Hamlet. He spoke understandingly and musically, and was always dominant. Mr. de Lange played the King and Mr. Andrew Leigh Laertes for, I should say, the first and last times in their careers; they must have enjoyed themselves thoroughly. The play should certainly be published, but before it is published, it should be retranslated into as contemporary Elizabethan as is contrivable. It may then be read with profit, for out of these convertites there is much matter to be learned.

K

MR. BARRYMORE'S HAMLET
(1925)

If Mr. John Barrymore was more than a little anxious when he made his first appearance before an English audience in the part of Hamlet at the Haymarket Theatre the other night, he might at least have comforted himself with the reflection that his anxiety was shared by quite a lot of the critics in the front of the house, who perceived in the event a trial of their own excellence no less than of his. A new performance of *Hamlet* in a fashionable theatre has something of the portentous atmosphere of a Test Match. Everybody in the auditorium is on his very best intellectual behaviour. And everybody is much busier than usual trying to decide whether this is a great Hamlet, or a rank bad Hamlet, or merely a transitory, respectable Hamlet. The all-important thing is not to make a blunder—not to write a genius down an ass lest we should ourselves be written down asses by posterity—and not, on the other hand, to be delighted by false fire, like a green girl!

I verily believe that a man of observation, strolling by chance into the auditorium of the Haymarket during the first interval and scrutinizing the faces of the critics, might have divined by their gravity that the play toward must be *Hamlet*. Whether they had come to bury Barrymore or to praise him would have been more difficult to decide, and it may be that the observed would have been no less perplexed on this point than the observer. My own feeling (not to beat about the bush) was that the execution of Mr. Barrymore's Hamlet far excelled its conception. The meaning of the words came through, a mercy deserving the warmest gratitude. But if the thoughts were the thoughts of Hamlet, they were not thought in Hamlet's way. The true temper of the character did not emerge.

Hamlet's trouble was that he couldn't ever stop thinking—Mr. Barrymore's was that he ever had to begin. And if Hamlets must be labelled, then I should call this a Wittenberg Hamlet—a Hamlet who was not by birth a thinker, a Hamlet who suffered from no rush of philosophy to the head, but a Hamlet who was capable of concentration and who had had philosophy dinned into him by university professors.

Mr. Barrymore spoke deliberately, he showed you each idea in the making, like a slow-motion picture. But while a slow-motion picture of a flash of lightning might reveal many fascinating mysteries, it would not present a true picture of a flash of lightning. And Hamlet's brain was a lightning brain, an intensely emotional brain, a brain that leapt in the dark and suffered sudden revulsions, a fevered brain that drove him to cry (and not to ponder): "Fie on't!" and "Pah!" and "Foh!" and "Ha!" and "O God! O God!" When Hamlet exclaimed: "O what a rogue and peasant slave am I!" it was an exclamation, not an explanation. Therefore, I do not feel satisfied when I hear Mr. Barrymore utter it as one who is bent, at all costs, on finding exactly the right words in which to accuse himself. "O," he seems to say, "what a—what am I? A rogue? Yes, yes, a rogue!—O, what a rogue and—no, not vagabond. I am not a vagabond, nor am I a villain, but—yes, that is the word, I am a peasant-slave—O what a *rogue* and *peasant-slave* am I!" He does not merely think things, he thinks them out, like a good boy. And this habit of thinking out everything leads sometimes to unfortunate results. It is quite clear that the idea of mouse-trapping the King must have entered Hamlet's head just before he asked the First Player whether, for the performance of *The Murder of Gonzago*, he can study a new speech of some dozen or sixteen lines. But when Mr. Barrymore comes, in his succeeding soliloquy, to the lines beginning, "I have heard, That guilty creatures sitting at a play", he beats them out as though now, for the first time, the plan of action has occurred to him. And when, still fifteen lines further on, he says: "The play's the thing, Wherein I'll catch the conscience of the King", it is again as though he has only just been struck by the notion.

Mr. Barrymore acts with intensely realistic feeling. If he is not the right living creature, he is a living creature. What he lacks is mercury. I could have wished, too, that he had put on a more antic disposition and that, after his encounter with the Ghost, he had presented himself to the rest of the Court more dishevelled in appearance, in manner, and in mind. For it seems to me that, under cover of pretending to be mad, Hamlet really does go a little mad, losing his self-control, letting himself rip, and saying things that surprise and perhaps even appal him. His motley releases him. Fancy dress is never quite as fancy as we pretend, for after all, we do want to put it on. And so Hamlet heaps insults on the head of Polonius and the others which he has long yearned to utter, but which he would never have uttered had he not been assured that his manner would convince the listener that he was a stark, staring lunatic.

An admirable Osric by Mr. Frederick Cooper and an Ophelia by Miss Fay Compton whose moods must needs be pitied, deserve high praise. What a diabolically clever actress Miss Compton is!—I say diabolically because I often find it difficult to persuade myself, as I watch her, that she is really feeling anything, and yet how skilfully she emerges from almost every ordeal! But *the* performance of the piece is Mr. Courtenay Thorpe's Ghost, whose elocution is not only immaculate and opulent in the variety of its harmonies, but who gives one the rare impression of a soul in torment. The first scene of all, in which the Ghost does not appear at the Haymarket, was more beautifully and understandingly given than I have yet seen it, and for this some of the credit must undoubtedly go to the bare, dignified, and imposing setting designed by Mr. Robert Edmund Jones, who is in the direct line of descent from Mr. Gordon Craig and who, having created his atmosphere, permits himself no distracting flourish. Indeed, for the setting alone this production is worth a visit.

As for the version employed, it is a disconcerting, rather namby-pamby version, with much of the strength diluted, and much of the length curtailed. But it is hard to say how *Hamlet* can be most satisfactorily cut, for, long as it is, every word of it seems to be essential, and until we are prepared to sit and listen for five hours or so, we must sit and suffer in our glory. At the close, as presented on the stage, it just degenerates into Famous Scenes from the Play. We wonder what on earth is happening and whether Shakespeare did not get rather tired before the finish. But it is not Shakespeare who tired. The fault is in ourselves. You need to be in training to see the whole of *Hamlet* —so why not train? After all, the performance is quite as exciting as running in a race or throwing a hammer. Perhaps if we began instead of ending the day with *Hamlet*, by which I mean the whole of *Hamlet*, we should leave the theatre refreshed rather than prostrated.

HAMLET GOES SLOW
(1925)

What an exhilarating experience it would be to see *Hamlet* for the first time without ever having read a word of it, without ever having come across a single quotation from it or a single illustration, without knowing beforehand whether Hamlet's uncle finally traps Hamlet or Hamlet traps his uncle, without even the ghost of a notion whether the title of the play is the name of a man or a synonym for village! Is there anybody of mature age and average intelligence in England to-day who can claim this rare adventure? If not, can anyone of mature age and average intelligence who has grown up in complete Hamlet-ignorance be discovered—and if not discoverable, then shall not some babe be reared with this especial end in view, that we may take him, a virgin Hamleteer, to see the play for the first time when he is, say, thirty?—that we may sit by him, that we may observe his reactions, and that we may hearken to his account of his impressions?

In this way we might come by a criticism not only fresher but more significant than any that has been written of the play during the past fortnight or (to be bold) during the past century. For after all, plays, with their surprises of plot, of psychology, of language, are written to be seen not twice, but once, and to be seen by people who have not heard the story and been familiarized with the characters beforehand.

We are so familiar with Hamlet to-day, there has been so much discussion about him and about the play, that we have got into a rather pitiful confusion, and are no longer capable of seeing him clearly. Nine people out of ten agree that he was, at any rate, an abnormally irresolute fellow, a notable example of action thwarted by thought, for all the world as though any average man, having heard that his uncle had murdered his father, would go straight off and plunge a dagger into his uncle's heart. But would not that, after all, be an abnormal course to follow? And is it not possible that the idea of regarding

Hamlet as incorrigibly irresolute would entirely fail to enter the mind of our virgin spectator? He might even regard Hamlet as abnormally active in the pursuit of his purpose. If Hamlet was to kill his uncle, it was clear that he must have more damning proof of guilt before he could justify himself in the eyes of the Court. "The Ghost said so" is rather a weak defence; what ghosts tell of murderers is scarcely evidence.

And how promptly Hamlet sets about procuring the evidence he requires! No sooner has the Ghost vanished from the ramparts than Hamlet resolves to feign madness in order that he may the more easily compass his ends. No sooner have the Players appeared on the scene than he resolves to trap his uncle with a mimic play. No sooner has he trapped his uncle than he draws his sword to execute his revenge, which is delayed by the very pertinent reflection that if he does it pat while the usurper is praying, the usurper will go straight to Heaven, whereas his own father was consigned to sulphurous flames with all his imperfections on his head. When, a few minutes later, in his mother's chamber, he believes his uncle to be hiding behind the arras—an avuncular habit he has noticed in the past—he thrusts his rapier straight through the curtains; the fact that he kills Polonius, and not his uncle, does not make his action any the less immediate. It is true that Hamlet does not really like the job—what normal human being would? But after this resolute taking-off of the wrong man, he might not unreasonably have protested against the Ghost's reference to his "almost blunted purpose". Or so our virgin Hamleteer might not illogically argue.

The audience on the first night of Mr. John Barrymore's production at the Haymarket Theatre a fortnight ago knew, of course, all about Hamlet. It arrived armed *cap-à-pie* with prejudices and preconceptions concerning the character, with the consequence that its primary enjoyment was inevitably, to some extent, overcast by comparisons with the might-have-beens and ought-to-bes of its imagination.

But if it knew all about Hamlet, it knew little about Mr. Barrymore except that he was an American star, and that was all to the good. An actor with whom we are not familiar has a much better chance of creating an effective illusion than an actor we know through and through; for, good as the old familiar faces may be, we all too easily recognize their old tricks under new conditions; nor can we escape prejudices and preconceptions concerning the ability of an actor with whom we are familiar; so that, whether these prejudices and preconceptions be justified or falsified, in the very act of recognizing justification or admitting falsification the illusion becomes blurred. For this reason, then, alone, it was probably more satisfactory to see Mr. Barrymore's Hamlet than it would have been to see Mr. Tearle's or Mr. Lang's or Mr. Faber's. The mystery surrounding it made the illusion all the more convincing. True, we did not let Mr. Barrymore off our delight at discovering that he had brought over no American accent, but only for a few moments did that make him the less real and alive. And very real and alive Mr. Barrymore was, very intelligent in utterance, an unmistakable coiner of thought.

But there are ways and ways of coining thought. You can coin laboriously and you can coin in a flash, and Mr. Barrymore's laborious way seemed to me to be the wrong one. If Hamlet was the greatest thinker in literature, he was also the most multitudinous, or—to kill two birds with a single stone—tumultitudinous. He thought by inspiration, not by perseverance. But Mr. Barrymore gave us a persevering rather than an inspired thinker, a two-and-two makes four soliloquizer, a man who tackled problems instead of a man whom problems were always attacking. The result of this was that the character came out, somehow, too small, lacked fire, elasticity, flow. And I think it was largely due to the tardiness of Mr. Barrymore's utterance that in a performance lasting nearly four hours we got, comparatively, so little of the play. The more I see Shakespeare's plays, the more convinced I become that they need a small, intimate theatre, in which rapidity of utterance is easily caught by every member of the audience. The Haymarket is not particularly large, but in the dress circle I was too far away, and it may be that Mr. Barrymore, cutting his cloth according to his measure, was taking me and the less fortunate "gods" into account.

Of the other performances, the finest seemed to me to be Mr. Courtenay Thorpe's Ghost, which was praised in such fitting terms by Mr. Bernard Shaw thirty years ago that I cannot do better than recommend you to look it up in his published criticisms. Mr. Malcolm Keen's King and Miss Constance Collier's Queen both seemed only half alive and mere echoes of old traditions; Mr. George Relph and Mr. Ian Fleming as Horatio and Laertes lacked grace and were too much like echoes of the Greenroom Club; Mr. Herbert Waring's Polonius, being executed as anything but a comic character, missed fire. It would not at all surprise me to learn that Polonius and the First Gravedigger were doubled by the same actor in the original production. Miss Fay Compton's Ophelia was, on the other hand, beautifully done. Another piece of acting of great merit was Mr. Frederick Cooper's Osric, a charming little fop who did not seem, for once, bent on making the most of slight but flashy opportunities.

Mr. Robert Edmund Jones's setting was superb. It gave one a sense of space and a sense of tragedy, it rigorously eliminated inessentials, it facilitated continuity. In conclusion, just a few points that struck me by the way. Why say "porcupine" when the text says "porpentine"? Why pronounce "adieu" French fashion when Shakespeare, who often uses it as a rhyme to "you", obviously intended it to be so pronounced? Why keep the Ghost off the stage until Hamlet sees him? And is it credible that Hamlet really pulled out a pocketbook after the Ghost scene and wrote down "A-man-may-smile-and-smile-and-be-a-villain"—shouldn't these tables be imaginary? Again, why accompany the play scene with *Coq d'Or* harmonies? But this play scene, with two actors to mime the action and two more to speak the words—again *Coq d'Or* fashion—was most impressively done. For the first time in my experience, *The Mouse-Trap*, which I had always set down as the worst play Shakespeare ever wrote, proved entirely thrilling.

HAMLET FROM THE ROOTS
(1930)

Let me exhort you to go to see John Gielgud as Hamlet at the Queen's. Here is a Hamlet to rank with the best—a young, living, bitter, brilliant, thought-ridden, wretched Hamlet—a Hamlet who has bad dreams—a Hamlet who cannot do the deed because he unpacks his heart with words and continually gets the satisfaction in imagination which he should reserve for action. Mr. Gielgud is splendid. Acknowledge him. Give him his due as the best Hamlet of this generation.

This Hamlet packed the Old Vic night after night. It should pack the Queen's week after week. Almost every line is spoken by Mr. Gielgud from the roots. Let the actor take care of the roots and the flower will take care of itself. How many popular performances are just cut flowers that can live only in the vase-water of public appreciation! I would commend, too, the beautiful Ophelia of Adele Dixon.

SIMULTANEOUS HAMLETS
(1930)

It must be a long time since two Hamlets have appeared simultaneously in the West End. It must be longer still since two Hamlets have appeared simultaneously in the West End and at neighbouring theatres. But the other day it was possible, at a single glance, to behold *Hamlet* boards outside the Queen's and *Hamlet* boards outside the Globe. An experience so unaccustomed that at first one suspected an optical illusion.

It was not, however, an optical illusion. It was not even a coincidence. For the embarrassment of Shakespearean riches which has fallen on the West End, we have largely to thank the taste of one man: Mr. Maurice Browne.

True, Mr. Cochran is responsible for half the International Season at the Globe, which has given us, among other excitements, Herr Moissi as the Prince of Denmark. But Mr. Browne is responsible for the other half. He is also entirely responsible for bringing Mr. John Gielgud and the Old Vic company to the Queen's. He is responsible again for *Othello* at the Savoy.

Two Hamlets at the same time are by no means one Hamlet too many. It is hard to see this play without being overwhelmed by its magnificence. And there are as many ways of playing Hamlet as there are of spelling the name of Shakespeare himself—which is no mean estimate, for in *The Autograph of William Shakespeare*, written by a

Philadelphian professor sixty years ago, no fewer than four thousand different possible ways of spelling the poet's name were laboriously listed. Over which of these four thousand ways of playing Hamlet is the right way, critics will never cease disputing. Herr Moissi, conscious of many possibilities, asks why he should limit himself to a single conception of the part. "I seldom", he says, "feel twice the same way about it—the Hamlet within me changes from day to day, as I change, as the world changes." He adds that it is not an actor's business to present a conception of a character, but to live it.

Herr Moissi has many valuable qualities. He can take the stage in a soliloquy like an actor who is not suffering from claustrophobia. He can seize on a moment and make a memorable thing of it, as he seizes on the moment when Polonius insensitively comments on the tears in the First Player's eyes, hushing the old man for his unseasonable admiration, yet himself (when he is alone) enlarging on the same miracle in more befitting terms. This is excellent. But Herr Moissi's Hamlet is a hand-to-mouth Hamlet, a Hamlet seizing the scraps he finds most appetizing, rather than a sustained and lucid character. He does not, like many actors, fall into the error of the pianist who uses the loud pedal to conceal his technical deficiencies. But his persistent use of the soft pedal, when the part fails to stimulate him, is unsatisfactory. At first I thought it might be an art concealing art. On closer acquaintance it seemed to be rather the revelation of a peculiar apathy.

Herr Moissi is at his best in the more hectic passages of excitement. But if I had to describe this Hamlet in one adjective, I should describe it as a soft Hamlet—and then, since one adjective will not suffice, I should add a Hamlet of sweet bells jangled out of tune. Out of tune poor Hamlet most certainly was once he had encountered his father's ghost. But how sweet, one sometimes wonders, were the bells even before that fateful meeting?

Certain features of this German production were highly to be commended. I have never seen a more convincing ghost. He really did look like a spook. Nor have I ever seen the opening dialogue on the ramparts invested at once with more vitality and mystery. Horatio's sceptical attitude was brought out strongly and his panting terror, once the ghost had appeared, made a fine contrast. The First Player delivered his speech most excellently in the Ercles vein, and silly old Polonius, weeping one moment, laughing the next, and doddering always, struck exactly the right note. The last part of the play, however, went for nothing, because it had been so murderously cut. I had always thought that the Germans were more respectful to Shakespeare than we are, but apparently it is not so. How refreshing it is to see on the programme of the Old Vic production at the Queen's Theatre next door: "*Hamlet* (Cut Version)". A well-cut version, but cut. Whenever a cut version of Shakespeare is presented on the stage, it would be well for producers to make a similar acknowledgment.

And now—although he is an Englishman—I must say a few words of Mr. John Gielgud, whose Hamlet is a really superb, vital, pitiable John-o'-dreams, never seeking to nobilify, never under-stressing the quick bitterness and brutality of this crawler between heaven and earth. The sooner we get away from the tradition that Hamlet was a charming young fellow in unfortunate circumstances the better. There is too much zest in his ugly behaviour to Ophelia, in his violent behaviour to his mother, in his bullyragging behaviour to Rosen-krantz and Guildenstern, in his insulting behaviour to Polonius, to be palmed off as pure antic disposition. I will warrant that he made some of the young fellows at Wittenberg suffer in the old days, and I should rather like to know whether, when his father was alive, he addressed many more words to him than he did to his uncle after his uncle had taken his father's place.

But this has taken me from Mr. Gielgud, whom I would praise for the salt in the dry tears of his performance, for the eyes that seem so sunk with want of sleep, and for the living meaning with which he invests almost every word he speaks. I would exhort all who read these words to see this performance. It is one that makes even dramatic critics applaud.

AN ORDEAL FOR MR. TEARLE
(1931)

To play the part of Hamlet is, even for the most illustrious actor after months of the most painstaking preparation, invariably an ordeal. To play it at twenty-four hours' notice, as Mr. Godfrey Tearle played it at the Haymarket Theatre, must be an even more harrowing experience and might be described as a nightmare but for the merciful fact that in such a crisis there is no time for sleep. The full story of the hubbub in the company created by the collapse of Mr. Ainley's voice on the very eve of production has yet to be revealed. But it is clear that if ever an actor deserved applause and allowances for stepping into a breach, that actor is Mr. Tearle. His performance was an act of heroism—and something more: a shining example to the whole theatrical profession.

For, after all, exceptions excepted, should not every English actor worth his salt be prepared to play the part of Hamlet at twenty-four hours' notice? It occurs to me that if I were a theatrical manager and if a young actor came to me for an engagement, I should take his breath away by asking, "Are you ready to play Hamlet for me to-morrow night?" If he said he wasn't, I should send him about his business. If he said he was, I should then seriously consider his qualifications for the part of the butler in my forthcoming comedy. Moreover, I should expect him there and then to stand up and give me a sample of his technique in any one of Hamlet's speeches I might care to name—expect it no less reasonably than Hamlet himself expected the First Player to reel off every word of Æneas' tale to Dido, even though it occurred in a play which was caviare to the general.

Mr. Tearle emerged from his test with considerable credit. He never halted for a word. He delivered himself of a sound and effective performance under conditions which (bating everybody's readiness to make allowances) could hardly have been more cruel. Half the spectators appeared to be suffering, or to be on the point of suffering, or to have recently recovered from suffering, influenza. One felt that in Queen Elizabeth's day, when the plague was the thing, the Haymarket would have been summarily closed not on account of the indisposition of the star actor but on account of the indisposition of the audience. Poor Mr. Tearle might well have imagined that he was acting in a hospital.

I have said that we were all ready to make allowances. I dare say there were a good many present who superstitiously believed that *because* Mr. Tearle had taken on the part at such short notice, his performance was, *ipso facto*, bound to be an epoch-making histrionic event. It was not, however, a night of miracles. Here was a serviceable all-round performance of a great play, with Mr. Tearle bearing the brunt of the burden bravely but not brilliantly on his shoulders. It was in his tenderest passages that he was most effective—notably his scene with his mother and his more melting moments with Ophelia. He was never bad. He was, however, a bit of a Dobbin. Where he failed most seriously was in conveying the bitterness in Hamlet's composition, the acidity of the tears shed by his heart, the storm of thoughts by which his brain was besieged, the charming and alarming impetuousness of his nature, the exclamatoriness of the man.

Mr. Tearle's elocution was good and his emphasis sensible, save in one or two surprising instances. When Hamlet inquires of Rosencrantz and Guildenstern whether they have come to see him of their own accord, and when he asks, "Is it a free visitation?" I cannot understand why the word "visitation" should be stressed. Nor, when he declares that the commandment of the Ghost "all alone shall live within the book and volume of my brain", can I understand why there should be a great underlining of the word "volume", as though it had something to do with size.

Of the other performances, none will live all alone within the book and volume of my brain, although Miss Fay Compton's Ophelia, turning thought and affliction, passion, hell itself, to favour and to prettiness, has a fine moment at the close of the mad scene when she gets to the flaxen poll. Mr. Herbert Waring plays Polonius entirely for dignity and not at all for humour, which is, I think, a mistake; for Polonius is connected, if distantly, with Pandarus and Justice Shallow. Mr. Malcolm Keen makes a very possible King. Miss Irene Vanbrugh as the Queen is quite out of her element, for even in modern costume it is always comedy that has been her strong card. Mr. Tom Reynolds tosses a pretty skull as the First Gravedigger, and Mr. Norman Page as the Second pleased me better than anybody in the cast.

A word of praise for Mr. Baliol Holloway's Ghost which is only permitted to make an appearance when it speaks because, paradoxically, modern producers, being no longer superstitious, are afraid of ghosts. But to represent an unholy ghost by a shaft of light (which is usually reserved for the Divine) when he is off the stage, and then to wrap him in complete gloom when he comes on, seems rather contradictory. But contradictions are, of course, bound to follow as soon as Shakespeare's own stage directions are ignored.

MR. GIELGUD'S SECOND HAMLET
(1934)

It is a long time since a London auditorium has been enlivened by such loud cheers as greeted Mr. John Gielgud last week after his first performance as Hamlet at the New Theatre. Probably there is no actor now on our stage, possibly there is no actress, with a following so large, enthusiastic and uncritical. It is comforting, therefore, to reflect that, unlike many popularities, Mr. Gielgud is an actor of fine taste and great ambition who needs must act the highest when he sees it, and that he is not likely to lead his supporters, as he so easily could, astray.

Mr. Gielgud's Hamlet is, by general consent, the best Hamlet seen since the war. It is a romantic, not a classical Hamlet, a Hamlet bitter with the saltness of tears he does not shed, a Hamlet passing all his predecessors in adoration of his dead father. I have never seen this intense father-worship more beautifully emphasized than it is by Mr. Gielgud at the start of the play—rightly emphasized, for the text demands it, and the poignancy of Hamlet's failure to avenge his father in more than words is tremendously enhanced.

There has, however, been one post-war Hamlet superior to Mr. Gielgud's Hamlet at the New, and that was Mr. Gielgud's Hamlet at the Old Vic four years ago. Something vital has gone out of his performance, which has become more facile and more naturalistic and which now speaks many of the speeches too trippingly on the tongue, so that often we do not get the full value of the surprising words and thoughts. The feeling is there, but we are not always convinced that this Hamlet would have been able to say these things if he had not learnt them by heart.

Now how are we to account for this decline? Certainly not by old age. Mr. Gielgud is only thirty. Nor can I put it down to misjudgement on my own part, having found an intelligent actor, an intelligent producer, and an intelligent critic (the only three people with whom I have discussed the performance) to agree with me. But I think I can give two reasonable explanations.

In the first place, when Mr. Gielgud played Hamlet before, he was not producing the whole play as at the New. This is probably too much for any human being to undertake. You cannot do justice to your own Hamlet if you are thinking half the time about the right way to play Ophelia and Polonius and the Gravediggers, with scenery, lighting, effects, and the other multitudinous harassing details that must crowd a producer's mind.

In the second place, when Mr. Gielgud played Hamlet before, he was playing Shakespearean part after Shakespearean part, so that he was thoroughly soaked in the playwright's convention and point of view. This is invaluable when you are interpreting playwrights who are not contemporary. You need to be not only in practice but in that *kind* of practice. And I'll wager that on the last night at the New, Mr. Gielgud's Hamlet will be twice as exciting as it was on the first.

For the rest, the acting is fair to middling. It includes Miss Laura Cowie's curiously impressive Queen, Mr. Frank Vosper's bilious King, and a good solid Horatio by Mr. Jack Hawkins. Miss Jessica Tandy's Ophelia is like a naughty little girl who has been stealing the jam. The décor by Motley is extremely beautiful but too dominant for those who favour three boards and a passion.

MIND THE STEP
(1935)

There are many ways of doing Shakespeare. One of the most popular these days is Shakespeare with Steps. At the Westminster last week the Dublin Gate Theatre gave us Shakespeare with Steps in the Dark. This must be thrilling for the actors. So thrilling that, although the play was *Hamlet*, it would have been excusable if one of them had burst into *Macbeth* and cried, "That is a step on which I must fall down or else o'erleap".

I was glad to see the ghost of Hamlet's father brought on in the closet scene—so often in modern productions he is here reduced to a voice off-stage, thus making Hamlet seem really loony. It was, however, a pity that the ghost should have been the only thing visible, for with Hamlet and Gertrude plunged into pitch dark, such lines as "But look, amazement on thy mother sits", and Gertrude's exclamation at the spectacle of Hamlet's hair standing on end, became almost laughable.

The outstanding thing in this production was, inevitably and satisfactorily, Mr. Michael Macliammoir's Hamlet. It had youth, vigour of mind, the self-contempt that seeks compensation in rudeness to others, and direct attack, not being embellished with those hundred-and-one little touches that are apt to make Shakespearean acting so over-subtle. Good elocution, too, with no Irish accent—if only Englishmen could speak Irish as well as Irishmen can speak English, then we might see Mr. John Gielgud and Miss Gwen Ffrangçon-Davies in *The Playboy of the Western World*.

MR. LAURENCE OLIVIER'S HAMLET
(1937)

Although Hamlet is one of the most varied and complex characters ever created, it is the custom, when a new actor plays the part, to distinguish his performance by a simple adjectival label: Mr. A is a Gloomy Hamlet; Mr. B is a Scholarly Hamlet; Mr. C is a Bitter Hamlet; Mr. D is a Royal Hamlet; Mr. E is a Rude Hamlet; Messrs. F, G and H are Poetical, Tempestuous, and Stark Mad Hamlets.

So they are written down. So they are recollected. What of the latest Hamlet, now being given us by Laurence Olivier at the Old Vic? It is spry—it is sinewy—it is capable of kangaroo-like leaps. Probably it will go down to posterity as an Athletic Hamlet. But I, personally, shall always think of it as a Handsome Hamlet—not that Mr. Olivier for one moment exploits or ever has exploited his good looks. It would not in the least surprise me to be told that he regards them as a millstone. But there they are. As the soliloquies proceed, I ask myself: "Could a man who looks like that think like that?" Or: "Could a man who thinks like that look like that?" This, assuredly, is not the face of one who has bad dreams, or who toys with the idea of suicide. (After which, Mr. Olivier will probably write to tell me that he does both!)

There was a suggestion beforehand that this was to be an Ernest Jones Hamlet—that is to say, a Hamlet in love with his mother, and therefore incapable of behaving as a lover should towards Ophelia. This, however, did not emerge in performance. Mr. Olivier's interpretation of Hamlet seemed no more psycho-analytical than George Howe's excellent performance of Polonius, or Alec Guiness's brilliant little sketch of Osric. Indeed, it struck me that if D'Artagnan (no friend of Freud) had played Hamlet, he might have given a performance not unlike Mr. Olivier's, which is at its best in moments of excitability.

Yet these moments of excitability are not always the most satisfactory, for in conveying the general impression, Mr. Olivier scamps the detail, and words that should speak volumes convey almost nothing at all.

This is notably the case after the play scene—which, by the way, is basely acted, with deliberate intent, as though by Bottom and Thisbe, and no less basely mocked, as though by the Court of Theseus. When Mr. Guthrie introduced his strollers without a woman in the company, we applauded his understanding and good sense. But when the appearance of a boy as the player-queen was immediately hooted and jeered at by the stage spectators, what a departure from Shakespearean intention was there! Never in the whole history of *Hamlet* can this play-scene have been more astonishingly misinterpreted.

Nevertheless, praise to the Old Vic. For how good it is to see
Hamlet given to us in its entirety, and so making sense all through.
Let us have done for ever with mangled versions that convert the last
half of the evening into little more than a series of incomprehensible
excerpts. How Mr. Olivier must feel around midnight on Saturdays,
after giving a matinée as well as an evening performance, I shrink
to contemplate. But it is a great feat—and none gamer for a feat than
he.

KING LEAR

SOUND AND FURY
(1922)

KING LEAR was revived at the Old Vic on March 20. The company seemed a little spent after its exertions in *Peer Gynt*. Perhaps
As You Like It would have been a more comfortable play to fall back
on. But in any case *King Lear* is, under modern conditions, an almost
uncrackable nut. Its vastness and its grandeur, bridled in a picture-
frame, dwindle to a kind of cramped restlessness. Little of the poetry
succeeded in bridging the perilous gulf of the Old Vic orchestra. And
why, when actors play madmen, do they become so operatic? Only
too often the spoken word becomes mere sound and fury, signifying
nothing.

Sanity may be incoherent more excusably, for we can generally
guess its meaning. When the sane man says, "Will you pass the
——", we may hand him the salt without listening for the last word.
But we must listen carefully to the last word of the madman, lest it
should be "moon" or "differential calculus". The sequence of thought
in madness is so strange and subtle that the actor should be at particular
pains to clarify the psychology. Lear and Edgar rampaged, stage
thunder and lightning worked overtime, spectators were in Paradise,
auditors in pandemonium. Russell Thorndike seemed like a dancing
jack with the string extra vigorously jerked. But it was refreshing to
find that he did not (like Henry Baynton) treat the contemplated tri-
partition of Lear's kingdom as the first act of his developing insanity.

Some critics carp at this stupendous play, objecting that Lear was a
silly old dodderer who deserved all he got. Does this make his frenzy
any the less awful, or the words he speaks any the less astonishing
and revealing? But, meeting such critics on their own curiously-chosen
ground, it may be pointed out that by the common law of ancient
Britain freeholds of inheritance were not generally devisable by will;
they were assignable only by formal delivery of the possession thereof
in the tenant's lifetime. Since Lear had no male issue, his kingdom
would have been divided *equally* between his three daughters on his
death, if he had not disposed of it beforehand. And Cordelia being his
favourite daughter, he wished her to have more than her sisters.
"What can you say," he asks her, "to draw a third *more opulent* than

your sisters?" All this is, of course, comparatively unimportant, but
not a bad stick to beat a donkey with.

The performance of outstanding distinction at the Old Vic was
Andrew Leigh's light, tragic Fool. Mr. Leigh is a born Elizabethan
clown; quick, humorous, graceful, alive and plebeian enough to
suggest a fundamental camaraderie with the groundlings. Shakespeare's clowns must have addressed themselves to the audience more
than did any of his other characters. Mr. Leigh's delivery in *King Lear*
was a thought too rapid, so that we lost a few of the gems. It is true
that most of the remarks of the clowns are interjectory, and so should
be thrown in lightly, to avoid holding up the action. But the Fool in
Lear is the chorus of the play, not to be dismissed with a "So la,
so la".

PROBLEM FOR YOUTH
(1931)

The Old Vic is concluding a memorable season with a production
of Shakespeare's titanic tragedy, *King Lear*. It has been said that if it
were possible to exhibit the actual Lear of Shakespeare on the stage,
the performance would be forbidden by law. It is a fact that for ten
years *King Lear* was withheld from the stage in consequence of the
mental derangement of George III, to be revived very soon after his
death. But even then it was not the actual *Lear* of Shakespeare that
was revived. For a hundred and fifty years managers favoured a
wretched distortion of the play by Nahum Tate, who brought in a
marriage between Cordelia and Edgar at the end and made the old
king recover his health and bless the "celestial" pair. This was the
version in which David Garrick took the town by storm.

At the Old Vic it is, of course, the *Lear* of Shakespeare that they
present and the Lear of Shakespeare that John Gielgud valiantly
essays. But what an undertaking for a young man to cope with! First,
he must be an old man. Next, he must be an old man who is hearty and
roystering, which is much harder, if you are young, than to be an old
man who is weak and decrepit. And after that he must mark an abrupt
decline from senile heartiness to senile decay—a decline not wrought
by age or by misfortune alone, but by a shattering combination of
the two. There must be magic, indeed, for a lusty shoot to transform
itself into an old oak struck by lightning.

Mr. Gielgud is a fine actor but, in the circumstances, it is not
surprising that I should have left the Old Vic hoping that I should
be alive in twenty years to see him play the part again. At present he
is inclined to be too declamatory. But he has his exciting flashes.
One is in that superb cry "I am cut to the brains!" And the whole of
the re-encounter with Cordelia is beautifully done. He leaves the Old
Vic to seek good, if not better, companions with credit.[1]

[1] Mr. Gielgud's next appearance was in *The Good Companions*.

I suppose he *must* leave the Old Vic. Yet I am reminded of a correspondence between Macready and Phelps when Macready was acting at Drury Lane in the West End and Phelps at Sadler's Wells in the East. "My dear Phelps," wrote Macready, "Why not come to the West —a great actor like you? Surely there is room for two!" To which Phelps replied: "My dear Macready, How kind of you to think of me! I am very happy at the East End of London. I cannot act as well off as I can on the stage, so I will stop where I am."

LEAR TWICE NIGHTLY
(1934)

A young actor unknown to fame is performing a feat unparalleled in theatrical history. To play King Lear is a forbidding labour for the most experienced star. To play it at the age of twenty-two is a colossal act of daring. But to play it, as William Devlin is playing it at the Westminster Theatre, *twice nightly*[1]—well, that has never been done before and will probably never be done again. Why are there no headlines in the Press, as for non-stop dancers and long-distance flyers? I understand that late last night Mr. Devlin was still alive.

It is pretty obvious that Mr. Devlin could not do what he is doing if he were a Salvini. Salvini refused to act Othello more than three times a week, and then never on two consecutive nights. Yet when I saw Mr. Devlin at the 9.15 house I was considerably impressed by his performance. It is grand in scale and intelligently planned. If there are no great moments, if the detail does not excite, the words are finely-spoken and the character comes out strong and true. Mr. Devlin is a surprise worth watching.

For two-thirds of the performance *King Lear* goes excellently. If some of the acting is weak, the producer, Hugh Hunt, has not failed in his direction. Here is a Cordelia who strikes (being a chip of the old block) a note of defiance and is not all maidenly modesty. Here is a Fool who is something more than a commentator and whose pathetic tremors heighten our sense of the dramatic situation.

But let us never, never, never, never, never have Shakespeare twice nightly again if it means versions such as this. Fancy putting on a great play with its greatest scene violently omitted! Not a word do we get of the overwhelming encounter between Lear gone mad and Gloucester blind. Compared with this sadistic cut, the plucking out of Gloucester's eyes becomes an act of subtle, tender, and delicate temperance. Who will help me to found a Society for the Prevention of Cruelty to Shakespeare?

[1] I learnt later that Mr. Devlin played Lear twice nightly only on certain nights.

LEAR TO THE RESCUE
(1940)

In these days of artistic as well as every other kind of crisis, high praise is due to the gallant stars who have rallied voluntarily to the cause of Shakespeare. Headed by Mr. John Gielgud, who could command as big a salary as any actor in England, and who is always thinking of the theatre first and himself afterwards, they are appearing for next to nothing at the Old Vic because they realize that the battle of the Old Vic is one we cannot afford to lose. And if *The Tempest*, shortly due, packs the house as it has been packed by *King Lear*, they may find it hard to resist extending the programme, which was originally limited to these two plays. In any event, they have, for the time being, put Shakespeare and the Old Vic on their feet again. They have restored the self-respect of the theatre. And although it may be a pity that it should require stars to do this—an equally fine performance given by a company of nonentities might easily have been a complete flop—all honour to them.

Has anybody ever made a success of Lear since Garrick? Garrick must have been tremendous. "I have heard", wrote Hazlitt, "that once, when Garrick was acting Lear, the spectators in the front row of the pit, not being able to see him well in the kneeling scene, where he utters the curse, rose up, when those behind them, not willing to interrupt the scene by remonstrating, immediately rose up too, and in this manner the whole pit rose up, without uttering a syllable, so that you might hear a pin drop." Mr. Gielgud's Lear is, inevitably, something less than this. The make-up is magnificent. The voice, when first heard, seems to have no connection with it, lacking depth and richness. But once you have grown accustomed to that, the feeling and variety of tone he puts into the opening scenes, the clarity of the meaning behind every word, are matters for rejoicing. Does he ride the storm? No; those amazing outpourings lose themselves in the wild open-air theatre. But in the scene with Gloucester on the cliff Mr. Gielgud rises to the top of his performance, which, if lacking in the ultimate note of sympathy—we feel for the words Lear speaks rather than for Lear himself—is a fine achievement.

What of the others? Mr. Hawkins as Edmund gives, I think, the most completely satisfactory performance, humorous, rascally, commanding. Mr. Haggard's Fool is intensely irritating. If I don't know how this part should be played, I do know that it should not be played like Puck. Mr. Hannen and Mr. Casson are thoroughly efficient as Gloucester and Kent; Mr. Harris gives poor Tom's outpourings without the gabble that usually makes them completely unintelligible; there is a very clever performance of the Steward by Mr. Somers. Miss Tandy is not up to Cordelia. She seems to have no reserves and to be making a commendable effort. Miss Compton and Miss Nesbitt

L

are well enough as Goneril and Regan, parts most actresses have
hitherto played entirely with their nostrils. For the rest, good enough.
For the whole, very good indeed. Which, where a performance of this
great and difficult play is concerned, is pretty remarkable.

MR. WOLFIT'S KING LEAR
(1944)

Mr. Donald Wolfit has completed his Spring Exhibition of Old
Masters at the Scala Theatre with a revival of *King Lear*. His performance of this part is not a patch on his Volpone or his Othello, but no
experienced playgoer will be surprised at that. To be every inch a
Lear is almost as rare as to be every inch a Cleopatra. (Has Shakespeare's
Cleopatra ever given satisfaction on the stage?) Nor, for the matter of
that, can Lear be measured by inches.

The opening is masterfully handled. The recognition of Cordelia
near the end is beautifully done. The comparative failure of the rest
is crystallized in Mr. Wolfit's rendering of the line "I am cut to the
brains", which comes out in a trickle of pain too whining for such a
gash and has a negative instead of a positive quality. If it is Lear's
tragedy that he loses his wits, it should be our gain that the process
is attended by revelation after revelation beyond the scope of reason-
fettered sanity. The human earthquake is there but not the treasures it
ejects. Too often Mr. Wolfit becomes involved in his own tune,
which governs and obscures the thoughts instead of emerging directly
from them. Too often we are able to predict the next note, which should
be no more predictable than the next astonishing and unforeseeable
word.

OTHELLO

TWO *OTHELLOS*
(1922)

DURING the month January 15—February 15, dramatic critics
were invited to attend performances of Shakespeare's plays at
the Savoy Theatre and the Old Vic. At the Savoy Mr. Baynton presented matinées of *King Lear, Julius Caesar, Othello, Romeo and Juliet* and
The Taming of the Shrew. As an actor he revealed some stature but little
depth; as a producer he did not scruple to commit *lèse*-Shakespeare.
His sins were the usual sins of omission and rearrangement, but
they were committed so much more flagrantly than usual that they
were detected by even the most illiterate critics. I do not remember
that any editor has ever been bold enough to "cut" Shakespeare's
Sonnets; but if such a daring spirit were to delete a couple of lines
from one sonnet (on the ground of impropriety), a couple of lines from
another (on the ground of unintelligibility), and a couple of lines
from a third (on the ground of limited space), he would hardly make him-

self more ridiculous than does the tailor and cutter of Shakespeare's plays.

The framework of a soundly-constructed play is as fundamentally important as the framework of a soundly-constructed sonnet. The excision of a single short link-scene may deprive the whole of grace, sense, or assonance. If you cut, you may as well add. To lop off Shakespeare's nose is no more humane than to give him a false one. And Mr. Baynton, having stabbed Shakespeare through and through with his blue pencil, might just as well have gone on to dress the wounds. Having eliminated the street meeting between Brabantio and Othello, he might no more absurdly have repaired the breach by writing a few lines to explain their apparently coincidental appearance in the council chamber. But no modern producer of Shakespeare has the courage of his sacrilege. His best conscience is not "to leave'd undone" but "to keep't unknown". He realizes that if he sets about joining the new flats, he will be caught out even by critics who now pass his "cuts" without comment because they are not familiar with the plays in the original.

Nevertheless, if Mr. Baynton persists in his present methods of production, there is only one sound thing for him to do, and that is to re-write the whole of (say) *Othello* honestly and coherently according to his lights. If he objects to such "indelicacies" as "goats and monkeys", "I'll chop her into messes", etc., he had better tone down the rest of the play in keeping with his excisions, make Othello miss his footing by the bedside, and so qualify the smothering of Desdemona as an accident.

Othello at the Old Vic was a very different affair. Here Mr. Atkins started with the theory, not that he must confine the play within the limits of a given production, but that he must extend the production to suit the requirements of a given play. For the first time in my experience I saw the whole of *Othello*, with all its magnificent propotions and overwhelming catastrophies unimpaired. I could not approve of an interval just before Othello's fit; of the labourings of the Old Vic Iago, with his whistling exit and his repetition of "All things shall be well"; of the neglect on the part of Roderigo to defeat his favour with an usurped beard. But Cassio for once remembered his beard, and Othello for once remembered his complexion. In Shakespeare's view (I take it) Othello had his points in spite of the fact that he was pot-black, just as Shylock had his points in spite of the fact that he was full-Jew.

It was difficult to feel the southern blood racing thro gh Mr. Wilfrid Walter's veins, but he experienced his agonies of mind at first hand and, for a northern Othello, would be hard to beat. Miss Florence Buckton, whom Mr. Atkins should be careful never to cast for romantic parts, was at her very best as Æmilia, and Mr. Andrew Leigh added another little masterpiece to his growing gallery of clowns. The remarkable point in the Old Vic performances is the triumph of good production over inferior acting.

It would, perhaps, be going too far to say that if you look after the production, the acting will look after itself. But it is, nevertheless, a fact that the whole of *Othello* given by competent amateurs would be far more satisfactory than half of it given by efficiently-controlled stars.

A NORTHERN OTHELLO
(1924)

Even the most northern Othello cannot fail to move an audience to pity. Mr. Ion Swinley, now playing the part at the Old Vic, is a very northern Othello indeed. In the big scenes we are deeply stirred. But that he does not quite understand, or cannot quite interpret, the soul of the Moor is evident from his handling of some of the earlier encounters. Othello should have intense command and a kind of genteel, filleted grandeur: that Mr. Swinley revealed neither may not have been due to lack of perception. But there were moments when he showed that, while the blood of Othello did not flow in his veins, he did not even know the kind of blood that should have been flowing.

An example may be cited in the senate-scene, when Brabantio says "I heredo give thee that with all my heart", etc. Desdemona is naturally distraught under her composure. A great effort of self-control is necessary to carry her through the situation. At this point she stretches back her hand, as if for moral support, to Othello, who would be acutely conscious of her state of mind. It is right in this scene that Othello should be supremely dignified and that he should not display to the magnificoes his innermost feelings. But when Desdemona stretches that hand back, it is clear what Othello's response would be. His own hand would leap to the encounter. His grip would be on her like a flash of lightning. Mr. Swinley's hand moved slowly towards Desdemona's and took it calmly—a northern hand to the last knuckle.

All through Othello's suave splendour in these opening scenes, there should peep little excitable uncontrollabilities. Mr. Swinley does not lose control of himself for the tenth part of a second. Another obvious opportunity was missed in the Cassio scene. It is natural that Othello's love for Cassio should cause him to cashier his officer more in sorrow than in anger, and it is clear from the text that his "never more be officer of mine" should be uttered in this spirit. But when, on these words, Desdemona enters and Othello, having exclaimed, "Look if my gentle love be not raised up", rounds on Cassio with "I'll make thee an example!" and so sweeps off, it is clear that this is another of those uncontrollable ebullitions which are like the spurting of blood from a pricked artery, and that the words should leap from his mouth like a hot flame. Mr. Swinley uttered them in a low tone, as you or I or any Englishman in plus-fours might utter them. He was not Othello—but he served.

The Iago of Mr. George Hayes was a good understanding piece of acting, not very subtle, and rather under-played. Mr. Hayes is naturally

a florid actor, and not long ago suffered rather badly from mephis-
tophelianism. He has now curbed this spirit, with the result that he
has become one of our best Shakespearean actors, but his Iago seems
to suffer from a fear lest, given an inch, it should take an ell. The
Desdemona of Miss Marie Ney, a newcomer, seemed to me to be
totally devoid of feeling, and it lacked—what Shakespeare's heroines
have always most lamentably lacked at the Old Vic—breeding. The
most finished performance was Mr. Andrew Leigh's oriental Clown.
But I cannot believe that this Clown was really intended by Shakespeare to be orientalized, any more than I can believe that Othello
was intended to appear in a Turkish bath-wrap. I always feel that he
needs a piece of soap and a sponge in his hand to complete the picture
satisfactorily.

A BACK-STAGE TRAGEDY
(1930)

In the matter of presenting Shakespeare, producers appear to be
bent on trying every way but the way visualized by the poet himself.
It is common knowledge that in Shakespeare's day the stage thrust
out its long, rude tongue into the auditorium, so that it was surrounded on three sides by spectators, in whose very midst the players,
as large as life and twice as dramatic, declaimed the mighty lines and
bodied forth the mighty passions bestowed upon them. Since there
was no proscenium arch, the players were not figures in a framed
picture. When Othello raged round the boards, he raged not in two
dimensions, but in three. When he fell into his trance, his position,
relative to the spectators, was very much that of a boxer taking the
count. Propinquity, which disenchants the view, put him on his
histrionic mettle. It also helped him to take fire from his audience,
and his audience to take fire from him. I don't suppose the groundlings
actually cried "Go it, Othello!" like louts at a football match. But
that must have been very much the spirit of the performance: a spirit
of intense and unremitting give-and-take.

Whether this sort of acting is generally desirable or not, it is the
sort of acting for which Shakespeare wrote his plays. It is also the sort
of acting wilfully obstructed by the presenters of *Othello* at the Savoy
Theatre, where the piece is now being performed on a stage which
seems to have been devised for the especial purpose of contradicting
all the most important implications of the Elizabethan platform.
Mr. James Pryde is, we all know, an artist of considerable merit, but
he is also an artist undertaking a job for which he has served no
rigorous apprenticeship. He comes to the theatre from the outer world.
He brings with him a host of non-theatrical preconceptions. And not
unnaturally, being a painter of pictures, he does all he can to emphasize
the pictorial aspect of the production, with consequences which would
kill the finest acting stone dead.

For what do we find? We find that, instead of the actor being among the audience as of old, he is now pushed as far back from it as possible. Five broad steps, where the actors fear to tread, lead from a front stage (which is used for what may be regarded as the minor scenes) to a back stage, with an extra proscenium frame of its own. And on this back stage, which is inevitably but a strip, we behold, as through the wrong end of a pair of opera-glasses, Iago instilling his poison into Othello's ear, Cassio bemoaning the loss of his reputation, Desdemona being distantly smothered in her bed.

This may please Mr. Pryde, and it may please Miss Ellen Van Volkenburg, the producer, who has specialized in puppets; but turn him into a puppet, and Othello's occupation's gone indeed.

Mr. Paul Robeson, who plays the part of Othello, and who appears to be a man of unusual intelligence, hit the nail on the head in an interview which he gave the day after the first performance. "Unless", he said, "I can feel that the audience is really terrified as Iago is, unless the audience is alarmed lest I should really leap over the footlights and come among them, wild with rage and jealousy, I feel I am not getting across." That is exactly the right spirit—and it is exactly the spirit fostered by the Elizabethan platform stage. But what a leap Mr. Robeson would have to make to get among the audience from the very back of the stage in the Savoy Theatre! How he must long to get down to the footlights, and how cruel it is of Mr. Pryde and Miss Van Volkenburg to keep him so far away from them!

Whether Mr. Robeson would be a satisfactory Othello under better conditions is another matter. Personally, I do not believe that he would. He seemed to me on the first night to be lacking in certain highly important qualifications for the part. For one thing, he lacked command. He was the under-dog from the start. The cares of "Old Man River" were still upon him. He was a member of a subject race, still dragging the chains of his ancestors. He was not noble enough. He was not stark enough. He did not tower. He seemed to me a very depressed Othello.

The fact that he is a negro did not assist him. True, he is the first performer of the part I have seen who faithfully answers to the description of "the thick lips". But that is a small matter. Shakespeare wrote this part for a white man to play and Mr. Robeson is not far wrong when he says that "Shakespeare is always right".

All Mr. Robeson's views on the matter are excellent. He learned his part wisely from the original text, with the original spelling and the original punctuation; an example that should be followed by all Shakespearean actors. "I think," says Mr. Robeson, "the contrast between Shakespeare's original and the 'cut' version which I had to learn prevented me from seeing Othello as a complete personality. Every line of the play builds up character, and where the lines were cut I felt the gap." One suspects that Mr. Robeson might be an ideal producer for this tragedy.

If the part of Othello is cut, it is not cut nearly so heavily as that of Iago, some of whose finest soliloquies are reduced to the most lame and impotent proportions. Is it not amazing that great lines should be thrown on the dust-heap in order to allow time for two extremely arty and Tilly-Loschy ladies to posture about the stage in an interlude which has nothing to do with the play and which would have been hissed off the boards by any audience with a grain of good feeling and bad manners?

But, quite apart from the diminution in length, I have rarely seen a less conspicuous or impressive Iago than that of Mr. Maurice Browne who, looking rather like Hamlet, appeared to be cut out for anything but villainy. He spoke his part without a trace of relish.

Miss Peggy Ashcroft plays Desdemona with sincerity and feeling. She does not endow the part with glamour and is, perhaps, a little on the vegetarian side. Nevertheless, that exquisite scene in which Desdemona prepares herself for bed is intensely moving; partly because, for a wonder, it is played as near the footlights as possible.

But credit is due to Miss Ashcroft and to Miss Sybil Thorndike, whose Emilia is the best piece of acting in the production. This may be a Garden City production, but there is nothing Garden City about Miss Thorndike, who might in the circumstances be welcomed (to quote the excellent Colley Cibber) if she outdid all her previous outdoings. Miss Thorndike is no apostle of the Little Theatre Movement. She is the apostle of a Big Theatre Movement. Her performances may be unequal, but she goes for it with a will. And I must say, it *is* nice to see *something* lively in *Othello*.

MISS EVANS AGAIN
(1932)

Othello at the Old Vic should be seen. Some faults it has, including the most honest Iago ever exhibited on any stage. Mr. Ralph Richardson is too radically agreeable to be cast for any but sympathetic parts. Mr. Wilfrid Walter's Othello, like so many Othellos, disappoints in the earlier scenes. Once he gets to the jealousy he makes a fine wounded animal, less concerned with foaming at the mouth than with intense suffering, which is as it should be. We could wish for more vitality, but the performance is piteous and notable.

As for the Emilia of Miss Edith Evans, it is magnificent. Never have I seen an Emilia to approach it. Miss Evans it is who makes the last scene the most tragic in the play. That four-times-repeated cry of "My husband?" is a revelation. When she cries, "Help, help, ho, help: The Moor has killed my mistress. Murder, murder!" I don't believe Mrs. Siddons could touch her. It is like a bellow from the mouth of Melpomene herself.

OTHELLO WAS A BLACK MAN
(1933)

If anyone to-day were to be asked what Shakespeare's play *Othello* is about, probably the first thing he would answer would be Jealousy. That, of course, would be perfectly accurate. Whether you agree or not with Macaulay's opinion that "*Othello* is, perhaps, the greatest work in the world", you can hardly fail to agree that it is the world's greatest play about jealousy. Such an agonizing picture does it present of this most degrading of all emotions that audiences may sometimes wonder why they should voluntarily subject themselves to the acute suffering which an adequate performance must inevitably inflict.

But if an Elizabethan had been asked what *Othello* was about, what would *he* have answered? I do not believe that he would have begun by describing it as an epic of jealousy, any more than I believe that if some great playwright were to produce a masterpiece on the nursery rhyme of the lady who loved a swine and who received only a monosyllabic "Hunc!" in answer to her endearments, you would begin by describing it as an epic of unrequited love. Until the theme had become so familiar as to seem almost commonplace, you would say, Here is a play about a lady who fell in love with a pig. And in the same way I believe Elizabethans first thought of *Othello* as a play about a black man who married a white woman. Jealousy, after all, is as old as the hills, but marriage between a sooty Moor and a snowy Venetian was a stark new sensation, which probably appealed to Shakespeare as just the thing to set before the Elizabethan groundlings who revelled in Websterian horrors.

The blackness of Othello is a point repeatedly emphasized in the text of the play, yet it is a point which has been blunted in nearly all latter-day productions, the Othellos of the twentieth century resorting to something very like "sunbronze" for their make-up. Whence these fears? Why have actors and producers been as afraid of an all-black Othello as a child is of a bogey? Partly, no doubt, because they know that Moors are not pot-black and because, in spite of Shakespeare's constant harping on Othello's sootiness, they have considered truth to history and geography more important than truth to Shakespeare. Partly because the popular actors of to-day want to look nice in order that they may be loved for themselves alone. Partly, again, because they feel that a pot-black make-up would deal a death-blow to facial expression—and so Othello has been ruined just as Greek plays are ruined because producers are afraid of masks, which also are inimical to facial expression, and to be commended in Greek tragedy on that very account. It was not ever so. We have no positive information as to the complexion affected by Richard Burbage, who originally created the part, but we do know that the actors who succeeded him—Betterton, Quin, Mossop, Barry, Garrick, John Kemble—all played Othello

with faces as black as that of Brudder Bones. It was reserved for
Edmund Kean to innovate the substitution of light brown, thus
making hay of the Duke's parting words—"Your son-in-law is far
more fair than black"—since it rendered them almost as true physically
as they were spiritually. Incidentally, it may be observed that this
change, made that the audience might more easily mark the workings
of Othello's features, was largely due to alterations in the interior
construction of our theatres, which involved the disappearance of
the apron stage and so thrust our actors farther and farther away from
the audience.

The love of Desdemona for Othello was an extraordinary
phenomenon. If it is not presented as an extraordinary phenomenon,
and if Othello's appearance is such that all the girls in the auditorium
feel Desdemona to have done a very natural, not to say enviable thing,
then Othello is deprived of his Achilles heel, and Iago is deprived of
one of the most effective weapons in his armoury. Othello must have
a skin that will account at once for his intense idealization of Desdemona and for his easy inflammability by the suggestion, at the
crucial moment, that Desdemona may, after all, be possessed by an
abnormal appetite. Consider the task Shakespeare set himself. It was
a task very different from that which confronted him when he sat
down to create Master Ford in *The Merry Wives of Windsor*. Here he
wrote out of an impulse to make the jealous husband appear ridiculous.

It was a task very different from that which confronted him when he
sat down to create Leontes in the opening scene of *The Winter's Tale*.
Here he wrote out of an impulse to make the jealous husband appear
mean and contemptible. These were fairly simple problems, which
any of Shakespeare's contemporaries might have tackled with success.
But to write a play about a husband who, married to a woman
of Desdemona's unswerving sweetness and purity, suspects her of
infidelity, proceeds to the most violent and debasing extremes of
jealousy, foams at the mouth, has fits on the floor, strikes her in
public, and ends by smothering her to death—to do this and to make
the audience *sorry* for the jealous husband all the while—here was a
task of amazing difficulty, which only a genius driven by an over-
mastering impulse could accomplish.

How did Shakespeare do it? Listen to the play carefully and you
will see. You will see how he begins by choosing a black man for his
jealous husband, because the colour of Othello's complexion, once he
comes to suspect, will, in itself, be a torturing ground for suspicion,
and so will help to condone his error. Make Othello a white man and
who, strawberry-spotted handkerchief and all, will be sorry for him?
He ought, we shall then say, to have known better.

You will see how Shakespeare loses no time in establishing what
may be called the sanctity of Othello's love for Desdemona and hers
for him. Whatever the other characters may hint, and whatever modern
psychologists may protest, it is perfectly clear before the first act is

over that Desdemona *wasn't* a queer girl for loving a black man; if she were, we might say, Serve her right—which would be fatal. It is also clear that Othello loves Desdemona *better* than most husbands love most wives, which wins our sympathy again.

You will see what a great general Othello is and how highly-respected. You will see how lightly he tosses aside the first insinuations made by Iago and how reluctant he is to be shaken. But you will also see how, in Iago, Shakespeare has been careful to create a character of such mephistophelian art and craft, that Othello becomes like a child in his hands—and how, if only by contrast, the deviltry of Iago sets off the nobility of Othello's nature.

Fully to explore the means employed by Shakespeare to make us sympathize with Othello would require a separate article, including an examination of the original story by Cinthio on which the play was based and in which Desdemona was not smothered, but beaten to death with a stocking full of sand—an episode again modified by Shakespeare on behalf of his hero. If we did not like Othello himself, the play would be insupportable. Even as it stands, it is sometimes very hard to bear—but we do bear it, and we are glad to bear it, because we come out of it better than we went in.

Yet how better? Why are we attracted to tragedy? What is the explanation? It lies, I think, in the fact that, just as we do not get enough happiness out of life, so we do not get enough anguish. In the hue and cry after virtue and contentment and civilization, we stifle our grief, suppress our baser passions, refuse to have our cry out or our hate out. But pain, like pleasure, will be paid one time or another, and we are drawn to tragedies such as *Othello* because they flush the channels that have been clogged by self-control.

And as it is with us, so it was with Shakespeare. I do not believe that he could possibly have written *Othello* if he had not, at some time or other, suffered the torments of jealousy. I do not believe that he would ever have *wanted* to write *Othello* if he had not endeavoured, at some time or other, to bottle up the green-eyed monster. Poor Shakespeare! Refusing to be jealous is even worse than jealousy itself. But if it ends in a masterpiece like *Othello*, it is, indeed, suffering not in vain.

ANTONY AND CLEOPATRA

MISS EVANS AS CLEOPATRA
(1925)

TO describe Shakespeare's *Antony and Cleopatra* as the richest love play in the English language is, I think, to launch a pretty safe superlative. There may be love plays more beautiful: for my own part, I prefer *Romeo and Juliet*, which touches my heart, where *Antony and Cleopatra* only stirs my blood. I cannot take part in *Antony and Cleopatra*, for I have never dreamed, and never shall dream now, of the Serpent of Old Nile; while Antony does nothing to make me feel that there, but for the grace of God, or the rancour of the Devil, goes a dramatic critic. I realize, however, that *Romeo and Juliet* is to *Antony and Cleopatra* as a lyric to an epic. That the Alexandrian tragedy should be so rarely staged is a sad commentary on English acting. For of all Shakespeare's heroines, none is more calculated than Cleopatra to expose the mean resources of the actress audacious enough to essay this part; and the actresses and the managers, aware of this, let well alone.

Playgoers will swallow a Desdemona, or an Ophelia, or even a Juliet who is merely sweet, as they will swallow a Lady Macbeth who is merely stark. But they will boggle at a Shakespearean Cleopatra who is merely any one thing, because the Shakespearean Cleopatra is so obviously infinite in her variety. She is royal. She is riggish. She is vain. She is vulgar. She is cruel. She is cowardly. She is a born commander. She is a born slave. She is innately faithful. She is innately deceitful—deceitful even to the man she worships so passionately that she would rather die than live after him. Twenty times a day she will pretend for a lover's trifle the death she is constant-marble to encounter for the greater thing that trifle symbolizes. She trades in love—but it must never be forgotten that she truly loves her trade. Because Cleopatra employs all the arts of a common, shifty courtesan to keep Antony's affection—the very arts she used, with less accomplishment, in her Caesarean salad days; because she lies to Antony even as she lies with him; because she loves the love game as much as the lover; the playgoer is sometimes misled into the suspicion that, with Antony away, she will try her skill anew with Octavius. But that is not Shakespeare's Cleopatra, who is at once the most shrewdly practical and hedonistically enthusiastic lover in drama. The love game demands that she shall die for Antony, and she dies for him with a spirit as uplifted as that of any patriot who, playing the patriotism game, acts the spy, falsifies the intelligence, hurls the stinkbomb, and dies magnificently for his country, committing suicide rather than be taken by the enemy.

This Cleopatra is, of course, a sensual creature, but, like all Shakespeare's heroines, she is strictly true to the man she loves, and if Dolabella expects any return for his services, he must know just where he stands when he hears Miss Edith Evans at the Old Vic say those six words, "Dolabella, I shall *remain* your debtor"—and wonderfully Miss Evans says them. But Shakespeare, as usual, is in difficulties between the character handed down to him and the character he desires to make of it. Cleopatra, in the most queenly and unexceptionable way, offers her hand to Thyreus, Caesar's messenger, to kiss. That Antony, on seeing this, should fly into a passion, call Cleopatra names, and shout that he has been abused, suggests that, whereas Shakespeare's whitewash might do for Shakespeare, it would not do for Shakespeare's Antony. It may be that, in his mind's eye, Shakespeare saw a Cleopatra who, having sought to hold Antony fast at critical moments by keeping him on the hop—but never giving real cause for jealousy—was now compelled to suffer the slings and arrows of a jealousy she had not attempted to arouse. If this be so, Miss Evans's performance does not help to clarify the point, for one of the short-comings of her Cleopatra is that it does not suggest innate deceitfulness.

Another shortcoming is that, while it is superbly sensuous, it is not possessed of a physical devil. The artist in love is before our eyes, not the passionate devotee. Miss Evans convinces me that Cleopatra loved Antony, but she does not convince me that Antony loved Cleopatra, for she presents no Egyptian dish, no morsel for a monarch, there are a hundred actresses who could convey this more successfully than Miss Evans—it is, indeed, only for this that they are on the stage at all. Antony cries that they will have another gaudy night, but as they leave the stage, I wonder whether it will be so very gaudy after all—this quite apart from the fact that the orchestra at the Old Vic seems to think it the appropriate moment to strike up with a dirge.

Yet what a wonderful piece of acting this Cleopatra is, all the same! There is not an actress on our stage to-day who could hold a candle to Miss Evans in her furies, her collapses, her recoveries, her languors, her lashings, her laments; not an actress who can strike a blow, nurse a daydream, or wheedle an asp like her. How she illuminates the text, revealing beauties undreamed of by the reader—which is surely the business of the Shakespearean theatre. How tender, how beautiful in its groping for a thought to express a feeling is Miss Evans's delivery of "Sir, you and I must part—but that's not it." How she purrs over her libidinous dreams. And how she capsizes criticism in the amazing scene in which she hales the messenger up and down. First she is sensuously restless, calling for music, dismissing music for billiards, then changing from billiards to an angling project she does not intend to carry out, but it is an excuse for yet another image of Antony. Then the black look of hate that comes over her face when she fears the messenger's news, the outburst of uncontrollable passion, the blow, and the perfection with which the tumultuous distractions of the concluding speech are presented:

In praising Antony, I have disprais'd Caesar.
I am paid for it now.—Lead me from hence.—
I faint.—Oh, Iras, Charmian!—'Tis no matter!—
Go to the fellow, good Alexas, bid him
Report the feature of Octavia: her years,
Her inclination, let him not leave out
The colour of her hair. Bring me word quickly.—
Let him for ever go!—Let him not, Charmian!—

Though he be painted one way like a Gorgon,
The other way's a Mars.—Bid you Alexas
Bring me word how tall she is.—Pity me Charmian!—
But do not speak to me.—Lead me to my chamber.

A dozen changes in a dozen lines, so brilliantly executed by Miss Evans that one is left with wet palms, too much overwhelmed to join in the applause. This is the culminating point of her performance. In the succeeding scenes it sags, to rise again to great heights at the finish, but never quite as high as this.

Of Mr. Holloway's Antony on Monday night it was not possible to judge, for he (like only too many members of the audience) was troubled by a bad cough, and often could speak only with difficulty. It seemed to have the makings of a good, but from the point of those already familiar with Mr. Holloway's excellent method, not a very interesting performance. It lacked breeding and was a general risen from the ranks rather than born. It had too much of the roughness of Enobarbus. Enobarbus himself was stiff and uneasy, with a voice like planks creaking in a storm. Few of the minor parts were even passably played.

As for the production, it might almost have been a Benson production. Let us leave it at that statement of fact, with this reminder: that a Cleopatra who calls for her laces to be cut and does not wear laces is not merely un-Elizabethan, but insane.

HIGH PASSION
(1930)

The Old Vic is the most important theatre in England. *Antony and Cleopatra* is the most magnificent love drama ever written. Harcourt Williams is the most understanding producer of Shakespeare we have had for years. John Gielgud is our most oncoming, deep-bitten tragedian. All of which indicates an immediate visit to the Waterloo Road, where the Egypt of the Ptolemys and the Rome of the Caesars may be seen in Renaissance costume—a shrewd and convincing guess at the picture in the poet's mind when he wrote the play.

Mr. Gielgud's Antony begins ineffectively, but in the middle scenes he presents a superb psychological shipwreck. Mr. Gielgud is always at his best in bitterness and distraction. Dorothy Green's Cleopatra is on the correct grand scale, and, if it lacks inspiration, sustains the high romantic note. A word of praise, too, for Ralph Richardson.[1]

[1] Whose Enobarbus lingers in the memory more distinctly and satisfactorily than any of the other performances.

ANTONY ROARS AGAIN
(1934)

Mary Newcombe, the new leading lady at the Old Vic, looks like becoming popular. To start off as Cleopatra is a pretty big ordeal. But if Miss Newcombe is not the Cleopatra of our dreams—what single actress could be?—she speaks Shakespeare meaningly and relishes the fact that words are of different weights and shapes. Barring intermittent modern inflections that savour slightly of the service flat, her elocution is admirable. She is broad enough for the great parts. And what she speaks means what it is meant to mean and remains blank verse.

Miss Newcombe might have done even better with another Antony. Wilfrid Lawson certainly does not help her. I have never seen an Antony who appeared to be less in love with Cleopatra. I have never heard an Antony who made more noise. He "roars like the hornéd herd" and, despite this roaring, is so indistinct that it is impossible to tell whether he speaks his words intelligently or not. Let's guess he does.

CLEOPATRA MISMOUTHED
(1936)

Eugenie Leontovitch has not made a success in the part of Cleopatra at the New. This will hardly surprise those who heard Lopokova as Olivia or those who have heard Bergner as Rosalind. For these foreign accents, this mishandling or mismouthing of English, though pretty in its place, would deal death to Shakespeare's music even if the ears of the actresses were fully sensitive to that music, which they can't be. Let's have no more of it. If Yvonne Arnaud comes out as Lady Macbeth I shan't go. If Lucy Mannheim comes out as Henry V I shall resign.

Antony and Cleopatra contains the grandest music ever put into words. But Beethoven's Fifth Symphony picked out with one finger by a child on the piano would sound as like the real thing as "The soldier's pole is fall'n" or "I have immortal longings in me" when grappled with by Leontovitch. So busy is she trying to speak English, and so busy are we trying to understand her, that we hardly consider whether this Cleopatra is good or bad. My impression is, however, that it would be bad in any language and that the substitution of some squeaking Cleopatra to "boy" her greatness would not be half the catastrophe the heroine fears.

Although Cleopatra's dresses seem to have been made for the express purpose of tripping her up, most of the costumes designed by Komisarjevsky are unusually beautiful. But a foreign producer for an English production of Shakespeare seems to me again a bad springboard, each syllable mattering as well as each characterization. Immeasurably the best performance is Mr. Leon Quartermaine's Enobarbus. Mr. Donald Wolfit's Antony is solid and unimaginative. Why Menas chews like a gangster is hard to determine, since there is no advertisement for any chewing-gum on the programme. And why Shakespeare's careful arrangement of scenes is reshuffled, let those who think he didn't know his job explain. For the first time in all my experience I heard booing on the first night of a Shakespeare play.

RANDOM NOTES

The new season at the Old Vic opens with *Antony and Cleopatra*. This is a staggering play. It reels with passion—not the sweet young boy-and-girl passion of *Romeo and Juliet*, but violent, overstrained, suspicious, recriminative adult passion just past its prime. Hazlitt remarks that Shakespeare's genius has spread over *Antony and Cleopatra* a richness like the overflowing of the Nile. It is, indeed, a flood—an epic flood of sensuality and despair. It is also, with its forty-two scenes, one of the hardest nuts Shakespeare ever gave a producer to crack, while as for the task he set the actors, it is so herculean that he might almost have written the parts of the two lovers for the express purpose of ruining histrionic reputations.

Bernard Shaw, conducting his campaign against physical passion, has written perhaps more trenchantly against Antony and Cleopatra than against any other Shakespearean characters. "Shakespeare's *Antony and Cleopatra*", he says, "must needs be as intolerable to the true Puritan as it is vaguely distressing to the ordinary, healthy citizen, because, after giving a faithful picture of the soldier broken down by debauchery, and the typical wanton in whose arms such men perish, Shakespeare finally strains all his huge command of rhetoric and stage pathos to give a theatrical sublimity to the wretched end of the business, and to persuade foolish spectators that the world is well lost of the twain.

"Such falsehood is not to be borne except by the real Cleopatras and Antonys (they are to be found in every public-house), who would, no doubt, be glad to be transfigured by some poet as immortal lovers." Small wonder that when Mr. Shaw saw his favourite actress, Janet Achurch, turning from Nora Helmer to play Cleopatra he was infuriated into ridicule, declaring that he could not bear to see her "curving her wrists elegantly above Antony's head as if she were going to extract a globe of gold-fish and two rabbits from behind his ear". But that, after all, is only another way of saying what was said by the historic Victorian gentlewoman who, after seeing Cleopatra hale the Messenger up and down the stage, murmured in her neighbour's ear, "How different from the home life of our own dear Queen!"

So much (*pace* Mr. Shaw) has been written in praise of *Antony and Cleopatra* that it may be as well to take the high quality of this tragedy for granted. It begins magnificently. It goes on magnificently. It ends most magnificently of all. And herein it differs from some of Shakespeare's other great plays, which have a way of falling off at the finish. For example, *Hamlet* with its fencing bout and poisoned cups; *Julius Caesar* with its excursions and alarums; and even *Macbeth*, in spite of its great poetic flights, with its moving forest and sword-and-buckler play.

. . . . .

In some cases the swift succession of short scenes and the hurly-burly of battle which concludes the proceedings in a sort of grand assault-at-arms becomes downright tedious. That it was not tedious in Shakespeare's time is tolerably certain, not only because he was such a master of theatrical (as well as dramatic) effect, but also because he would hardly have repeated the formula so often if it had not worked. We must remember that, for the short scenes, his stage was adapted as ours is not. As for the fighting, I think we may take it that in an age when fencing-schools were as popular as lawn-tennis courts are now, and when the man in the Elizabethan tavern was as familiar with the technical jargon of the foils as the man in the Georgian club is familiar with the technical jargon of Contract Bridge, any self-respecting producer would see to it that the rapier-play was executed with the highest degree of skill. It may even have been the expectation of the final, helter-skelter dust-up that sustained some groundlings through the preliminary acts of poetry and psychology.

. . . . .

Even so, these fighting finishes can only be praised as effective sops to the public. They are not exciting as art. But in the plays which are free from them, and which are unencumbered by long recapitulations of past events, as the Friar's speech in *Romeo and Juliet*, what flashes of inspiration descended on Shakespeare again and again as he neared his end! It always seems to me that among the most impressive master-strokes in all Shakespeare is the scene at the end of *Antony and Cleopatra*, where the Clown, on the brink of the final catastrophe, brings Cleopatra his basket of figs. Here, after fifteen hundred lines, continuously sustained, of high heroic verse that scales the peaks, Shakespeare suddenly drops into the vale of prose, with an effect on the audience that is like the ominous, muffled beating of a funeral drum. "I wish you joy o' the worm." Superb as is the Porter's speech in *Macbeth*, thrilling as is the disregarded little scene with Cinna the Poet in *Julius Caesar*, this scene in *Antony and Cleopatra* seems to me an even finer illustration of the intense dramatic effect which may be achieved by the sudden introduction of a prose passage into a verse play at a critical moment. Dare one say that after the gaudy racket of the decasyllabic and hendecasyllabic line, the plain and infinitely variable rhythms of prose fall on the ears with a peculiarly sane and moving dignity? Remark, in any case, the intensification that may be produced by under-statement. "I wish you joy o' the worm." Of the worm, not the asp. That "worm" was an inspiration by which Shakespeare was so completely captured that he repeated the word nine times in the course of thirty-seven lines. Try reading the scene with the substitution of "asp" for "worm" and see how much it loses.

Immediately after the departure of the Clown, Shakespeare returns to verse. With Cleopatra's "immortal longings" we are on the peaks again. And as prose gained by following verse, so now verse seems to gain even more by following prose. But it wasn't, of course, deliberate on Shakespeare's part. It was instinctive. He wrote not with an object but from an impulse. And wrote not only with his hand but with his ear.

. . . . . .

Study the end of *Antony and Cleopatra*. Study the end of *Love's Labour's Lost*, where the introduction of the death-motive strikes one of the most exquisite and unexpected notes ever struck in a comedy. Study the end of *The Merchant of Venice*, where the whole of the last act is like a lovely musical harlequinade. Study even the very end of *The Comedy of Errors*—and then agree that Shakespeare knew better than anyone how to end a play, even if he did not always put that knowledge into practice.

SOME NOTES ON THE OLD VIC AND ITS UNSURPASSED SHAKESPEAREAN PRODUCTIONS
(1921)

ONE evening this autumn, at a symposium of dramatic critics, the writer of the present article was asked to name the most important theatre in London. Unhesitatingly he answered: "The Old Vic." And the assembled company endorsed his verdict. The question was an easy one to answer, because the greater number of our theatres have now completely lost their individuality. Time was when almost every theatre in the town bore the hallmark of a distinct artistic policy. But with the supersession of the actor by the commercial-manager, the specialist theatre has degenerated into an impersonal multiple store. No longer do we instinctively associate the Comedy with comedy, while music is a matter of accident in the Lyric. The Empire flutters from the kinema to the revue and back again; John Drinkwater transforms the Lyceum into a lecture-hall; the Gaiety becomes a

M

platform for Maeterlinckian metaphysics; and Mr. Sam Mayo's mother-in-law contends (successfully) with Euripidean demigods for possession of the Holborn Empire.

Meanwhile the theatre managed by Miss Lilian Baylis, on what is sometimes called the wrong side of Waterloo Bridge, holds with magnificent obstinacy on its well-worn course; and just as, by constant service and attention, one man may come to be regarded as another's greatest and most intimate friend, so the Old Vic, setting out with a declared purpose and assiduously directing its efforts toward a determined end, has come to be regarded as the prescriptive home of Shakespeare in the City of London. Nor will those who have intelligently marked the trend of Shakespearean production during the past quarter of a century grudge this theatre the position which it has attained. The Old Vic may not be Shakespeare's spiritual home: his spiritual home is the old Globe Theatre on the Bankside, where the environment was peculiarly adapted to the requirements of his plays.

The Old Vic may not provide the most suitable accommodation that could be devised for Shakespeare in modern times; even in the Waterloo Road it is often painfully apparent that Shakespeare yearns for the demolition of the proscenium arch and the restoration of the stall-scattering apron stage on which to stretch his legs. But it is nevertheless possible to praise the productions of Shakespeare's plays now given at the Royal Victoria Hall, for Mr. Robert Atkins has brought to bear on them a sympathy, an insight, and a fundamental appreciation of the essentially practical beauty of the poet's creations such as no other manager of the century has displayed.

For years Shakespeare has been nothing more than a dressed-up mummy, trailed ignominiously across the stage in a gaudy coach, preceded and succeeded by a flamboyant and irrelevant cortège, the purpose of which has been to divert the attention of the spectators from an idol no longer worshipped by the high-priests themselves. Thus, we have been given *A Midsummer Night's Dream* with real rabbits running round the Athenian woods, and the public has just loved the rabbits. Thus, we have been given *The Tempest* with an Ariel, like Peter Pan, on wires; and "Oh!" the public has murmured as Ariel has ascended into space, "What a heavenly play *The Tempest* is!" But now, at last, we seem to have set out on an intensely thrilling voyage of discovery, the rabbits are scurrying back into their burrows, Ariel at last is coming down to earth, and hope beats high in the hearts of all who pay heart-homage to Shakespeare. The productions at the Old Vic are swift, simple, and to the point; and if Mr. Atkins has yet far to travel before he reaches the only destination worth making for, he is well on the right road.

It is especially gratifying to be able to speak well of the work now done at the Old Vic, if only because the performances which were given there in the old days again and again reduced us to a state of such blank dismay that to have commended them would have been to betray the first principles of aesthetic criticism. It is true that the difficulties besetting the producer in those days were probably even greater than they are at the present time, but the business of a critic is, in our view, strictly with the finished product, and it is not for him to praise a work of art because the obstacles in the way of its achievement were hard to overcome. On that basis one might lavish the most flattering encomiums on an ear-rending performance of a sonata by a scraping violinist with a hook for an arm. Nor is it for a critic to praise a work of art because the "object" of it is commendable. On that basis one might lavish the most flattering encomiums on a vulgar ballad, incompetently sung by an amateur performer in aid of a worthy charity.

In short, that hard-worked phrase "in the circumstances," has nothing to do with the case. Aesthetically there is only one circumstance, and that is the circumstance of the direct and immediate impression, agreeable or disagreeable, created on the senses of the individual auditor or spectator. This is a point only too often ignored by professional critics. They may (being human) praise an insufficient artist because they happen to know that he is in financial trouble and that he has a wife and family to support; they may (being myopic) praise an insufficient performance of Shakespeare because they labour under the delusion that, Shakespeare being Shakespeare, any performance of any of his plays, however insufficient, is better than no performance at all.

A well-known writer confessed to us how, in the days of his self-conscious juvenility, he read right through the whole of *Paradise Lost*, paying not the least attention to the sense of those magnificent words, and scanning them at a great rate, merely that he might subsequently enjoy the pleasure of boasting that he had accomplished the feat. If there be any consistency in the critics who uphold that even a bad performance of Shakespeare deserves encouragement, they will be driven to commend that youthful indiscretion, which was, in reality, but a ridiculous, erratic and indefensible act of vainglory.

The critic who allows irrelevant considerations to sway his judgment will, in the end, almost invariably find himself hoist with his own petard; and here the Old Vic furnishes an illuminating case in point. Last season when Mr. Robert Atkins took over the practical management of the plays and the theatre emerged for the first time out of the rut of the commonplace, we were so deeply impressed by the excellence of the productions that we converted ourselves into a kind of honorary agent and passed from friend to friend, exhorting each of them to cross the river and see the miracle with his own eyes. But every time came back the same reply: "Ah, yes, the Old Vic! We know all about it! For some mysterious reason the critics have entered into a conspiracy of praise. We were taken in by them. We went there. We beheld the miracle. But, thank you! not again! We prefer reading Shakespeare." Vehemently we protested how we, even as they, had in the old days visited the Vic, and, even as they, gained little profit

M*

there. Earnestly we explained how Mr. Robert Atkins, with a wave of his wand, or an extra backward tilt of his bowler hat, had changed all that. Emphatically we asserted that critics in the past had not praised the Old Vic because they thought the performances given there good, but only because they thought the cause deserving; and that the praise they now bestowed was not for the deserving cause but for the deserving result. To no avail. Our friends were adamant. And if critics do not tell the truth, they cannot expect the discerning public to be guided by them. So, even to-day, there are many who cold-shoulder the Old Vic, its pitch having been queered by well-meant but inexcusable mendacity.

The only critical standard is the absolute standard; the failure of modern criticism is that it is comparative. Comparative standards are not easy to avoid. How many young critics have we seen setting out with the highest principles and the best intentions, scornful of their easy-going, slipshod comrades, resolved to praise only what is, in their own estimation, really worth praising, and to condemn all that deserves condemnation. But, alas! judged by any absolute or ultimate standard, what a pitiful handful of the plays produced to-day can be commended. "Bad!" writes a youthful critic. "Bad!" And again, "Bad!" He yearns for an opportunity to say "something nice". He grits his teeth and pens his tenth successive unfavourable verdict. What will his editor say? And won't his readers begin to set him down as a bit of a curmudgeon? His heart grows aweary of this little world.

And at last, from sheer fatigue, he yields a play more praise—just a shade, a mere shade—than in his inner consciousness he believes it to deserve. A poor play, perhaps, but, after all—better than last night's! And so the rot sets in. Bad plays become "not bad" plays, not quite good plays become "quite good", good plays become "great", and great plays—there's the rub! The sins of comparison come home to roost. Having glibly called *John Ferguson* "great", *Abraham Lincoln* "great", *A Bill of Divorcement* "great", what is he to say when, at long last, he meets the really great play of his dreams? There is nothing for him but to hide his head and to admit that comparisons are not only odious, but absurd. To compare one play with another is as absurd as it would be to compare a fugue by Bach with an oil-painting by Carpaccio, or the multiplication table with a caramel.

Let us then make it quite clear that when we praise the present productions at the excellent Old Vic, we mean just this: that they are the only productions of Shakespeare we have ever enjoyed. Sometimes we marvel at our enjoyment, for many of the actors are obviously inexperienced and many of the smaller parts are shakily interpreted. But the basis of the productions is so sound that every time we taste the real Shakespearean flavour as it cannot be tasted even in reprints of the First Folio or the Quartos; and the prospect that the Old Vic may come to an untimely end is one we contemplate with the liveliest apprehension and alarm. Yet this prospect must be contemplated if

we are to avert the catastrophe which now threatens the most important theatre in London—a theatre which has now produced no fewer
than thirty out of Shakespeare's thirty-seven plays, the whole thirty
of which it has been possible for the poor playgoer to view from the
Old Vic's fivepenny gallery for a sum less than the price charged for
a single stall at a frothy revue. The Old Vic just succeeds in paying
its way. But the building is an old one, and the L.C.C. has ordered
extensive structural alterations. Unfortunately these charges will
involve the dislodgement of the Old Vic's neighbour, Morley
College, for which the Old Vic will be under the obligation of providing a new home. And so the life of the Old Vic now depends on
whether it can furnish forth the £30,000 which these most inconvenient
and elaborate alterations are to cost. The theatre can lay its hands on
one-third of the sum. Twenty thousand pounds remains to be raised
by public subscription. And it will be to the eternal discredit of play-
going London if these £20,000 are not forthcoming.

SHAKESPEARE'S FUTURE
(1924)

THE apathetic response accorded by West End playgoers to the
invitation to attend the Cochran-Baylis Shakespeare Season at the
New Oxford Theatre is now historic. A great deal has been written
on the problem. Every writer has interpreted it according to his preconceptions. Shakespeare is obsolete. The public is asinine. We don't
know how to produce Shakespeare—we don't know how to act
him—we don't know how to manage him, or even how to advertise
him—the attack is from all sides. Some of these interpretations must,
however, be regarded with suspicion when it is remembered that
Shakespeare has been made a consistent commercial success on the
other side of the Thames by the very company now appearing at the
New Oxford. This, clearly, is not a case for "first principles."

What we have to do is to discover whether there is something
peculiarly Elizabethan in the atmosphere of the Old Vic, or whether
Surrey is superior to Middlesex, not only in cricket, but in culture. For my
own part, I am inclined to believe that if the Old Vic Company were
to persist at the New Oxford for month after month it would succeed
in making Shakespeare a permanent and profitable feature of that
theatre; and while the Old Vic Company will, of necessity, return to
its native shore, I am hoping that Mr. C. B. Cochran will not be
dashed by such empty seats as he may have espied. It seems to me that
Mr. Cochran might do quite a lot to restore to the Bard some of his
lost property—for just as Shakespeare has derived great benefit from
the erudite sensitiveness of Mr. William Poel and the masculine drive
of Mr. Robert Atkins, so he might gain a further advantage from the
jolly gamesomeness of Mr. Cochran, who, if he were to try his hand

personally at producing *Hamlet* or *As You Like It* or *Macbeth*, would, I feel sure, triumph in one respect over all the other Shakespearean producers now in the field.

As everybody knows, Mr. Cochran likes nothing better than what is known as a good fight. The Rodeo has been compared to the bear-baiting displays of Elizabeth's days: quite apart from the vexed question of cruelty to animals, which in both cases is incidental rather than essential, they cater for the same instinct. The boxing matches, again, that Mr. Cochran loves to organize may be compared to the fencing and wrestling contests so popular in the time of Elizabeth and James I. The rapier-play that occurs so frequently in the Shakespearean comedies and tragedies and histories was one of the sops thrown to the Rodeo and prize-ring public of those days, and we may be sure that it was executed skilfully enough on the stage to present a highly exciting and technically brilliant spectacle. If Mr. Cochran were to produce a modern play with a boxing match in it, we may be sure that he would give us something more than a succession of namby-pamby pats. And I cannot think that he would countenance for one moment the feeble duellos that render modern Shakespearean performances so ludicrous at what should be their most breathless moments.

Mr. Cochran would see to it that the public was given—as Shakespeare meant it to be given—a jolly good fight for its money. If he had the managing of the set-to between Charles and Orlando, you may rest assured that it would be something like a set-to—no springboard for sniggers, with two perfect gentlemen doing their best not to inconvenience each other seriously. And you may rest assured that the battles which now bring so many of the tragedies and histories to such an inglorious conclusion would, under the influence of Mr. Cochran, be something like battles: if there were only a few combatants, at least they would lay about them with a will.

The importance of making the fights in Shakespeare really good fights will become all the more evident once they take place—as they surely must take place before very long now—in an arena rather than in a frame. The revival of the arena in the Russian theatre, the breaking down of the proscenium barriers by Reinhardt in Germany, cannot fail to have their effect in this country. And this, coupled with the fact that the production of Elizabethan plays has become about as Elizabethan as it dares become in Victorian theatres, and that it still remains disconcertingly unsatisfactory, suggests that Shakespeare may count on the restoration of his plays to a whole-hearted platform stage before very long. Mr. Atkins, for one, is chafing for a platform stage. He has found, by practical experiment, that it is as impossible to get the full effect of *Coriolanus* in a frame as it would be to get the full effect of *Chu Chin Chow* in a theatre designed so as to rule out the practicability of scenery. And it will be interesting to see what provision for the production of Elizabethan plays will be proposed by those who have the Shakespeare National Theatre in hand. If it is a theatre of the modern type, it will be a theatre in which adequate representations of Shakespeare cannot be given. If, on the other hand, it is a theatre of the Elizabethan type, it will be a theatre in which it is impossible to give an adequate representation of, say, *The Way of the World*. In reality, we need (at least) two theatres; if the proposed Whitehall site is granted by the Government, I understand that there would be enough space for two, back to back. This seems to be the only solution. If no provision of any kind is made for a platform stage, the theatre will not be so much a Shakespeare Memorial as a Shakespeare Mausoleum.

A real platform stage would confer many benefits on Shakespearean actors. Among the chief of these would be the Freedom of the Clown. The Elizabethan clown is hand-in-glove with the audience. Again and again he addresses the groundlings. At present this intimacy is severely hampered by the proscenium. The little apron at the Old Vic is a very poor apology for a platform, which throws the actor open to the spectators on three sides, but it is better than nothing, and it was on this apron that Mr. Hay Petrie, when playing Launce in *The Two Gentlemen of Verona* a few months ago, actually had the temerity to wink at a gentleman who gave a belated laugh in a private box. This liberty on the part of Mr. Petrie—a liberty he could never have taken from the back of the stage—created a small sensation among the critics. Mr. Petrie was getting out of hand. Mr. Petrie was losing his head. To me, however, it seemed to be the most brilliant, as it was the most daring, of all Mr. Petrie's brilliant and daring inspirations. It is, indeed, the most important thing that has happened at the Old Vic during the past year. The sooner we realize the kinship between Launce and Alfred Lester, the sooner we shall be likely to get Shakespearean clowns of the calibre of Kempe and Tarleton. And if ever Mr. Petrie finds himself on a platform stage, hobnobbing with Tom and Dick and Harry, he will find himself impelled, I fancy, to do something more than wink.

In the meantime, go to see him at the New Oxford—for you will not be able to see him at the Old Vic next season. He has sent in his resignation, and it is possible that he will be swamped before long in the vast West End morass out of which clever actors can only extricate themselves occasionally "by kind permission of" the management.

STRATFORD'S OPPORTUNITY
(1926)

THE destruction by fire of the Memorial Theatre in Stratford-on-Avon is one of the most cheering catastrophes ever left unpredicted by Old Moore. Whether it was purely accidental, or whether it was the work of some benevolent incendiary with a real passion for Shake-speare, we shall never know for certain.

On the whole, however, it appears more likely to have been an Act of God than of any of those gentlemen who reveal the measure of their Shakespearean enthusiasm by declaring at regular intervals, on public platforms, with all the authority of committee-members possessing inside information, that "our beloved poet" has done more to knit the British Empire together than all the Colonial Secre-taries of the nineteenth century rolled into one.

It was not because the Memorial Theatre was an ugly and an inconvenient building that it needed burning, but because it was the wrong kind of theatre for Shakespeare, and because its disappearance paves the way for the erection of the right kind of theatre for Shake-speare at last: that is to say, a theatre not too large, with no proscenium frame, and with a platform or apron thrust so boldly into the auditorium that it abolishes what would normally be the first fourteen or fifteen rows of stalls. This is the stage, surrounded on three sides by the audience, for which Shakespeare wrote his plays—a stage on which the actors performed, not in the two-dimensional convention of the picture gallery, but the three-dimensional convention of a circus, bringing Hamlet and Mercutio and Cleopatra and Volumnia to life in the very midst of the attending playgoers.

We never see Shakespeare's plays as Shakespeare intended them to be seen, because there is no theatre in England built for the purpose, and because modern theatres built for other purposes present diffi-culties that defy adaptation. And so insistent has become the demand for a really Shakespearean theatre that it is hard to see how it can now be ignored in Shakespeare's own birthplace.

London is a harder nut to crack. Sites are expensive. Shakespeare is a commercial quicksand. Subsidization is still a dream. But in Stratford the case is different. The prosperity of the town depends so largely on the possession of a Shakespearean theatre that a new one is to be built at once, and I suggest that this prosperity will be more considerable if the new theatre is constructed on the ancient than if it is constructed on the modern plan.

For Stratford flourishes by virtue of its visible Shakespeareanism. Visitors flock there not merely because there Shakespeare was born, but because the Stratfordians have been at pains to preserve, as far as possible, the old buildings just as they were in Shakespeare's time. The custom of the shops and of the hotels waxes in proportion to the illusion that here indeed Shakespeare did once walk, and here indeed Anne Hathaway did once keel the pot.

Shakespeare, it is true, walked many and many a time down Fleet Street, but we find it difficult to feel this, because our eyes seem to contradict the fact. We go to Stratford to see something different that will conjure up a vision of William's Ghost.

And hitherto one of the conspicuous weaknesses of Stratford's appeal has been the fact that in the theatre, which should be its greatest strength, we have been offered productions of Shakespeare's plays in no way different or more Shakespearean than those we may see at the Old Vic and elsewhere.

A festival is organized. The most widely advertised feature of the festival is the Shakespeare season at the Memorial Theatre. We book our rooms. We entrain for Stratford. And when we get there and go to the theatre we find that, for all the theatre can offer us, we might just as well have stayed at home and gone to Miss Baylis's *Julius Caesar* or Mr. Ainley's *Much Ado*.

It is on this account that I, for one, resist the temptations of Stratfordian festivals. But if I knew that, by going to Stratford, I should be able to see authentically Shakespearean productions peculiar to the town and not to be seen anywhere else in the world, then what a fascinating centre I should consider it, and what a regular visitor I should be! And there are thousands more in the same case.

Sceptics may declare that the clamour for an Elizabethan theatre is purely archaic, and that modern costume is the only wear. With this view my intelligence has not a shred of sympathy. When I go to see the operas of Gilbert and Sullivan, I rejoice in the D'Oyly Carte monopoly, thanks to which the spirit of the original productions has hitherto been so staunchly preserved. One day the copyrights will run out, and Tom, Dick and Harry will get to work, and in a couple of hundred years productions of *The Mikado* and *Iolanthe* will have so divagated from the old D'Oyly Carte traditions that charges of archaism and antiquarianism will be levelled against those who are perspicacious enough to point out that Sullivan's music no longer sounds as it should sound, because it is consigned to an orchestra of forty saxophones, and that Gilbert's words no longer make the public laugh, because they are roared through a megaphone.

Attempts to popularize the operas will be made by giving them lavish fifty-thousand-pound productions. Or Koko and the Duke of Plaza-Toro and Elsie Maynard will be rigged out in the dress of the twenty-second century. Or the Fourth Dimensionalists will step fiercely into the breach, and the constitutionally go-ahead critics, together with the critics who are constitutionally afraid of getting left behind, will explain to the bewildered public how delighted poor dear Gilbert and poor dear Sullivan would have been could they only have witnessed one of these esoteric Fourth Dimensional productions.

Thus all sorts of wild theories will lead to all sorts of wild practices, and the only way that will remain untried will be the original D'Oyly Carte way—the old-fashioned way that must on no account be tried, lest it should be bruited abroad that the theatre is not progressing after all.

That is a pretty fair parallel of the case in which Shakespeare now stands. But with the demolition of the Memorial Theatre a golden opportunity for rescue is offered to the inhabitants of Stratford. Let us hope that they will not neglect it, for even if it were purely archaic, an Elizabethan theatre on the banks of the Avon would be the most lucrative new memorial they could erect. And it would not be merely archaic. It would be, aesthetically, the most valuable piece of machinery in the country.

"THE MAKING OF AN IMMORTAL"
(1928)

MANY years ago, when I was making my first acquaintance with the works of Mr. George Moore, I was transported with delight by the literary elegance and sly honesty of one of the most delicious volumes of reminiscences ever written: *The Confessions of a Young Man*. I don't suppose that one-tenth of the distinguished audience which assembled at the Arts Theatre the other night to see *The Making of an Immortal* had ever read that early work; and of those who had read it, I don't suppose that one-tenth recalled a certain passage on *Romeo and Juliet*, which was peculiarly apposite to the occasion. In this passage Mr. Moore told how he strayed into a theatre one night to see a performance of *Romeo and Juliet*, and how he had been distressed by the intervention of the actress's acutely feminine personality between the words of Juliet and the ears of the spectator, and how he had felt that the part should really be played, as in Shakespeare's own time, by a boy.

I have always remembered this passage, because I, too, have always felt that parts written expressly for boys to play would be best played by them. And because there are so few who hold this view and I have written so much at one time or another in favour of boy performers for Shakespeare's heroines, lately I have become a little self-conscious about it and have given my readers a rest. After all, it was only a theory. And after all, might there not be something in the objection of those who declared that the boys in Shakespeare's plays were especially trained for this purpose, and that modern boys would be unequal to the demands made upon them?

Well, Mr. Moore, ably assisted by Mr. Robert Atkins and Mr. Brian Glennie, has demonstrated that there is nothing in that objection at all. Before *The Making of an Immortal* had been in progress very long at the Arts Theatre, the audience was astonished to find a boy dressed in the farthingale of the original Juliet pouring out his true love's passion with such a pure, virgin feeling that the words achieved a new and rarefied beauty. In a few moments the case had been proved by practical demonstration. And if any manager of imagination and courage would, in the face of the success that drew such immediate and instinctive applause, now venture to present *Romeo and Juliet* at a West End theatre with Mr. Brian Glennie as Juliet, London would be provided with an aesthetic sensation of the best class—a sensation which might rank in history with that provided by the Infant Roscius.

The delivery of Juliet's "mask of night" speech by Mr. Glennie was the most important thing that has happened in the theatre for a long time; and that Mr. Moore had some inkling of this was suggested by the letter which he wrote in praise of the work of Mr. Glennie and of the other boys, and which was read at the conclusion of the second performance. If *The Making of an Immortal* had contained nothing else of value, it would have justified its existence. But it was an amiable little *jeu d'esprit*, and although I am so far from being a Baconian as to suspect all Baconians of being actuated by a "jealousy complex", I enjoyed much of Mr. Moore's play as "tittle-tattle" of a very amusing, if rather obscure, type. The play was almost as much a tilt at Shakespeare as Shaw's *Dark Lady of the Sonnets*. Here he was presented, not as an inspired thief, but as an inveterate money-maker—an Elizabethan theatrical manager whose understanding of art was pretty much on a level with that of most modern theatrical managers. The making of an immortal consisted of the announcement by Bacon and Jonson that Shakespeare was the author of the seditious *Richard II*, which had sent Queen Elizabeth into a fury. This announcement allayed the fury, since the Queen held the sedition to be of small importance if it did not emanate from any man of high position.

But I could not quite make out who, according to Mr. Moore's play, was supposed to be the author of the works attributed to Shakespeare which preceded *Richard II*. If they were by Shakespeare, then to take *Richard II* away from him seemed rather pointless. If they were not by Shakespeare, then the making of an immortal must have occurred long before the incidents presented by Mr. Moore.

The cast assembled to perform Mr. Moore's little play was a fine tribute to his reputation. Miss Sybil Thorndike was at her best as Queen Elizabeth. What an up and down actress she is! Since it is my duty as a critic to distinguish the cause of her "ups" from the cause of her "downs", I would suggest that she is inclined to be at her best when she is exercising a severe restraint on her emotions. When she holds herself in, she can be very fine indeed. When she lets herself go, she is less impressive. This is probably due to the fact that in real life she is so full of enthusiasm that restraint on the stage comes to her as the relief that is experienced by many other actresses when they perform parts that are emotional.

In addition to Miss Thorndike, there was Mr. Charles Laughton as Ben Jonson—a richly suggestive picture, but revealing traces of hasty composition. Mr. Laughton is not always sure of his words, and an actor who is not sure of his words cannot be sure of anything.

Mr. Malcolm Keen as Richard Burbage was not in form. Perhaps it is not easy for an actor to play an actor off the stage, and perhaps he would have found it easier if he had merely been required to give us an impression of Burbage's Hamlet rather than of Burbage's Burbage. But Mr. Leslie Faber as Bacon—one of the most despicable figures in the history of England—was excellent, and Mr. Charles Carson made a nice nincompoop of the Bard.

With Mr. Edmund Gwenn and Mr. Hay Petrie in small parts, the author was well served. But it was the boy actor who served him best. The Old Vic has lately made history by capturing Edith Evans and Jean Forbes-Robertson. Why not capture Brian Glennie to follow in their footsteps?

HOW SHAKESPEARE KEPT THE CENSOR BUSY
(1933)

A FEW weeks ago, when *King John* was being performed by the O.U.D.S. at the New Theatre in Oxford, members of the audience were surprised by a sudden interruption in the middle of one of the scenes. The actor playing the part of the king had just spoken the lines:

> "Oh, when the last accompt 'twixt heaven and earth
> Is to be made, then shall this hand and seal
> Witness against us to damnation"

when a gentleman in front, unable to contain himself any longer, rose from his seat and shouted, "I must protest against the use of swear words in this theatre." Whereupon he was politely but firmly requested to leave, and the performance continued without further disturbance.

It is to be hoped that no listener will be prompted by similar feelings to switch his wireless off abruptly at some dramatic moment during the broadcast of *Coriolanus* this week. Having anxiously examined the text of the play, I am happy to find that neither the word to which exception was taken at Oxford, nor any variant of it, occurs. *Coriolanus* is peculiarly free from anything that could be complained of on the ground of profanity. This may be due in part to the fact that it is one of Shakespeare's pagan tragedies. But since these pagan tragedies all abound in anachronisms, we cannot be sure that *Coriolanus* was always as unexceptionable as it is in the only authoritative text that has come down to us—the text of the First Folio, published in 1623.

Just as the plays of modern authors are subjected to an official censorship, so were the plays of Shakespeare in the reigns of Queen Elizabeth and King James I. The Master of the Revels, executing his duties under the direction of the Lord Chamberlain, supervised all plays given in public and blue-pencilled whatever he chose. Again and again he blue-pencilled words written by Shakespeare, because they were held to be seditious or libellous or indecent or offensive to foreign nations or (most often) profane.

Among the various Acts passed from time to time to define and enlarge the powers of the licensing authorities was *An Acte to Restraine Abuses of Players*, in which it was laid down that—

". . . if at any tyme or tymes, after the end of this present Session of Parliament, any person or persons doe or shall in any Stage play, Interlude, Shewe, Maygame, or Pageant jestingly or pro-phanely speake or use the holy Name of God or of Christ Jesus, or of the Holy Ghoste, or of the Trinitie, which are not to be spoken but with feare and reverence [? such person or persons] shall forfeite for everie such Offence by hym or them committed Tenne Pounds."

This particular Act was passed in 1606. It affected not only performances of plays, but also their publication in book form. And so, by comparing editions of Shakespeare's plays printed before the passing of the Act with editions of the same plays printed after-wards, it is possible to see just how Shakespeare's text was altered to suit the Censor.

We find, for one thiug, that where Shakespeare originally wrote "God", it was again and again changed to "Heaven". Thus, where Cassio had said, " 'Fore God, an excellent song," he was made to say, " 'Fore Heaven, an excellent song", and where Hotspur had said, "By God, he shall not have a Scot of them", he was made to say, "By Heaven, he shall not have a Scot of them". "God give thee the spirit of understanding" was watered down to "Maist thou have the spirit of understanding". Words like "Zounds" and " 'Sblood" were omitted altogether or replaced by such weak equivalents as "By my troth" or "By this hand". And quotations from the Scriptures were eliminated or disguised, so that "Wisdom cries out in the streets and no man regards it" became, simply, "No man regards it", while in Shallow's "Death, as the Psalmist saith, is certain" the words "as the Psalmist saith" were suppressed.

But it was not, as I have indicated, on the ground of profanity alone that the censorship of Shakespeare's day interfered with his plays. More than once Shakespeare was required to change the names of his characters. We have the Censor to thank for Falstaff, for when Shakespeare first wrote *Henry IV*, this fat and cowardly knight was called Sir John Oldcastle. Oldcastle he would have remained to this day had not Sir John Oldcastle been an ancestor of Lord Cobham, whose influence was as great as his indignation. So Oldcastle became Falstaff, and the reference to him as "my old lad of the castle" became a mystery to be elucidated by commentators.

Was it out of mischief that, when Shakespeare wrote *The Merry Wives of Windsor*, his third Falstaff play, he made Master Ford take the name of Master Brooke—the family name of the Cobhams? Whether or no, he had to change it again, for Brooke became Broome —and Shakespeare's puns were again upset.

Nations, it would seem, are no less susceptible to insults than individuals. The Captain Jamy episode, which disappeared from *Henry V*, seems to have been censored out of regard for our Scottish neighbours, over whose dignity King James was naturally sensitive. Two passages which were left out of *Hamlet* are believed to have been suppressed through fear lest they should offend Anne of Denmark; while in *Much Ado about Nothing* political considerations, involved by the presence of foreign ambassadors, are held to have been responsible for the excision of the sally about dressing like "a German from the waist downward, all slops, and a Spaniard from the hip upward, no doublet."

From the indications given—and they are only a small part of the story—it will be gathered that Shakespeare kept the Censor a good deal busier than either of them might have wished. But of all his troubles, by far the most interesting occurred in connection with *Richard II*, in which performance of the famous Deposition Scene was forbidden during Elizabeth's reign. The fate of Richard II had always haunted Elizabeth, who had been terrified of suffering a similar fate ever since a Papal Bull of Excommunication and Deposition against her had been published in Rome in 1570. Since the publication of this Bull made it the duty of every Roman Catholic in England to attempt her overthrow, the last thing Elizabeth desired was that her subjects should be reminded of the possibility. "I am Richard II," she is reported to have said, "know ye not that?"

That the association did not exist in the mind of Elizabeth alone is clear from the fact that on the very day preceding the Essex rising the rebel leaders paid Augustine Phillips, a leading member of Shakespeare's company, forty shillings to revive *Richard II* at the Globe Theatre. Whether Elizabeth was exaggerating when, a few months later, she complained that the piece had been played at the period of the rebellion "forty times in the open streets and houses," with seditious intent, can only be conjectured.

It was not until the fourth edition of *Richard II* came out in 1608 that the deposing of the king, omitted from the first three editions, was included in the text. The censoring of this highly important scene, which runs to 165 lines, must have come as a severe blow. To compensate for the gap in time and dramatic interest suddenly created, it may well have been necessary to insert something else in a hurry. I have a pet theory that the Aumerle episode, which consists of abominable doggerel, and is widely recognized as not by Shakespeare, was hastily composed by some hack, or bodily lifted out of some older play to fill the breach.

That attempts were hastily made on the eve of production to make good the ravages of the Censor is suggested by the manuscript of *Sir Thomas More*, in the British Museum. This play, which had been copied out for submission to Sir Edmund Tilney, the Master of the Revels, was so heavily marked by him for amendment that no fewer than five authors were summoned to the rescue, one rewriting one scene, and one another. For this, posterity may be profoundly grateful, since paleographic experts have, within comparatively recent years, identified one of the hands as that of Shakespeare himself.

INDEX